REINVENTING
FINANCIAL AID

THE EDUCATIONAL INNOVATIONS SERIES

The Educational Innovations series explores a wide range of current school reform efforts. Individual volumes examine entrepreneurial efforts and unorthodox approaches, highlighting reforms that have met with success and strategies that have attracted widespread attention. The series aims to disrupt the status quo and inject new ideas into contemporary education debates.

Series edited by Frederick M. Hess

Other books in this series:

The Strategic Management of Charter Schools
by Peter Frumkin, Bruno V. Manno, and Nell Edgington

Customized Schooling
Edited by Frederick M. Hess and Bruno V. Manno

Bringing School Reform to Scale
by Heather Zavadsky

What Next?
Edited by Mary Cullinane and Frederick M. Hess

Between Public and Private
Edited by Katrina E. Bulkley, Jeffrey R. Henig, and Henry M. Levin

Stretching the School Dollar
Edited by Frederick M. Hess and Eric Osberg

School Turnarounds: The Essential Role of Districts
by Heather Zavadsky

Stretching the Higher Education Dollar
Edited by Andrew P. Kelly and Kevin Carey

Cage-Busting Leadership
by Frederick M. Hess

Teacher Quality 2.0: Toward a New Era in Education Reform
Edited by Frederick M. Hess and Michael Q. McShane

REINVENTING FINANCIAL AID

Charting a New Course to College Affordability

Edited by

ANDREW P. KELLY AND SARA GOLDRICK-RAB

Harvard Education Press
Cambridge, Massachusetts

Library of Congress Control Number 2014935204

Paperback ISBN 978-1-61250-714-9
Library Edition ISBN 978-1-61250-715-6

Published by Harvard Education Press,
an imprint of the Harvard Education Publishing Group

Harvard Education Press
8 Story Street
Cambridge, MA 02138

Cover Design: Steven Pisano
Cover Photo: Christian Beirle González/Moment/Getty Images
The typefaces used in this book are Minion Pro and Myriad Pro

Contents

Foreword   **vii**

    Martha J. Kanter

Introduction   **1**

    Andrew P. Kelly and Sara Goldrick-Rab

1   **Designing Research to Provide the "Actionable Knowledge" Needed to Improve Student Aid Program Performance**   **13**

    David S. Mundel

2   **The Politics of Student Aid**   **33**

    Daniel Madzelan

3   **The Promise of "Promise" Programs**   **55**

    Rodney J. Andrews

4   **From FAFSA to Facebook**   **75**

    The Role of Technology in Navigating the Financial Aid Process

    Regina Deil-Amen and Cecilia Rios-Aguilar

5   **Incentivizing Success**   **101**

    Lessons from Experimenting with Incentive-Based Grants

    Lashawn Richburg-Hayes

6   **Reforming Repayment**   **127**

    Using Income-Related Loans to Reduce Default

    Nicholas W. Hillman

7   **Rethinking Institutional Aid**   **149**
    Implications for Affordability, Access, and the Effectiveness of
    Federal Student Aid
        Lesley J. Turner

8   **Managing Risk, Reaping Reward**   **171**
    The Case for a Comprehensive Income-Based Student Loan System
        Stephen Crawford and Robert Sheets

9   **Making College Affordable**   **191**
    The Case for an Institution-Focused Approach to Federal Student Aid
        Sara Goldrick-Rab, Lauren Schudde, and Jacob Stampen

Conclusion   **207**
        Andrew P. Kelly and Sara Goldrick-Rab

Notes   **225**

Acknowledgments   **257**

About the Editors   **259**

About the Contributors   **261**

Index   **267**

Foreword

American history can reveal what is often difficult to see, let alone learn from, in the passing blur of daily events. Looking back over five decades, at various times when our nation was spiraling down into the depths of a recession or emerging even stronger on the other side of one, it's clear that the values and ideals that formed our nation continue to guide what we want for tomorrow and what we do today: to best educate the American people.

Research over the last fifty years tells us that education for all has yielded a healthier society, a more productive work force, a surge of innovation (technological and otherwise), new models of entrepreneurship, and boundless competition from the markets that drive economic growth. Research has also revealed the sometimes intentional, but often unintended, consequences of each of these forces that together have excluded large portions of our people from acquiring a quality education and, accordingly, from the promise of the American Dream. For example, the failures resulting from a host of education innovations that have been tried and showcased are rarely discussed and hardly ever make it to the front page. A second example: millions of Americans take advantage of student financial aid but never complete college. What has been happening, and why?

In setting the context for this influential book about student financial aid, it is important to remember that educational opportunity is increasingly significant in today's world. We know that education positively influences the success of our nation. But we still don't know enough about how to improve our system of education. We haven't uncovered or explored the right incentives that will drive students to perform to the best of their abilities and to develop their unique capacities to learn, to grow, and ultimately to work and contribute to society. We don't have nearly enough research about what works in higher education, and we have hardly any research on the interaction of federal, state, and institutional forces—to say nothing of individual student behaviors—that, taken together, shape the success of our student aid system. We celebrate small gains, and we tirelessly keep looking for the breakthroughs that will lift what I've often called the "top 100 percent of Americans" to greater levels of educational attainment.

Our Founding Fathers heralded what we have inherited today—the value of educating every American so that he or she may reach his or her potential as citizen, as worker, and as a person of moral character. Literally and figuratively, education powers the heart, soul, and future of our democratic society. Helping the common people aspire to greater achievements through education is a hallmark of the character of America today. And we have been at it for a very long time.

In a letter to George Wythe, his mentor and our nation's first professor of law at the College of William and Mary, Thomas Jefferson, then minister of France, opined on the proposed Northwest Ordinance, which was codified into the law of the land a year later:

> I think by far the most important bill in our whole code is that for the diffusion of knowledge among the people. No other sure foundation can be devised, for the preservation of freedom and happiness . . . Preach, my dear Sir, a crusade against ignorance, establish and improve the law for educating the common people.[1]

Three-quarters of a century later, President Lincoln signed into law the Morrill Act of 1862, officially titled "An Act Donating public lands to the several States and [Territories] which may provide colleges for the benefit of agriculture and the Mechanic arts."[2] In passing the Morrill Act, political leaders of that era marked the federal government's first commitment to ensuring Americans the opportunity for public higher education in what we now know as the land grant colleges and universities that invigorate our nation.

More than eight decades later, following two world wars, President Truman's Commission on Higher Education put forward the nation's first goals for higher education, namely

> to bring to all the people of the Nation:
> - Education for a fuller realization of democracy in every phase of living
> - Education directly and explicitly for international understanding and cooperation

- Education for the application of creative imagination and trained intelligence to the solution of social problems and to the administration of public affairs

The Truman Commission report reiterated Jefferson's call:

Education is by far the biggest and the most hopeful of the Nation's enterprises. Long ago our people recognized that *education for all* is not only democracy's obligation but its necessity. Education is the foundation of democratic liberties. Without an educated citizenry alert to preserve and extend freedom, it would not long endure.[3] (emphasis added)

In fact, five years later, in his 1952 commencement address at Howard University, President Truman told the graduating class:

I wish I could say to you who are graduating today that no opportunity to use your skills and knowledge would ever be denied you. I can say this: I know what it means not to have opportunity. I wasn't able to go to college at all. I had to stay at home and work on the family farm. You have been able to get the college education that is so important to everyone in this country. Some of us are denied opportunity for economic reasons. Others are denied opportunity because of racial prejudice and discrimination. I want to see things worked out so that everyone who is capable of it receives a good education.[4]

By 1952, the United States had grown to 157 million people, up from just 34 million at the time of the Morrill Act. Within five years, we would add five million more Americans, all of whom would have a shot at an education. That same year, we also welcomed home millions of World War II veterans, many of whom were able to access a college education thanks to the federal GI Bill.

Fast-forward to today. The United States is home to an estimated 320 million people—diverse newborns from all backgrounds and cultures, youth, the working class, disconnected and unemployed young people and adults, and the baby boomers who are aging out of the work force in droves. The U.S. Census Bureau reports that we will grow to approximately 400 million residents by 2050.[5]

In government, public policy, industry, and philanthropy circles, we are seeking all manner of reforms to keep higher education within the reach of every American. College costs are spiraling up at a time when families are questioning whether it is affordable for their children today or their grandchildren tomorrow. While many believe that the federal and student loan and grant programs are not sustainable, and are seeking a quick fix to a long-standing, complex problem, Andrew P. Kelly and Sara Goldrick-Rab ask us to take the long view in considering reforms to reshape student aid policy for the twenty-first century. They agree wholeheartedly that without reform, the growing number of Americans seeking education beyond high school will be excluded from the promise of the American Dream, as Jefferson, Lincoln, and Truman warned over the last two centuries. President Obama has taken up the same call to action as our forefathers, and it is almost certain that future administrations will grapple with policy reforms that have benefited from the range of deep thought and perspective displayed by the prominent authors in this book.

Kelly and Goldrick-Rab reference today's gridlock in Congress; the layers of federal, state, and institutional bureaucracy that overwhelm simple, good, productive policy making; the competing constituencies, each holding onto individual advantages without regard to what may be better for all; and the paramount needs of the burgeoning middle class, with special attention to those most in need of opportunity. They ask us to reacquaint ourselves with our history, hold back from snap judgments (all too common in government), and carefully think through the well-articulated views of the renowned scholars and practitioners who share new ideas about how to reform student aid.

Reinventing Financial Aid calls upon us to remember the recent past—the first term of the Obama administration when the higher education, banking, and student loan lobbyists decried the advent of Direct lending which had been in the works for more than twenty years, echoing the long and contentious process that produced the Morrill Act. The promise of efficiency and simplification eventually convinced Congress to support SAFRA—the Student Aid and Fiscal Responsibility Act that enabled the federal government to bypass lenders and make loans directly to students. When President Obama signed SAFRA into law as part of the health care reform legislation, it ended bank subsidies, saving the government $68 billion over eleven years and providing $36 billion of the savings in additional funding for the Pell Grant Program, thereby increasing higher education opportunity for low-income, economically disadvantaged students.

Since then, America's colleges and universities have welcomed more than nine million students to the doors of higher education, up from six million in 2008, marking more than a 50 percent increase for the most financially needy students in our nation. Increasing public disclosure on the performance of higher education on various student aid-related metrics—such as student loan cohort default and repayment rates as well as simplification of the Free Application for Federal Student Aid (FAFSA)—represent some initial steps toward major reform of our student aid programs.[6]

However, as the editors and chapter authors detail, policy reform needs the best thinkers of our nation to put forward sustainable student financial aid proposals based on solid evidence from credible studies of unquestionable scholarship. Successful reform, as the authors note, requires long-term thinking and hard work: leaders must come up with evidence-based proposals, experiment with those ideas, and then agree on a path forward to buck the status quo and improve the student aid system.

This is an important book that holds great promise in shaping student aid policy for the twenty-first century. It is especially instructive that its two editors have found common ground from opposing points of view on their topic to produce this book. Would that our nation's political and policy leaders might follow their example.

I have known and admired both of these scholars since I arrived in Washington, DC, five years ago to work as President Obama's Under Secretary of Education. From divergent perspectives, Drs. Kelly and Goldrick-Rab well understand the successes and follies of government policy making, and they have amalgamated their best thinking with that of their distinguished colleagues who have authored the various chapters in this book. From this work, let us ask that members of Congress, the administration, policy makers, and higher education stakeholders from across our public and private sectors think as hard about sustaining the future of American higher education as the co-editors of this significant book have done. In doing so, our nation will surely "avail [to itself] of those talents which nature has sown as liberally among the poor as among the rich, which perish without use, if not sought for and cultivated."[7] *Reinventing Financial Aid* helps us understand our responsibility as a nation to ensure that the top 100 percent of Americans seeking higher education will have that opportunity through the centuries ahead.

—Martha J. Kanter
Under Secretary of Education (2009–2013)
U.S. Department of Education

Introduction

Andrew P. Kelly and Sara Goldrick-Rab

Years from now, historians may denote the start of the twenty-first century as a turning point in the history of student financial aid. Crippling student debt, a weak economic recovery, and skyrocketing bills for college attendance are putting financial aid programs at the center of a national debate about college affordability. News reports warn of a generation of students "drowning in debt" and an inflating "higher education bubble" with student loans as the new subprime mortgage. A recent *Newsweek* cover story even asked bluntly "Is College a Lousy Investment?"

This is not the first time that Americans have questioned the value of a college degree. In fact, each recession brings such doubts.[1] But the size, scope, and growth rate of the student debt problem—an estimated $1 trillion, almost triple the amount ten years ago—and the relentless increase in college tuition have combined to create a sense of urgency. Moreover, stagnant family incomes and tightening public budgets contribute to the distress and generate public outcry. The combination of strong educational ambitions and the high price of college attendance are hitting Americans in their pocketbooks, and policy makers are taking notice.

But the standard policy response to these concerns—spending more money on financial aid—is unlikely to solve these pressing problems. Nor will it put the country on a sustainable path toward providing an affordable postsecondary education to the masses of people who want it. Instead, we argue that policy makers need to begin asking tough questions about student financial aid programs and how they affect students *and* educational institutions. Why is college increasingly unaffordable even though spending on financial aid has never been higher? How does aid affect the prospects that recipients will complete a degree? Is it possible to rethink aid programs to support colleges and universities in becoming more effective at helping all incoming students complete their intended degrees?

Unfortunately, though additional spending on financial aid is often politically popular, it is risky to push for fundamental reforms to the way financial aid is designed and delivered. Powerful interests in all political camps favor the status quo. Every member of Congress has a college in his or her district, and most have more than one. Federal student aid programs are the lifeblood of these schools. And frankly, many people simply feel good about helping needy students go to college. They worry that altering existing programs will simply lead to their demise, setting aside a persistent problem: the current aid system does nothing to contain college costs, leaves even the poorest students with a great deal of unmet financial need, and as such supports students as they begin college without doing nearly enough to help them finish degrees.

We point out these problems in an effort to improve the effectiveness of financial aid and make college *more* affordable—not in an effort to demolish financial aid programs or undo very real progress made in terms of college access over the last thirty years. The nature of the problem has been apparent for almost a decade. For example, in 2006 the blue-ribbon commission convened under Margaret Spellings, George W. Bush's secretary of education, called for holding colleges and universities accountable for how well they serve their students and for simplifying the financial aid application process. The commission's recommendations went nowhere, but it drew an important line in the sand.

Despite being from the opposite party, the next administration has also come to question the traditional approach to student aid. In his first State of the Union address, President Obama promised Americans that "we will provide the support necessary for you to complete college and meet a new goal: by 2020, America will once again have the highest proportion of college graduates in the world."[2] Since that time, the president has remained a top champion of the student aid system but is now adamant that long-term reforms are urgently needed. Four-and-a-half years after taking office, in 2013, he bluntly told Americans, "The path we're on now is unsustainable for our students and our economy."[3]

In many ways, President Obama's call for reform reflects his experience with the structural issues that have blunted the impact of student aid programs over the past half century. Upon taking office, the president and his administration immediately identified postsecondary education and the federal financial aid programs that fund it as important catalysts to get the country moving again. He challenged Americans to get at least a year of postsecondary education and pledged to provide the aid necessary to do so.

And provide support he did. From 2009 to 2011, the president oversaw an unprecedented expansion of the federal Pell Grant program—the cornerstone of the country's student aid system. Federal spending on Pell nearly doubled, going from $18.3 billion in 2008–2009 to $35.7 billion in 2010–2011. The maximum grant award increased from $4,730 to $5,550, and the number of recipients reached 9.4 million in 2013, double what it was in 2006.[4] In total, the government spent almost $200 billion on the Pell Grant program since 2008. Before America could go back to work, it was going back to college.

All that spending kept out-of-pocket costs paid by families stable, at least temporarily. Data from the College Board show that while the published price of tuition jumped between 2008 and 2011 in response to state funding cuts and hard-hit endowments, what students paid after grants and scholarships ("net price") remained flat or declined. According to the College Board's analysts, it was the "unusually large increases" in the Pell Grant program and tax credits that helped to "[relieve] the burden on students."[5] But the large increase in Pell spending did not go on forever, and soon reached a plateau. As soon as that happened, the net price paid by families rose again because states and institutions were doing very little to help. Even though the maximum Pell Grant is larger than ever, its purchasing power has reached an all-time low, washed out by the relentless tide of rising college costs. When originally conceived, the grant covered almost 75 percent of the annual costs of attending a public four-year college or university; today it covers barely one-third. In other words, the federal government is spending more than ever, yet college is far less affordable for needy students than it has been in the past.

By 2012, a frustrated president had changed his tune. In his State of the Union, he officially put colleges "on notice" and told them they must do more to keep higher education affordable. In the summer of 2013, he warned that "families and taxpayers can't just keep paying more and more and more into an undisciplined system where costs just keep on going up and up and up. We'll never have enough loan money, we'll never have enough grant money to keep up with costs that are going up 5, 6, 7 percent a year. We've got to get more out of what we pay for."[6]

The president went on to propose fundamental changes to the way the government doles out student aid. Under his plan colleges would receive financial aid dollars based not only on how many students they enroll, but how well they perform on a set of performance measures, such as the proportion of low-income students they enroll and whether those students are able to pay off their loans.

The plan faces long political odds. But it is a harbinger of things to come. The days of simply spending more on financial aid and hoping for the best are over. Students and families need more effective assistance. The question now is not *whether* aid programs need to change, but *how* they should be changed to meet the demands of a new century. Doing so will entail more than tweaking existing programs or layering new ones onto the old system—the preferred approach up to this point.

This book is designed to put bolder and more far-reaching ideas on the table. The goal is not to propose a single agenda or build consensus around a specific set of recommendations. Rather, we set out to assemble a collection of research that pushes leaders to think beyond the shortsighted, deadline-driven, and evidence-free policy making that has characterized student aid "reform" in the past. The chapters that follow lay the groundwork for the kind of long-term reform effort that will be necessary to shore up educational opportunity and financial sustainability for decades, not just the next fiscal year. Such an effort requires that we acknowledge where aid programs have failed to live up to expectations, that we revisit age-old assumptions about incentives and policy design that have not been borne out, and that we carefully experiment with new grant and loan models and study their outcomes. That process starts with a sense of what the problems are and how we got here.

NEW CHALLENGES AND OLD TOOLS

What is most remarkable about the president's 2013 proposal is how long it took to get to this point. Nearly fifty years after the current student aid system was designed, federal policy makers, advocates, and prominent foundations are recognizing the need for change. But the signs of trouble have been brewing for some time. As the landscape of higher education changed dramatically over the past half century, federal aid programs designed in the 1960s and 1970s have failed to change with it.

Prior to the Higher Education Act of 1965, states were primarily responsible for funding higher education. Federal forays into student aid via the GI Bill and the National Defense Education Act, while important, were limited compared to today's programs. But the Great Society era placed education at the center of the country's efforts to eradicate poverty, and the Higher Education Act of 1965 ushered in a new federal role in promoting college access for needy students. In the years that followed, reauthorizations expanded the federal footprint, creating the foundational grant program in 1972 that would become known as the Pell Grant, and later expanding the student loan program to cover a broader group of families in 1978.

What started out as a modest stream of funding designed to help the neediest students attend college has slowly grown to be one of the primary means of financing higher education. The growth in the size of the programs tells the story. For instance, in 1977 the federal government spent $5.7 billion (in 2012 dollars) on Pell Grants to fund 2 million students. Thirty-five years later, the Pell program served 9.4 million students and grew to a price tag of $35 billion per year.[7] The expansion is even more dramatic for student loans. In 1995–1996 the federal government disbursed $34.2 billion in student loan money (in 2012 dollars), and about one-quarter of all bachelor's degree recipients borrowed.[8] By 2003–2004 new disbursements reached $51.9 billion (in 2012 dollars).[9] Less than ten years later, in 2011–2012, 40 percent of undergraduates took out federal student loans, and in 2013, new loan volume exceeded $100 billion.[10] Moreover, in 2011–2012 federal spending on all financial aid (including tax credits) topped $170 billion, or about 70 percent of the total aid provided by states, institutions, private grants, and the federal government.

In the space of forty-five years the federal government has gone from peripheral player to main partner in the financing of higher education. But this transition did not happen in a vacuum. Rather, the expanding federal footprint influenced the behavior of other stakeholders—states, families, and institutions themselves. For instance, as federal aid increased, states retreated from their traditional role as the primary funder of higher education. To make up for declining state revenue, public institutions raised their tuition prices. In 1981, average state funding per full-time equivalent student (FTE) was $8,400, while the average public tuition was $2,400 (in

2012 dollars). Fast-forward to today, and the shift in financial responsibility is striking: average state funding per FTE is $6,600, and average public tuition is nearly $8,900.[11] In the past decade alone, published tuition, fees, and room and board expenses at public four-year institutions have gone up 45 percent.[12]

The story is certainly not limited to the public sector. When reforms made student loans more accessible to the middle class in the late 1970s, private colleges and universities began to dramatically raise their tuition. The trend picked up steam in the 1980s and 1990s; between 1983 and 1998, tuition prices at private nonprofit colleges increased 76 percent after adjusting for inflation.[13] Competition for students and the chase for higher rankings drove private campuses to increase spending on amenities. Elite flagship public campuses followed suit. Students and families, for their part, have been willing to pay higher tuition bills with the help of student loans, often equating higher prices with higher quality and seeking out the campuses with the nicest facilities and student life.[14] But the race to attract affluent students has meant higher and higher prices for all, including those least able to pay.

The result has been a predictable pattern: when tuition prices rise, federal policy makers call for more generous federal aid programs to ensure access. Increases in federal student aid, in turn, provide even less incentive for institutions to maintain low tuition or for states to maintain public investments. Whether federal aid programs "cause" higher tuition prices has been the subject of heated debate, with researchers disagreeing over whether there is robust evidence of a causal link. But this debate only serves to distract from the more basic problem: federal aid policies are powerless to keep tuition prices low or encourage state investments. So even as federal aid programs have grown more generous, tuition prices have increased at a faster clip, sapping their purchasing power.

Not surprisingly, program outcomes have not lived up to expectations. More people than ever are attending college, but attainment gaps between income groups have actually grown over time. A recent study comparing college access and degree completion across income groups found that students from the lowest income quartile who were born in 1980 were more likely to enroll in and graduate from college than similar students born in the 1960s. But students from the top income quartile made much larger gains in both categories over that period, meaning low-income students fell further behind their more affluent peers.[15] These income gaps continue to hold even among academic high achievers. In other words, educational inequality based on family income has gotten worse, not better, as federal aid programs have expanded.

Questions as to whether aid programs are working as intended have been around for some time. But concerns about mounting student debt and tight public budgets have added a sense of urgency to these discussions. Data from the Federal Reserve Bank of New York show that outstanding student debt has topped $1 trillion, with an average debt load of about $25,000. To be sure, most borrowers owe less than $25,000, and only a small percentage have the six-figure debts that have captivated the media. But small balances can still pose a problem for young workers, and delinquency rates are also on the rise. The Federal Reserve Bank data show that 12 percent of student loans are ninety days delinquent, a higher rate than among credit cards.[16] For context, at the height of the recent mortgage crisis, delinquency rates reached 10.1 percent.[17] The Consumer Financial Protection Bureau recently reported that 22 percent of federal loan borrowers in repayment are either in default or forbearance.[18] These troubling numbers have led to panicked talk of a "student loan bubble" and placed aid reform squarely on the agenda.

THE CHALLENGE OF REFORM

The stage is set for far-reaching financial aid reform. In response to discouraging outcomes and tight federal budgets, advocates, researchers, and foundations have increasingly campaigned for change. "Stated plainly," Lumina Foundation President Jamie Merisotis said recently, "the current student financing model is broken."[19] In a speech commemorating the 150th anniversary of the Morrill Act, Bill Gates told the Association of Public and Land-Grant Universities that "aid should be structured to provide incentives—for institutions and students—to raise college completion rates . . . We cannot be agnostic about whether aid subsidizes failure or success."[20]

Unfortunately, policy debates have typically focused on maintaining existing programs and making small and shortsighted tweaks to award levels and interest rates rather than meaningful reform. For example, politicians spent eighteen months posturing over the interest rate on newly issued subsidized Stafford loans in 2012 and 2013. The changes would have done nothing to help current borrowers, and estimates suggested that allowing the rate to rise would have saved new borrowers about $9 a month at a price tag of $6 billion to taxpayers. Similarly, the Obama administration has spent considerable time and political capital on expanding the Income-Based Repayment program (IBR), where qualifying borrowers pay 10 percent of their income over twenty years, at which point the debt is forgiven. The focus on struggling borrowers is understandable, but IBR also ignores the root cause of the problem—high college costs—and may even exacerbate it.

These small-bore efforts are rarely promising or sustainable because they fail to address the fundamental tensions and conflicting incentives that underlie the financial aid system. For example, while policy makers want to ensure that out-of-pocket costs do not deter students from attending college, they do not fully grasp how generous student loan programs affect the incentives of colleges and states to provide aid. Similarly, they want students to finish their degrees, yet orient the system around enrollment—not completion. And while former students bemoan debt loads and call for more generous repayment options, the root problems of tuition costs and uncertain returns often lack a visible constituency. Prospective students and their families have been told that almost any investment is worth it, while borrowers are understandably more concerned with paying off their debts than reforming the whole system.

For their part, organized interests like the higher education trade associations have sought to protect the status quo above all else. Colleges and universities, most of whose business models rely on the current system, have little reason to change existing programs and often find common cause with student advocates who push for more aid funding. And elected officials benefit politically from supporting policies that provide aid to students and families, even if those policies may not be the most effective or efficient investment of resources.

Most troubling, perhaps, is that there has not been robust experimentation with financial aid programs with an eye toward how to improve them. Unlike other areas of social policy, where experimental evaluations of policy outcomes have become de rigueur, federal financial aid programs have never been subjected to this kind of scrutiny, nor has there been a concerted effort to test alternative ways of designing and delivering aid. As a result, we simply do not know enough about which kinds of financial aid programs work best, for which students, and in what ways. As Stanford economist Eric Bettinger remarked in 2012, "There is surprisingly little research on how need-based aid programs affect students' collegiate outcomes."[21] A recent review of the literature pointed out that the evidence is even thinner on student loans: "[Loans] are likely to remain a key component of student aid packages, yet almost no evidence exists about their effects on college enrollment and completion."[22] This lack of research and development—quietly supported by college trade associations for fear of what evaluation might bring—hamstrings efforts to improve program performance.

In fairness, recent calls for reform have not completely ignored the need for more research and experimentation on how changes could improve student success. Efforts such as the College Board's Rethinking Student Aid project and the recent Reimagining Aid Design and Delivery initiative by the Bill and Melinda Gates Foundation have placed student outcomes at the center of reform debates. But even here, policy recommendations tend to focus on affecting targeted policy changes for the short term—how we can simplify the Free Application for Federal Student Aid (FAFSA) and increase institutional accountability in the next reauthorization of the Higher Education Act. These questions are important, but they stop short of tackling the structural problems that underlie disappointing program outcomes.

A WAY FORWARD

Clearly, the time has come to explore reforms that go beyond the system as it is currently designed and the assumptions on which it was built. The popularity of existing programs and political clout of the constituencies that protect them have often made it difficult to think about what could be. But redesigning the financial aid system to reflect the demands of a new century and ensure that public money is spent wisely will require more creativity, rigorous research, and political bravery than has been the norm. This book provides leaders with a place to start on such an agenda.

But meaningful reform will also require frank debate and, often, disagreement among stakeholders with different political and disciplinary perspectives. To identify, test, and refine reform ideas, leaders will need input from the various corners of the higher education policy sector. The problem is simply too large, complex, and politically difficult to rely on one perspective.

This book reflects that kind of collaboration. The editors approach student aid policy and reform from very distinct points of view. Andrew directs a research center at a conservative Washington think tank, while Sara is a left-leaning sociologist within a top education school at a flagship public university where she directs a research laboratory aimed at creating more hope and identifying productive solutions for the future of higher education. In general, Andrew favors market-based solutions to problems of higher education financing, access, and success. Sara would prefer a system of universal public higher education to the patchwork, expensive public/ private system we have now. Likewise, as the chapters that follow illustrate, the book's contributors come at questions of student reform from very different perspectives and professional experiences. Some authors are bright young researchers, while others are veteran educational policy makers who have been involved in student aid policy for decades. Each chapter brings a unique perspective, and some feature a new voice in the field.

However, the common thread that runs throughout is a sense that the current system is not serving students' or taxpayers' interests particularly well, that it often privileges the interests of institutions over those of other stakeholders, and that policy makers have little guidance on how to reform the system. From there, the point is to take a hard look at promising new ideas and uncover common ground and areas of disagreement. In contrast to much of the recent work on student aid, which is geared toward the next reauthorization of the Higher Education Act, this book takes a longer view that will inform the reauthorizations that are ten or fifteen years away.

The book is laid out in three broad sections, beginning with two chapters that provide a critical history of the development of financial aid policy and the abject lack of research and development on aid programs. To reform these programs for the future, policy makers must learn from the past. The second section examines ongoing contemporary efforts to rethink the design of student aid programs—from performance-based scholarships to income-based loans to the use of technology to boost community college students' awareness of aid opportunities. Most of these efforts are still somewhat new, but they provide an empirical look at how they are faring on the ground. The final section grapples with the ways in which federal aid policy affects the behaviors of individuals, states, and institutions. Each chapter in the final section calls for significant revision to the current incentive structure created by aid programs.

Section one kicks off with a chapter by David Mundel, veteran observer of federal aid policies. He looks at the often-disappointing results of federal aid efforts and argues that these outcomes are due, in part, to a failure to engage in the research and development efforts necessary to improve performance. Given the disappointing results of current student aid policies, the limited understanding of the effects of these and alternative policies, and the increasing likelihood of future funding constraints, policy makers must develop a research agenda in order to avoid continued disappointments in the future. In the second chapter, Daniel Madzelan, a thirty-year veteran of the U.S. Department of Education, explores the political dynamics of aid reform. Madzelan provides a first-person review of the history and development of federal student aid programs including the Pell Grant, student loans, and tax credits. He reminds us that aid reform is not a new idea, and that contemporary debates tend to repeat old ideas while running up against the same political barriers to change.

Section two provides a window into innovations in financial aid that are taking root right now. It begins with an examination of so-called Promise Programs—locally funded scholarships that guarantee aid to students who attend public schools in a particular locality. Rodney J. Andrews, a professor of economics at the University of Texas at Dallas, examines the early evidence on these programs and highlights the features that distinguish them from other aid programs. Andrews outlines concerns about financial sustainability and some of the lessons we might learn from Promise Programs about the effects aid opportunities can have on K–12 schools and students. In chapter four, Regina Deil-Amen of the University of Arizona and Cecilia Rios-Aguilar of Claremont Graduate University look at how the digital revolution may help students navigate the complicated process of applying for (and re-upping) federal aid. The authors use a large-scale study of a widely used social networking application to identify the most common financial aid challenges students face, exploring the promise and limits of technology to solve enduring information and access issues.

The fifth chapter moves on to examine how new types of aid programs might affect the behavior of individual students. Lashawn Richburg-Hayes with MDRC summarizes findings from a series of experiments on performance-based scholarships—aid programs that are tied to student success on a series of academic benchmarks. The author cautions that while early results suggest that incentive-based grants can result in a larger proportion of students meeting academic benchmarks, policy makers should not simply graft these lessons onto existing federal programs like the Pell Grant without considering potential unintended consequences.

Chapter six examines how student loan policies continue to affect students after they leave school, when it comes time to repay their loans. Nicholas Hillman of the University of Wisconsin-Madison finds that within three years of entering repayment, one in ten borrowers defaults on his or her federal student loans. Hillman goes on to discuss options for improving the student loan repayment process and proposes a simplified income-based repayment approach.

The final section of the book grapples with the incentives that current aid policies create for states and institutions and how to change them. In chapter seven, University of Maryland professor Lesley Turner looks at how institutions distribute their own student aid dollars via scholarships and tuition discounts. In particular, the chapter focuses on the extent to which institutional aid is awarded based on need versus merit and how federal need-based aid (like Pell Grants) might crowd out the former. Are there policies that might help combat this substitution effect?

In chapter eight, Stephen Crawford, research professor at George Washington University, and Robert Sheets, former director of research at Business Innovation Services at the University of Illinois at Urbana-Champaign, argue for dramatic changes to student loans. In particular, they argue that we must augment the goals of the student loan program to include return on investment and managing risk. To promote these goals, the authors propose a more dynamic loan system where eligibility, loan limits, and interest rates would be tailored to reflect a variety of factors including institution and program choice, expected earnings, and academic performance once enrolled.

In the final chapter of the section, the authors encourage policy makers to rethink the initial decision to structure federal student aid as a voucher distributed to students. Authors Sara Goldrick-Rab of the University of Wisconsin-Madison, Lauren Schudde of Teachers College Columbia University, and Jacob Stampen of the University of Wisconsin-Madison ask whether directing federal aid to institutions, rather than students, would create more effective institutional accountability and more control over college costs. The last chapter concludes the volume by drawing out the implications for policy and identifying important areas of agreement and disagreement among the editors and the contributors.

Collectively, these contributions challenge leaders to think beyond how to fulfill next year's budget constraint or please one special interest or another. Most importantly, they question the assumption that the aid programs inherited from the 1960s and 1970s can be sustained through minor changes. Rather than coaxing old policy tools to accomplish new challenges, policy makers, researchers, and policy advocates may need to entertain different approaches to achieving college affordability. In order to create the financial aid system needed for the twenty-first century, exploration and testing of fresh policy ideas must begin today.

1

Designing Research to Provide the "Actionable Knowledge" Needed to Improve Student Aid Program Performance

David S. Mundel

INTRODUCTION*

Federal support for higher education began with the Morrill Act of 1862 that provided land grants to states remaining in the Union "to support the creation of colleges that teach such branches of learning as are related to agriculture and the mechanic arts . . . in order to promote the liberal and practical education *of the industrial classes*"[1] (emphasis added). This focus of federal support for higher education on equalizing opportunity for lower-income youth continues to the present.[2]

Over time, aid to college students (instead of institutions) has become the major form of federal support, and the focus of aid has been broadened to include middle-income youth and older, independent students. Federal support for students began in 1935, when the National Youth Administration supported jobs for students. Subsequently, the post–World War II and Korean War GI Bills dramatically increased support for students.

The modern era of student aid began in the late 1950s with the establishment of the first federal student loan program. In the 1960s additional student aid programs were authorized and funded, including an extension of eligibility for Social Security benefits to 18- to 21-year-old dependents attending college full-time, as well as the Federal Work-Study, the Guaranteed Student Loan, and the Educational Opportunity Grant programs. In

* I would like to thank W. Lee Hansen (University of Wisconsin–Madison) for his help and guidance on this chapter.

the 1970s further expansion occurred with the creation of the Basic Educational Opportunity Grant (later called Pell Grant) program. The scope of federal student aid was later expanded to include support for many middle-income students, and new benefits were provided through the tax system. More recently the focus of federal aid has been broadened to include raising persistence and completion rates.

Currently, federal student aid provides over $170 billion in support for higher education.[3] Federally subsidized and guaranteed loans account for the majority of this support (over 60 percent). Grant programs—including Pell and veterans' programs—account for an additional 28 percent, while tax benefits account for another 11 percent of aid to students and parents.

The results of these aid programs have been disappointing throughout much of this modern era.[4] Many of the problems they addressed continue to be significant,[5] and some have grown worse. During these same years, attention to the design and funding of federal aid has remained episodic and opportunistic in spite of the programs' growth. Although there have been increases in research-based evidence that could, if used, improve the student aid program performance, this knowledge has remained limited, and the use of this knowledge when developing policy has been even more limited.

Clearly what is needed to improve student aid policies and practices is a problem-focused body of *actionable knowledge*.[6] Although policy makers, foundations, advocates, and others have called for improving student financial aid programs, only a relatively small amount of actionable knowledge is available to assist in this process. When compared to the research-based evidence available in other policy domains—for example, health care and defense—the paucity of actionable knowledge about student aid is striking.

Actionable knowledge in the field of student aid reform needs to be directed toward understanding the behavioral impacts of potential policy changes rather than simply assessing which individuals and institutions receive aid—the focus of much of current analysis. That is, the research should include assessments of the impact of aid programs on the behavior of potential students and of the institutions affecting student aid policy outcomes, including middle and secondary schools, colleges, and state governments. In addition, it is necessary to better understand the impact of changing demographic, economic, sociological, and political contexts on aid program performance. It should be noted that actionable knowledge does not need to be based solely on empirical data, and if results or findings are based on data, the results need not be highly statistically significant or fully conclusive to be important.[7] Fully conclusive knowledge is rarely achievable or available, particularly in a timely manner.

This chapter is intended to help chart a course for increasing the availability and use of such knowledge. To do so, we must first understand the history of the longstanding and continuing problems that federal student aid policy makers have tried to solve as well as the reasons why our understanding of these problems has remained so limited. Second, we need to understand the role that underperforming research and development (R&D) and policy-making processes have played in establishing these limitations.

In addition, the chapter includes a preliminary list of topics that should be addressed to establish a research foundation that can support future efforts to reform student aid policies, programs, and practices. Absent such a systematic R&D effort, student aid programs will continue to fall well short of our goals for increasing equality of opportunity and the quality and competitiveness of our nation's labor force.

LESSONS LEARNED: FACTORS THAT HAVE LIMITED STUDENT AID PROGRAMS' PERFORMANCE

A variety of market and nonmarket problems,[8] as well as changes in contexts within which the higher education sector operates,[9] have affected the performance of federal student aid policies during the last fifty years of increasing federal involvement in this sphere. Although researchers and policy makers have addressed several of these factors, many of their negative impacts on performance continue. Furthermore, several potentially important factors have not been addressed by either research or policy.

Market Problems or Failures

The rationale underlying much of the growth in federal student aid that began in the 1960s rested on the concept of market failure. Simply stated, private markets do not operate in ways that lead to the optimal level of a society's investment in higher or postsecondary education. The importance of market failures was brought to general attention by Milton Friedman in his 1962 book *Capitalism and Freedom*.[10] Friedman and other economists proposed and studied several remedies for these market failures, including: government subsidies to stimulate overall increases in college attendance; subsidized or guaranteed student loans to overcome constraints on students' ability to borrow funds; need-based grants and supplemental education and counseling services for youth from economically disadvantaged, lower-income families; and improved information to assist potential students and their parents who lacked the knowledge needed to make effective college-going decisions.

Early projections of the effectiveness of the resulting system of federal student aid rested on several believed but unexamined assumptions, as well as on other assumptions that were neither explicit nor addressed. These poorly understood assumptions were related to the behaviors of high school graduates and their parents, of colleges and universities, and of state governments—that is, the customers, suppliers, and supporters of the nation's higher education system.

The following are some of the assumptions regarding the responsiveness of potential students and their parents to student aid:

- Many qualified, lower-income high school graduates who would not otherwise attend college would respond to the price reductions created by student aid.
- Some poorly qualified youth would increase their qualification for college-going as a result of the increased affordability created by student aid.
- Aid programs would stimulate newly enrolled students to be successful in college (mirroring the persistence and completion rates of other enrollees).
- Most targeted, prospective students and their parents would be able to understand and navigate the process of applying for financial aid.

Assumptions regarding the responsiveness of colleges and universities to student aid included the following:

- Institutions would seek to enroll aided students from lower-income families.
- Institutions would not substitute federal aid for aid that they had previously provided to students.
- Institutions would not increase their list prices in response to student aid.
- Proprietary institutions would continue to represent a small segment of the higher education system in response to increased and more portable student aid.

In addition, it was assumed that increases in federal support for student aid would not cause the other principal funders of the nation's colleges and universities—state governments and middle- and upper-income parents—to reduce their support of colleges and students.[11]

The disappointing results of federal student aid programs indicate that many of these underlying assumptions were, at least partially, inaccurate.[12] A review of the policy debate surrounding the initial creation of many of the existing student aid programs indicates that many underlying assumptions remained unquestioned when new student aid initiatives were introduced in the 1960s. Subsequently, when programs were redesigned, expanded, and supplanted, the validity of most of these assumptions remained unexamined.

Nonmarket Problems or Failures

Just as Friedman brought to public attention the importance of market failures, several social scientists—including RAND economist Charles Wolf Jr. and Harvard political scientist Graham Allison—elaborated sets of nonmarket or government failures.[13] Although this literature did not address either the higher education system or student aid, a review of the several nonmarket factors indicates that many have been sources of the disappointing performance of student aid. In addition, scholars argued that the efficacy of government activities aimed at offsetting private market failures is likely to be reduced by these nonmarket or government failures.

This literature identified several types of nonmarket failures, many of which appear to have influenced student aid policy performance, including: internalities and private goals that affect organizational behaviors within private for-profit enterprises, private nonprofit institutions, and governmental organizations; limited competitive processes that create monopoly-like positions and unequal distributions of political power between large, organized actors and individual market participants; failure of nonmarket organizations (especially those with monopoly-like positions) to address redundant and rising costs; externalities or unintended and negative consequences; and inequalities of information and access that restrict political and claimant participation.

Several of these nonmarket failures appear to have restricted federal student aid program performance, for reasons such as those listed below.[14]

- The ability of student aid programs to accomplish stated goals depends on complex inter-institutional connections and collaborations within the highly fragmented and decentralized education system, but these connections are weak (particularly between colleges and high schools), and there are few incentives for creating or strengthening them.

- The responses of states (as highly political and bureaucratic organizations) to federal student aid initiatives are uncertain and heterogeneous (and unlikely to be similar to the responses of classical, market-oriented organizations). Furthermore, state responses are likely to be affected by issues lying well outside of higher education, such as societal and political trends and changes in the costs of publicly financed medical and criminal justice activities. State responses to federal policy changes are likely to be slower and more erratic than those of less complex institutions.

- Colleges and universities are also likely to respond to changes in federal student aid in ways that differ from other, more market-focused enterprises.[15] In part this is due to the complexity of these institutions' goals (e.g., preferences for higher ability students who positively affect college rankings, students who are easier to educate, and legacy applicants). These goals are likely to limit their responsiveness to students targeted by financial aid. Furthermore, many institutions may and often do prefer to use institutional resources for purposes other than supplementing federal aid.[16]

- The complex and shared governance and management systems that dominate the higher education sector (particularly its private not-for-profit and public institutions) also impact institutional responsiveness to changes in federal aid policies. These systems both slow and modify institutional responsiveness. In some cases, these systems appear to influence the allocation of institutional resources and attention toward objectives that are at odds with the enrollment and success of federally aided students. Finally, colleges use nonmarket mechanisms—for example, accrediting agencies, state licensure entities, and political lobbying—to protect their positions or create local or regional monopoly positions.

- Federal agencies and bureaucracies that control student aid also resemble market-based monopolies. These government organizations have strong desires for increases in resources and programmatic stability. As such, they press for continuation of standard operating procedures and against adaptive approaches involving greater levels of uncertainty and organizational change.

- Finally, the expanding scope and size of federal student aid programs have stimulated the creation and growth of constituencies and lobbying groups that tend to favor the same goals as those sought by federal operating agencies—maintenance and expansion of existing programs as opposed to new approaches. To the extent that these external constituencies administer aid programs, their support of the responsible government bureaucracy may be conditioned on limited government control and regulation.

These nonmarket factors have received little if any attention in either research or policy debates surrounding new or changed aid policies. Furthermore, when attention has been directed toward these factors—for example, the decline of state support for need-based aid and low tuitions—significant policy changes have rarely been considered or adopted.

Changes in Economic and Political Contexts

One major contextual change in higher education during the last fifty years has been a decline in parental and state willingness to pay for college-going, resulting, in part, from the student-aid-induced shift toward student-based and/or -directed financing of college-going. These aid-stimulated changes became particularly strong when macroeconomic conditions affected parental and state funding capacities. It also seems plausible that this shift toward student-financed college-going has stimulated unanticipated increases in part-time and interrupted enrollment patterns. The growth of these enrollment patterns may, in part, be responsible for stagnant or declining rates of college persistence and completion.

Changes in the national and state political contexts have also influenced the performance of federal student aid. At the federal level, growing political fragmentation and partisanship have increased the pressure on program advocates to focus their energies on maintaining financial support for aid programs. As a result, attention directed toward improving performance has declined.[17] This decline in attention has probably been increased by the belief of many program advocates that raising performance concerns endangers continued financing. As a result, strategies for maintaining or improving program performance that would be useful during future periods of budget stringencies and reductions have remained largely undeveloped, unexamined, and/or untested.

WHAT DOES AVAILABLE RESEARCH TELL US ABOUT THE IMPACT OF STUDENT AID PROGRAMS?

During the past four decades, hundreds (if not thousands) of research papers and reports have been written about federal, state, institutional, and privately financed financial aid policies and programs. The results of this research have been assessed and summarized in several carefully conducted research reviews.[18] Many of these studies and reviews have included recommendations for improving the performance of federal and other student aid programs.

The impacts of these studies and reports—in terms of increases in understanding and implementations of more effective programs—have been limited. In part this is the result of the failure of the research to address several key factors affecting aid program performance. Furthermore, many research studies have not been accessible or understandable to important audiences—policy makers, their advisors, and journalists and others who inform these actors. The utility of numerous reports prepared by think tanks, advocacy groups, and foundations has also been reduced by their being advocacy documents that include little research or analysis.

Nevertheless, there is a growing body of research-based, actionable knowledge about the impact of student aid programs on potential college-goers. The following is a brief review of what we know and don't know about the effectiveness of current aid programs and potential new approaches.[19]

- There is a fairly substantial body of knowledge about the effect of net-of-grant prices on college-going among different groups of recent high school graduates. However, we know much less about the college-going effects of other forms of aid or combinations of types of aid. We also know little about the effect of aid on youth who have delayed college-going.
- We know that grant-induced reductions in net prices have larger positive impacts on college-going among lower-income youth and that these students, when aided, tend to enroll in lower-priced and less selective, public two-year and four-year colleges. Based on observations of natural experiments, we know that small and

continuing increases in Pell Grants that cause declines in net-of-grant prices at lower-priced colleges stimulate small increases in college-going among aided youth.[20] We also know that a growing number of lower-income grant recipients (including older adult students) have enrolled in for-profit, proprietary schools with high list prices. It is unclear whether these enrollment increases are the result of student responsiveness to aid, institutional marketing and recruiting, program offerings, or a lack of competitive offerings or efforts by traditional colleges.

- Research also indicates that there are small, short-term effects of grant-induced reductions in net price on college attendance and college choices. A more limited body of evidence suggests larger, enrollment-stimulating effects among lower-income adults (compared with the effects among lower-income youth). We have very little knowledge about the longer-term effects of lower list or net prices.

- Recent, more rigorous studies have indicated that efforts providing lower-income students and their families with customized or individualized information, targeted counseling and mentoring services, and assistance with complex financial aid application processes[21] can substantially increase college-going rates (particularly among young women).[22] This suggests that combining these types of programs with price-reducing grants would be more effective than grant programs alone.[23]

- We have essentially no evidence about the potential impact of student aid on students, parents, teachers, and counselors during middle and early high school years. It is clear that the formation of college-going orientations, expectations, and behaviors originate during these years, but there is little evidence regarding whether early knowledge of the availability of student aid, and/or the uncertainties associated with the absence aid guarantees, have an effect on college attendance rates and patterns.[24]

- Although foundations, policy makers, and researchers have paid increasing attention to the importance of college persistence, success, and completion, there is little research-based evidence regarding the effect of student aid on these outcomes. A recent experiment in Wisconsin suggests that providing increased aid to Pell Grant recipients enrolled in the state's public colleges and universities has a small positive effect on persistence and time to degree, particularly among lower-income Pell Grant recipients attending less selective colleges.[25] But it is not known whether this type of aid would affect these outcomes in other states or how such a supplementary aid program could be structured to have a larger effect.

- In general, the research on persistence, time to completion, and degree or certificate completion suggests that students who receive federal aid tend to have the same outcomes as non-aided students who enroll in the same colleges. If aid changes the college choices of aid recipients, making them more likely to enroll in colleges that have higher overall levels of student success, then aid would be likely to stimulate increases in postsecondary success among aided students. If, on the other hand, aid stimulates students who would have otherwise enrolled in colleges with better student outcomes to enroll in lower performing schools, aid may actually stimulate lower average rates of success.

- The evidence regarding the impact of student aid on college prices is not conclusive and is highly dependent on contextual factors.[26] Historically, federal grant and loan levels were relatively low, federal aid was highly targeted on a small group of lower-income students, and the funding capacities of states and college endowments were high. In this context, the impact of federal aid on college pricing decisions appeared to be small. Similarly, prior to the recent recession, when Pell awards to low-income students were growing slowly and steadily and state fiscal capacities were not seriously constrained, the list prices of public two-year colleges (the colleges most likely to be attended by newly enrolling, aided students) remained essentially constant, and net-of-grant prices facing these students declined.

- However, during the recent recession and the subsequent slow recovery, the impact of federal student aid on institutional pricing policies appears to have increased.[27] During these years, states' financial capacities declined and other activities became higher-priority targets for the limited available state support. At the same time, federal support for student aid grew as a result of the Pell Grant program being included in the economic stimulus package. In this context, it appears that federal grants and loans enabled (or perhaps caused) public colleges to increase their prices given their strong reliance on less available state support.

- Very little research has been directed toward understanding the impact of federal student aid on institutional and state offerings and activities, including those offerings and activities most related to student aid program effectiveness (e.g., education and counseling services, college recruiting and admission activities, and institution- and state-provided student aid). As a result, we know very little about the potential impact of federal student aid on these factors that influence college-going rates and success and may complement or decrease the direct effect of federal student aid.

Overall, this review of what we know indicates that the extent of available actionable knowledge regarding the impact of federal student aid is limited. We have some knowledge about the impact of federal student grant aid on the college-going behaviors of lower-income youth and young adults, but very little understanding of how other forms of aid affect college-going rates, patterns, and successes. We know even less about the impact of federal student aid on middle and high schools and their students. Similarly, we have little knowledge regarding the impact of federal aid on colleges and one of their most important sources of funds—state governments.

Perhaps most importantly, we know little about the direct impact of student aid programs and practices on students' noneducational activities (e.g., full- or part-time work) that are related to rates of college-going, persistence, and success. Equally importantly, we know little about the impact of federal aid on parental support of their children while they attend college.

Sources of Gaps in Available Knowledge

Conclusive research on higher education is difficult to conduct. The American higher education system (like the economy and society of which it is a part) is complex and interactive, making it difficult to assess the causes of outcomes. Carefully controlled and evaluated experiments designed to provide knowledge about the variety of potentially important causal relationships are costly and difficult to conduct. Naturally occurring experiments are difficult to assess because changes occur within a range of economic, social, demographic, cultural, and political contexts that may change simultaneously. Additional analytic interpretation problems result from the shared governance structures present in most higher education institutions, the multiplicity of college funding sources, and the fact that educational outputs and outcomes are the result of several simultaneous processes.

Regrettably, it is also clear that although the production or development of knowledge is one of the major objectives of the higher education system, many institutions and individuals in this system are not interested in being the focus of serious research. In fact, scholars attempting to conduct research on higher education often report major problems in obtaining data from their own institutions, data that could presumably help these institutions improve the performance of their own programs.

But a lack of research is not the only problem; there is an even greater lack of the "right" type of research. For example:

- Much of the research on student aid has been focused on describing the type of students that receive aid and how much aid they receive, rather than the behavioral changes that the expectation and receipt of aid may stimulate among potential students. Few research studies have focused on how the availability of aid and the expectations it may generate affect the behavior of potential college students, their parents, and the schools that they are attending.
- Much of the student aid research has been episodic (rather than replicative and cumulative) and methodologically weak.
- Little research has focused on the interactions among institutional, state, and federal student aid policies and the joint impact of these policies.
- Little research has focused on the impact of financial aid on the growing role of nontraditional students (older, independent students), nontraditional patterns of attendance (e.g., part-time and interrupted enrollment), and nontraditional institutions (e.g., proprietary).
- Most of the research efforts are relatively small, discipline-based (rather than problem-oriented) studies that rely on existing data sets rather than more focused, project-specific data. There have been fewer large-scale, multiyear, team projects (e.g., experiments) focused on major issues and the impact of policy alternatives.

The Role of the Funders

Foundations appear to be increasingly interested in immediate impact and advocacy rather than developing improved understanding and testing new initiatives. Funders appear to favor the possibility of new findings as opposed to replications and reexaminations that can improve confidence in what is known about what works and why. The federal agency that supports postsecondary educational research appears most interested in funding large-scale data collection efforts that generate descriptive studies with high reported levels of statistical significance. Support for serious but less conclusive studies that can generate substantively important, policy-relevant, causal findings (e.g., less statistically significant findings that nevertheless suggest policies or factors that provide higher levels of policy leverage) is much more limited.

In addition, the federal government and many other funders of research seem relatively uninterested in influencing the overall structure or operations of the research community in ways that could improve the quality, character, and utility of student aid research. For example, there is little funder effort aimed at expanding and speeding the sharing of data among researchers (as opposed to the hoarding of data until an investigator has had papers published).

The Role of the Research Community

As the academic marketplace has tightened, researchers have become even more focused on discipline- and publication-oriented projects to advance their careers. In addition, a focus on statistically significant findings often leads to research that is poorly interpreted and reported and of little policy relevance.[28] The difference between substantive and statistical significance is rarely addressed. Furthermore, if tests of statistical significance indicate less than sought-after certainties, many researchers report that there is no evidence of an effect, while others report that the research indicates an absence of effect (although neither of these conclusions is accurate). Finally, much of the research that indicates there is a modestly statistically significant effect is never reported or distributed—because it is either omitted from published papers and reports or reported in documents that are never published or shared.[29]

The Role of the Policy-Making Environment

As the federal role in student aid has grown and the bulk of the federal aid has been concentrated in a small number of large programs, the major funder of student aid research (the federal government) has become more conservative in its approach to research about these programs. As a result, federal research is oriented toward strengthening support for its dominant programs rather than improving performance through new strategies and approaches. This conservatism has reduced the supply of potentially disruptive research and development initiatives, leaving major gaps in available knowledge. As student aid policy making has become more dominated by partisan politics, entrenched bureaucracies, and advocacy organizations, the role of research-based analysis has declined. As a result of this decline, the research community's willingness to focus its research efforts on policy-relevant issues has also declined.

DESIGNING AN ACTIONABLE KNOWLEDGE RESEARCH AGENDA AIMED AT IMPROVING STUDENT AID PROGRAM PERFORMANCE

A search for value should underlie the design of the needed research agenda. A few basic principles can help guide this agenda toward the achievement of actionable knowledge, namely relevance, validity, and availability. Relevance refers to whether the research provides knowledge and information that can, if used, increase the likelihood of greater policy success and reduce the likelihood of policy failure or disappointment. Validity is related to the accuracy of predictions of policy performance based on this knowledge. Availability or accessibility refers to whether knowledge and information can be understood by potential users.

In assigning value to components of a research agenda, it is important to note that the results of research can be valuable throughout the knowledge development and policy processes (including design, development, testing, selection, implementation, operation, monitoring, and assessment). The search for value does not imply that each element of a research agenda needs to be directly related to a specific policy decision. In addition, the value of actionable knowledge based on empirical observations or data should not be based solely on whether a study's results are highly statistically significant. Highly statistically significant results are less influenced by random-sampling-induced errors, but less statistically significant results may be less affected by other sources of error,[30] and these results can provide important understandings of policy performance.

This knowledge can be based on student-aid-specific studies and research focused on other domains in which behaviors are, at least in part, analogous to behaviors that underlie actions affecting financial aid impacts.[31] Clearly, research techniques and reporting styles from other domains could be useful in student aid research.

The following types of research can provide actionable knowledge and are thus appropriate candidates for inclusion in an aid-focused research agenda.

Theory and Hypothesis Development and Articulation

As noted earlier, several important issues (e.g., the impact of nonmarket failures on aid program performance and the impact of aid policies on middle school and high school students and their parents) have not been addressed in research on student aid programs. As a result, the theories and hypotheses regarding these issues that are needed to provide a foundation for more directly relevant actionable knowledge are generally unavailable. In these areas, existing research needs to be reviewed and new theoretical research needs to be conducted to build a foundation of well-grounded theories and hypotheses that can inform policy design, development, and implementation processes. This work should include efforts aimed at incorporating theoretical constructs and hypotheses derived from other policy domains.

Empirical Research: Case Studies and Data-Driven Observational Studies

Carefully focused and conducted observational studies based on case studies (of individual as well as groups of organizations) and survey data (from student-aid-specific[32] and other data sets[33]) can provide basic insights and potentially useful actionable knowledge. In addition, combinations of these studies—for example, multiple case studies, multiple data sets, and mixed-methods research—can be particularly informative.[34]

Data-driven observational studies should not be limited to large data sets that are more likely to lead to statistically significant findings. Smaller, more focused data sets are likely to provide more accurate measurements of relevant variables and include complex or nuanced factors that can provide extremely important, policy-relevant insights. Large, operational data sets—"big data"—may lack carefully designed and selected samples, and may not include data on every important factor, but these data can provide important insights, particularly about the tails or outliers of distributions. An understanding of these outliers can provide insights regarding modes of policy failure, unintended and negative policy consequences, and factors that lead to higher levels of policy performance.

Studies based on small data sets, on highly targeted, special small surveys, and on existing data from previous surveys and operational collections, have important advantages that should be considered in the development of a research agenda. These studies are less expensive and are likely to provide results much more quickly.

Policy Design and Prototyping

This style of research is probably the most neglected component of public sector research programs, except in policy domains in which engineering issues dominate. Within most public domains, policy design occurs during the regulatory and operational planning processes, following the highly political program authorization process. In general, the political issues developed during the authorization process continue to affect subsequent program design activities. In addition, many aspects of the program design process take place in conservative bureaucratic contexts that are unsuited for the careful exploration of factors that should influence design choices.

Student aid program design should involve prototyping in which preliminary prototypes are iteratively developed, "built," and tested. This design, build, and test process will both improve program performance and produce knowledge.

Placing policy design and prototyping projects within the student aid research agenda can provide important benefits. These efforts are likely to raise important questions and uncertainties that need to be addressed early and openly. In addition, placing these efforts within the research domain may protect new initiatives from premature opposition by organizations and interests who seek to protect current programs and practices.

Carefully Evaluated and Documented Demonstrations

Demonstrations of existing and newly developed programs and activities can provide important information about performance influencing factors. The utility of the information and knowledge resulting from demonstrations is largely dependent on the quality and comprehensiveness of descriptive evaluations. Regrettably, many researchers discount and/or ignore knowledge gleaned from such demonstrations. Equally regrettably, many of the reviews of program demonstrations are less than thorough and careful. Placing demonstration reviews within a research-oriented, knowledge-development organization has the potential to raise the acceptance, rigor, and utility of these types of studies.

Experimental Studies

Experimental research can involve staged experiments comparing programmatic alternatives in carefully controlled contexts or quasi- or natural experiments, in which naturally occurring events and changes in program characteristics create experiment-like conditions. Relatively few staged experiments have been conducted, in part because they are expensive—they require careful design, sample selection, and data collection efforts. But these studies are also more likely to provide accurate assessments of causal consequences as well as accurate and well-documented data that can be analyzed by a variety of researchers using a range of analytic approaches.

Quasi-experiments tend to be less expensive and less valid. Few quasi-experiments have created well-documented databases that researchers can use in subsequent studies. In addition, most of these studies have failed to address major questions regarding the validity of their data and artificial control groups.

To be more useful, experimental studies should be implemented earlier when policy choices are less constrained and the data resulting from these studies are more likely to be used by a broader range of researchers.[35] To further the value of high-cost, staged experiments, funders should include explicit requirements and funding for activities that increase the sharing of experimentally derived data.

Program Monitoring, Review, and Assessment

Program monitoring, review, and assessment should be a component of a research agenda. These activities should not be solely the responsibility of the operational units of the Department of Education, because reports from such units are likely generally descriptive documents that lack assessment of outcomes, processes, and potential problems.

Program monitoring activities should include but not be limited to operational data—"big data." Monitoring data should include nonoperational surveys and other observations that can provide information patterns of program performance. Student-aid-oriented monitoring efforts should be expanded to include attitudinal studies of participants, nonparticipants, and other individuals and organizations whose behaviors influence program performance. These monitoring efforts should include assessments of contextual issues that appear to be affecting policy and program performance and the development of data sets that allow internal and external researchers to assess performance issues.

TARGETS FOR AN "ACTIONABLE KNOWLEDGE" STUDENT AID RESEARCH PROGRAM

An actionable knowledge student aid research program should be focused on the wide range of issues confronting such aid. Although a development of a full agenda is beyond the scope of this chapter, the following targets should be included in such an agenda:

- *Evaluation of the impact of recent changes in the Pell Grant program and student loan programs.* During the last few years, funding for and operating characteristics of these programs have changed dramatically.[36] The impact of these changes and the simultaneous changes in economic and demographic factors need to be an immediate focus of research.
- *Assessments of the impact of student aid programs on institutional, governmental, and parental behaviors and on opportunities to stimulate more collaborative or complementary behaviors.* These activities should include the development and assessment of alternative strategies for changing middle school, high school, and other precollege programs and services so that they complement and increase the performance of federal student aid programs.
- *Development and assessment of alternative strategies for better targeting of student aid resources on types of students and types of institutions whose behaviors are more likely to be changeable.* This research should focus on particular segments of lower-income youth and young adult populations and less selective, public four-year and two-year colleges.
- *Identification and scoping of future challenges likely to face the aid system, including contextual, demographic, and institutional challenges.*
- *The design, development, and assessment of possible financial-aid-based strategies for improving student persistence and success.*

- *Identification and assessment of possible changes in student aid policy that tailor programs toward new modes and patterns of attendance and instruction.*

Although an "actionable knowledge"-oriented research program focused on these and other important issues confronting the student aid policy makers can help to improve the performance of the nation's student aid system, it cannot, by itself, create this result. This result can only occur with complementary changes in the political, organizational, and institutional processes and practices in which research-based knowledge is used. Strategies for changing this use of knowledge are beyond the scope of this chapter.

2

The Politics of Student Aid

Daniel Madzelan

INTRODUCTION

In 1977, the Pulitzer Prize for general nonfiction went to *Beautiful Swimmers: Watermen, Crabs and the Chesapeake Bay*—a story about the Atlantic blue crab and the men who pursue them. The author, William W. Warner, was a General Schedule employee of the Smithsonian Institution in Washington, DC. He recounts a time in the late 1960s when an extremely poor early-season harvest had Maryland and Virginia officials accusing each other of mismanaging the Bay's resources to such an extent that a committee in the U.S. House of Representatives held hearings on the subject. Predictably, little was resolved, and by the end of the season the harvest had rebounded to its normal level. Warner notes one waterman was heard to remark, "Just goes to show, ain't no one person knows all there is to know about crabs."[1]

In 1978, a recent college graduate, I accepted the offer of a General Schedule position with the U.S. Office of Education, and was assigned to the Bureau of Student Financial Assistance. Entry-level professionals essentially serve a four-year apprenticeship, and during this time I worked on the campus-based student aid programs. Afterwards, and over time, I advanced to more responsible positions within the agency, where I most frequently worked on policy proposals for the programs administered by the Office of Postsecondary Education (OPE). Within a few years it became clear to me—and I hold this view today—that no one person knows all there is to know about federal student aid.

Given the scope and reach of the federal aid program, it is inevitable that a number of people know at least a little about the subject. However, explicit agreement on the program's purpose, which is essential to developing alternative approaches, may be elusive. Indeed, the plain language of the Higher

Education Act (HEA) merely describes each program; it does not offer specific outcomes that each program ought to achieve.

I am unable to identify any particular scheme for accomplishing important objectives. In my experience significant change has typically been a product of exploiting favorable circumstances. Thus the purpose of this chapter is to explore some of the groups and interests involved in making student aid policy, the political challenge of reforming aid to meet evolving federal goals, and the conditions under which policy change has occurred. It is an anecdotal, first-person account of the recent history and development of federal programs. It is not a comprehensive summary of that history, nor do I include advocacy groups or nongovernmental organizations in this discussion. I do draw on more than thirty years as a participant in the policy debates and political battles that shaped the evolution of federal aid programs—first from a back-row seat in the room where such decisions were made, later as a top decision maker in the policy development process.

Along the way I developed an appreciation for a simple fact: the line that separates student aid policy from that which is not student aid policy is neither bright, straight, nor stationary. Said a bit differently, there are many potential avenues for changing federal aid policy—HEA reauthorizations, the budget reconciliation process, administrative or regulatory changes within the executive branch—and many ways to change it, from tweaking eligibility and award formulas to simplifying existing processes to creating new aid policies or modifying existing ones. But each venue and each area of policy is subject to its own web of interests and political preferences, which often makes it difficult to make even small changes to anything already in place, let alone revisit any of the assumptions that underlie foundational programs like Pell Grants, student loans, or tax credits. As such, it has often been easier and more politically palatable to add new things—new grant and loan programs, repayment options, and tax breaks—than it has been to reform existing policies. This dynamic is by no means unique to federal student aid; indeed, federal policy tends to be difficult to change in many different sectors. But the fact that our main grant and loan programs look remarkably similar to how they did at their inception is a mark of how the politics of student aid make it difficult to change, even in the face of new demands.

I am hopeful that identifying past conditions favorable to change will help interested parties recognize future opportunities for achieving desired reforms.

THE PLAYERS

Like all good dramas, the politics of student aid features a cast of decision makers, each of whom brings their own preferences and objectives to policy debates.

The Executive Branch

As the presidency has grown in its power to set the domestic policy agenda for the country, the executive branch has become increasingly central to the direction of student aid. All administrations want to speak with a single voice when it comes to policy matters, but there are multiple voices within the executive branch. Historically, the Executive Office of the President— made up of the Office of Management and Budget (OMB), the Domestic Policy Council (DPC), and to some extent the National Economic Council (NEC)—has played a coordinating role, making sure that the various federal agencies were working to advance the president's overarching domestic policy agenda, or at least not work against it. While occasionally I observed these offices delve into the specifics of a student aid policy proposal, they seemed chiefly tasked with ensuring that specific proposals comported with the administration's overall domestic policy agenda.

Typically, the Department of Education, along with its subject-relevant program offices (Office of Postsecondary Education and Federal Student Aid) and staff offices (Undersecretary, Budget Service, and General Counsel), has had responsibility for developing the details of an administration's higher education policy proposals. The Department's day-to-day administration of existing aid programs makes it well positioned to understand the potential effects of new policy proposals. Increasing White House interest in the details of student aid policy is a recent trend, and perhaps inevitable given the increasing reach of the student aid programs.

Congress

Of course, Congress is the ultimate policy author. Historically, the authorizing committees had—and were very protective of—that responsibility. Until recently, higher education policy was typically revisited every six years via HEA reauthorization, with the authorizing committees in the driver's seat. And despite growing differences between the two parties during the late 1980s and 1990s, higher education policy making was typically bipartisan—the 1986, 1992, and 1998 reauthorization bills each passed with very large majorities.

But things have changed in recent years. First, as budget considerations have come to dominate policy discourse, the budget committees as well as the appropriators have taken on a more visible, obvious, and important role. And as the parties in Congress have become increasingly polarized and closely divided, the rhythm of routine reauthorizations has fallen by the wayside, and higher education deliberations have taken on a decidedly more partisan tone. Both of these developments seem to have shifted power away from the authorizing committees and opened up opportunities for other policy makers to shape aid programs.

The Pell Grant Program

Though the Pell Grant program is obviously not a political actor, its place at the top of student aid priorities makes it an important political force nonetheless. In particular, the Pell Grant maximum has become something of a sacred cow in student aid policy making. As such, when the program has faced a funding shortfall, leaders have often gone to great lengths to preserve the maximum grant, even if it meant tweaking the program in ways that might detract from other goals.

And shortfalls are not uncommon. The Pell Grant program may be unique among all domestic discretionary programs in that its funding is determined largely by annual appropriations, yet for individual beneficiaries—college students—the program performs as an entitlement. Appropriators rely on government estimates—from both the Department of Education and the Congressional Budget Office—of near-term student demand and program costs. The government's program cost estimation models work well in the absence of external shocks, especially increased unemployment due to general economic downturns. When the economy goes south, many out-of-work persons seek to acquire new job skills through postsecondary education, increasing the program's near-term demand. This unexpected increase in demand often outstrips the program appropriation, resulting in a funding shortfall. In general, Pell shortfalls have been addressed partly by supplemental and increased annual appropriations, and partly by economic recovery. Also, due to the forward-funding nature of the program, the Department can borrow from future appropriations to manage periods of funding shortfalls to ensure that every otherwise Pell-eligible student receives his or her grant.

Thus we have a program that swings between periods of expansion followed by periods of "treading water" where leaders scramble to plug shortfalls. But in their preoccupation with finding enough money to maintain the maximum grant, policy makers tend to spend little time thinking about broader reforms that may improve the efficiency or effectiveness of the program overall. As a result, outside of an increasingly large maximum grant and increased participation by individuals seeking to enhance job skills rather than pursuing academic degrees, the program looks much the way it did forty years ago.

Even in the absence of a shortfall, efforts to change programs are often evaluated on the basis of how they will affect a recipient of the maximum grant rather than the effect on the average recipient. A quick story from early in my career illustrates how the best-laid plans can fall victim to this kind of politics. In 1983, the Reagan administration's budget request proposed a significant increase in the Pell Grant maximum coupled with a simplification effort that consolidated several grant programs. The administration proposed a $3,000 maximum Pell—a two-thirds increase over the existing $1,800 maximum—paid for by eliminating the Supplemental Educational Opportunity Grant (SEOG) and the State Student Incentive Grant programs, as well as constraining Pell participation through changes to the student eligibility formula.

At the appropriations committee hearing, a member of Congress asked the Department's principal witness several questions. To paraphrase the exchange:

Member of Congress: What is the current Pell Grant maximum?
Department's Witness: $1,800.
Member: What is the current SEOG maximum grant?
Witness: $2,000.
Member: You propose a $3,000 Pell Grant but will zero out the SEOG
   award—where will needy students get the other $800?
Witness: (No answer).

Never mind the fact that the *average* Pell Grant and SEOG awards at that time were around $950 and $500, respectively, and that the additional money saved from phasing out SEOG would be reinvested in the Pell program.

The Congressman had made his point: maximum grant awards are politically important.

Change Is Difficult, But Not Impossible

In short, reforming student aid is a political challenge as well as a technical one, and political forces make it difficult to change student aid programs. While researchers and policy wonks often believe public policy problems can be "fixed" with technical solutions, those interested in reforming student aid must recognize and anticipate the political barriers to change. Certain aspects of aid programs—the maximum grant award or the student loan interest rate—take on political significance above and beyond their substantive importance for students or families.

But policy change has indeed occurred, and in the remainder of this chapter, I draw lessons about how these various forces have combined to shape student aid policy making in different eras and contexts. At times, leaders have capitalized on opportunities to change things; at others, the best of intentions have run aground on ideological differences and budgetary politics. I discuss these lessons in four sections, each of which describes a particular constellation of actors, preferences, and events that facilitated the efforts to change federal student aid programs.

First up is a description of how a presidential administration recognized and then leveraged a favorable budget and political environment to expand the direct loan program (the Student Loan Reform Act of 1993). Second is a discussion of how presidential leadership forged an approach to college financing via the income tax code. Third is an example of a comprehensive effort by the Department to lead the effort to change student financial aid program policy in the 1992 HEA reauthorization. Finally, I discuss how the increasing attention given to the maximum Pell Grant award over the last several years has prompted a shift toward using the annual budget process to advance policy goals.

Three themes emerge. First, student aid policy change can spring from any of several sources, and the nature and significance of that change is likely determined by its particular source; in recent years, presidential leadership has tended to drive such changes, especially by using the budget process to advance higher education policy goals. Second, conflict between the executive branch and Congress, as well as within both the Congress and executive branch, can impede reform efforts. And third, the nature of student aid policies is at least partly determined by the complex processes and diversity of interests that characterize the framework of these programs.

The resulting picture is of a policy process that is often ad hoc and driven by near-term political exigencies rather than by systematic policy development. Would-be reformers in positions of power should take heed of some hard-won lessons regarding student aid reform. I summarize those lessons in the conclusion.

WINDOWS OF OPPORTUNITY: EXPANDED DIRECT LENDING

Sometimes apparent serendipity is actually savvy politicians taking full advantage of opportunities that present themselves. Federal financial assistance programs are a case in point. For instance, Franklin Roosevelt, with victory certain in World War II, pushed the idea for the original GI Bill, which included education benefits for returning veterans. Similarly, Dwight Eisenhower, fearing the United States was falling behind the Soviet Union in the race for global supremacy, advocated for the National Defense Education Act, which authorized the first generally available federal student aid program—National Defense Student Loans (now Perkins Loans). Finally, Lyndon Johnson's Great Society agenda capitalized on an electoral mandate to enshrine federal support for postsecondary education via the Higher Education Act of 1965, which provided the foundation for the modern federal student aid program.

But presidents have played an increasingly pronounced role in higher education agenda-setting over the past two decades. President Clinton was particularly important in ushering in this evolution. Prior to the 1990s, no president under whom I served had articulated a coherent higher education policy agenda, and congressional leaders exerted the most control over the country's burgeoning student aid programs. Clinton, who promoted a vision of the "opportunity society" on the campaign trail, was the first, in my experience, to pursue a higher education agenda. He proposed—and achieved—an expansion of existing national service programs that would extend college aid to students in exchange for community service. A companion proposal—income-contingent loan repayment—was designed to help public sector and other lower-wage employees repay their student loans, thereby encouraging young people to pursue employment opportunities without regard to salary levels.

But one of Clinton's most far-reaching ideas was his support for a federal direct lending program for student loans. Prior to his inauguration, federal lending to college students was almost exclusively the domain of banks and other private lenders. These private organizations provided loan capital to student borrowers, and those loans were federally guaranteed.[2] The participation of private lenders in the guaranteed program was voluntary—the government encouraged lenders' participation through a set of financial incentives, including a market-based rate of return on their loans and guaranteed repayment in case of borrower default.[3] Notably, the 1992 HEA Amendments provided for a five-year demonstration program to test the feasibility of the government acting as a student loan lender, a policy proposal initiated by the George H. W. Bush administration.

After taking office, President Clinton promoted a more aggressive phase-in of direct lending such that it would replace the guaranteed loan program within five years. Doing so provoked a predictable response from the private lenders who benefited from the existing program and their allies in Congress. As a representative of the American Banker's Association remarked at the time, "We expect this plan to be just another failure in the Government's long history of taking over private enterprises."[4] Then Republican Jim Jeffords wondered aloud, "I question whether the hiring of 600 employees at the Department of Education will save money. It just doesn't make sense."[5] Expanding direct lending was hardly a slam dunk.

However, a fortunate confluence of three developments enabled President Clinton to push his shift toward direct lending. First, the Federal Credit Reform Act of 1990 (FCRA) changed the way the government priced its credit programs for program budget purposes. Previously, federal budgeting rules were heavily biased toward guaranteed lending because only the subsidies, not the loan principal, were considered government expenses. In contrast, direct lending required the government to "book" the entire loan principal at the time of origination in addition to any subsidy costs.[6] Under those rules, a $100 direct loan would show up in the budget as a cost of $100 even though the government would recover most of that money (with interest). The cost of the same amount lent as a guaranteed loan would only reflect the interest benefits paid by the government on behalf of students to private lenders and the cost of covering defaulted loans. FCRA recognized that the initial principal provided was not a true cost to the government because most of it would ultimately be repaid. Under the new law, pricing federal credit programs, whether guaranteed or direct, reflected the government's cash flows associated with the loans, thus eliminating the inherent bias toward guaranteed lending that prevailed up to that point. With the change, direct lending was no longer recorded as a cost to the government, but could indeed be a source of government revenue so long as the government acted as a responsible, profitable banker and "borrowed low and lent high."

The second development was Clinton's support for income-contingent loan repayment. Candidate Clinton called for reforms that would lessen the student loan repayment burden for graduates pursuing national and community service opportunities. This could be accomplished by tying loan repayment amounts to borrowers' incomes. Congress had created such an income-contingent program on a limited scale via a demonstration project in the 1986 HEA reauthorization. Four years later, however, the Department ended the program because it learned that individuals were extremely reluctant to disclose their personal income information. As such, a more successful income-contingent repayment policy required an independent, third-party verification or disclosure of a borrower's income. Direct lending by the Department of Education could facilitate such income verification via the Internal Revenue Service. After all, the IRS would deal with a single entity (the Department), not the thousands of guaranteed student loan lenders that existed at that time.

Third, the economy was weak in the early 1990s, and federal budget deficits were becoming a larger concern. Years of deficit spending were finally being noticed. Because the new FCRA accounting rules cast direct lending as a potential revenue source for the government, direct lending became an attractive option for policy makers increasingly preoccupied with the deficit and looking for ways to increase revenue without raising taxes.

The stage was set for a move to direct loans. First, FCRA made direct lending "affordable"—even profitable—with regard to the federal budget. Second, direct lending facilitated the third-party income verification, which was necessary for an efficient income-contingent repayment program, which in turn was critical to President Clinton's goal to promote public service. Third, Congress, and the country, had finally noticed the perils of continual deficit spending. A portion of the savings realized from expanding direct loans, which would also reduce spending in the guaranteed loan program, could be used for deficit reduction.

Seeing an opportunity, the Clinton administration formulated a plan to move to 100 percent direct lending within five years, and with the help of congressional allies built it into the 1993 budget reconciliation bill. A portion of the $6 billion savings went to student borrowers in the form of reduced loan costs, and the remainder went to deficit reduction.

Despite Democratic majorities in both houses of Congress—by a margin of forty-one seats in the House and six in the Senate—passing the 1993 reconciliation bill was not a given. Vice President Al Gore cast the deciding vote in an evenly split Senate. Similarly, a single vote ensured passage in the House. The Department then moved aggressively to enroll institutional participants in the expanded program's first year.

Windows of Opportunity Can Close—Quickly

The effort to expand direct lending also speaks to the difficulty of preserving and implementing controversial policy changes from one period to the next. Like most new laws, the passage of the legislation was only part of the battle; opponents found ways to frustrate the growth of direct lending. When the composition of Congress changed considerably a year or so later, the prospects for a complete transition to direct lending dimmed.

In 1994, Democrats lost their majority in the House of Representatives for the first time since the 80th Congress (1947–1949), and Republicans also took control of the Senate. While the new majority did not directly undo the growing direct lending program, they did identify a way to stunt its growth: slow federal funding for administrative costs because, after all, administering the program is an expense for both institutions and the Department of Education.

The original direct loan legislation provided for an administrative fee of ten dollars for each direct loan originated by a participating institution. But the new Congress eliminated it, hoping to dampen institutions' enthusiasm for converting to the direct loan program. In 2006, Congress eliminated mandatory funding for the Department's direct loan program administrative costs, subjecting these expenses to the annual appropriations process and the political battles therein. With Congress frustrating its growth, the direct loan program never achieved more than one-third of total federal student loan volume prior to the Obama administration.

Despite a fortunate confluence of events, the direct loan program was never fully phased in as originally intended. However, the partial implementation of the program in the mid-1990s did provide a toehold for the program and allowed policy makers to learn from the experience. The complete shift to direct lending in 2010 has its roots in this early program. Still, in 2010 it was turmoil in the financial markets and not intentional federal policy that pried a new window of opportunity wide open.

PRESIDENTIAL SWAY LEADS THE WAY: TAX CREDITS FOR HIGHER EDUCATION

When people think of financial aid, they tend to picture Pell Grants and student loans. But over the past fifteen years the federal government has delivered increasing amounts of higher education assistance via the tax code. While these tax credits are sometimes lost in discussions of student aid reform, the truth is they have grown to be a major part of the aid portfolio. When enacted in 1997, the Hope Scholarship and Lifetime Learning tax credits were expected to provide some $36 billion in college tuition assistance to lower- and middle-income families over ten years. Today, with the expansion in the program—now called the American Opportunity Tax Credit—provided by the American Taxpayer Relief Act of 2012, *annual* tax expenditures of $18 billion provide college tuition assistance, largely to middle-income families, due chiefly to generous income eligibility thresholds.

While tax credits for education were scarcely a new idea, targeted tax cuts were viewed much less favorably than general tax relief in the post-1986 tax reform era. But presidential leadership and growing pressure from middle-class voters were challenging that view. Prior to the mid-1990s there was little in the income tax code that provided benefits to families for higher education expenses, and those that did exist were complicated, narrowly focused, and underutilized, accounting for little in the way of federal tax expenditures. That would change.

In early 1996, with an election looming, President Clinton's campaign recognized that addressing college affordability would appeal to middle-income voters. The president's Council of Economic Advisors advocated using income tax credits to provide higher education financial assistance. In June of that year, the president announced two new tax credits: the Hope Scholarship for students and the Lifetime Learning tax credit for families.

The Hope Scholarship—rarely called a tax credit—would be a refundable tax credit available to students for each of the first two years of college. The goal, repeated often, was to "make the 13th and 14th years of education as universal to all Americans as the first 12 are today."[7] The value of the "scholarship" would be up to $1,500, indexed annually for inflation, and made available to "good" students, that is, those who maintained at least a B average and were drug free.

But within the administration some questioned the need for a new tax expenditure that would accomplish many of the same goals as the existing Title IV programs. In particular, the government already had in place a student aid delivery system in the Pell Grant program. So, the argument went, it would be more efficient—and popular with the higher education community—to simply add the resources to the Pell Grant program given its well-established delivery apparatus that was already familiar to colleges and universities. But others in the administration, perhaps more sensitive to the mood of new majorities in both houses of Congress, advocated an approach that could be sold to the legislature, and the American people, as a tax cut. In short, the administration signaled it would consider a Republican plan for a tax cut, but only if that plan cut taxes for families with college-age children. And this time, there would be no phase-in period for the new policy; the administration had learned with direct lending to insulate its policy from any near-term political turnover.

So, in summary, the administration proposed two tax credits: a Hope Scholarship valued up to $1,500 per student for undergraduates in their first or second years who were enrolled at least half-time, had maintained a B average, and were drug free; and a Lifetime Learning tax credit equal to 20 percent of a family's out-of-pocket tuition and fee expenses, up to a maximum of $10,000 of such expenses, for any postsecondary education or training by one or more family members. The Lifetime Learning tax credit covered undergraduate education beyond the second year as well as graduate-level and professional education, and even as little as a single course. These two tax credits, along with several smaller provisions including income deductibility of student loan interest paid, would account for the largest share of what would become the Taxpayer Relief Act of 1997 (TRA) that provided approximately $98 billion in tax relief.[8]

But the new credits were not without their detractors within the higher education community. The administration's proposal placed a new requirement on colleges and universities to report tuition and fee payments received from each of their students to the IRS. Furthermore, the initial proposal would have required schools to also determine and report whether each student had met the grade point average (GPA) requirement. Institutions complained vigorously about both administrative requirements. Higher education advocates were also quick to point out that though the administration was positioning the Hope Scholarship as a college access program, federal programs that promoted college access—most notably Pell Grants—made no reference to a student's academic qualifications. Any Hope Scholarship GPA requirement, they argued, would decrease college access.

The Treasury Department, however, was not about to back down on the new reporting requirements. Several months earlier a study from the Government Accountability Office (GAO) estimated that about one-fourth of all payments under the Earned Income Tax Credit were improperly claimed by taxpayers. The administration could ill afford a similar result—at best waste and abuse, and at worst outright fraud—in the administration of a new tax credit priced at $36 billion over ten years.

Ultimately the administration ceded the GPA requirement, but held fast to requiring reporting of tuition and fees paid. At a House Ways and Means Committee hearing on the proposed higher education tax credits, Treasury Secretary Robert Rubin played down the reporting requirement by holding up a pencil and a piece of paper and remarking that all colleges would need to comply with the new reporting requirement "will be the cost of a pencil, and then you qualify and you put it in an envelope and you send it back."[9]

But even with the reporting requirements, concerns about fraud and abuse in tax credit programs remained. The administration revised the proposed policy to eliminate the refundable aspect of the Hope Scholarship and use those savings to increase grant amounts for Pell recipients, reasonably confident that the higher education community would view this policy change, and the resources it freed up, favorably. The 11 percent increase in the maximum Pell Grant (to $3,000 from $2,700) would be, by far, the largest single-year increase since the program became available to all undergraduate students.

The higher education advocacy groups were generally (if not always enthusiastically) supportive of the administration's tax plan, though I recall the land-grant colleges and universities being especially supportive. They noted that it had been about twelve years since the Social Security education benefits for college students had been phased out, and that those resources had not been replaced. Additional student benefits delivered through the income tax system would certainly be better than no additional resources at all.

On the other hand, the American Association of State Colleges and Universities (AASCU) was decidedly cool to the idea and thus needed to be convinced that the policy was in the best interests of their students. I was asked to represent the Department at a meeting in the Roosevelt Room at the White House between senior administration and AASCU staff. The august setting was no accident—I sure was impressed by the display of Cavalry Flags from the Battle of San Juan Hill—and it sent a clear signal as to the purpose of the meeting: time to get on board with the president's proposal. Though I was not present for similar meetings with other higher education interests, it seems likely that the administration would have used this strategy to woo other groups into the coalition. Ultimately, the community—including the state colleges—would not pass up a significant increase in federal benefits for college students and their families, even if those benefits were not delivered through their colleges and universities via the existing student aid system.

It became increasingly clear that the administration's proposals for higher-education-based tax relief, coupled with proposals to balance the budget, would be successful. The president's efforts to use college tuition assistance as a means to provide tax relief to middle income taxpayers culminated in August 1997 when Clinton signed the Taxpayer Relief Act.[10]

Unintended Consequences?

The Clinton administration was intent on expanding college tuition assistance for families, and they chose to capitalize on the tax-cutting mood in Congress by using the income tax system to deliver new benefits. To insulate them from changes in the future, the Hope and Lifetime Learning tax credits were created as permanent parts of the income tax code. It took several years for increasing numbers of eligible taxpayers to learn of and claim these new benefits now available to them. As take-up rates increased, so did concerns that the complexity of the tax credits led fewer taxpayers to take advantage of them than were eligible to do so. The GAO as well as the Treasury Inspector General for Tax Administration issued reports citing this programmatic inefficiency. The incoming George W. Bush administration indicated it would look into streamlining the various tax benefits for higher education.

But the Bush administration made little effort; officials quickly realized that because of existing budget constraints, any modification to the tax credits that would reduce taxes for some would necessarily increase taxes for others. Even if policy makers were able to find the correct balance between winners and losers, being labeled an advocate for higher taxes was too big a political risk.

The Obama administration "solved" this dilemma by increasing tuition tax credits for taxpayers who were currently eligible, expanding the income eligibility thresholds to provide benefits to additional taxpayers, and giving it a new name—the American Opportunity Tax Credit (AOTC). But unlike the Hope Scholarship, the AOTC is not permanent, and it requires periodic renewal at substantial cost. If the latest round of policy making is any indication of things to come, though, the AOTC will be around for a while—it was renewed through 2017.

The Clinton administration pursued permanent change to the tax code because it preferred that approach to providing financial assistance to families with college students over one reliant upon the uncertainties of the annual appropriations process. But over time, it has become enormously difficult to change these tax policies, even if the goal is to redirect federal resources to the Title IV programs or simplify the system. As such, providing college tuition assistance via the tax code has hampered efforts to promote necessary changes in other programs.

THE DEPARTMENT FLEXES ITS POLICY-MAKING MUSCLE: THE 1992 HEA AMENDMENTS

In today's polarized Congress, where actual policy making is at a premium and battles between the legislative and executive branches have become the norm, it can be easy to forget instances when the policy-making process actually functioned quite well. The 1992 HEA Amendments were a case in point.

Overall, the congressional effort on the 1992 amendments is often remembered for its focus on establishing new compliance and oversight provisions to combat abuses in the for-profit college sector and guarantee the integrity of the programs overall. In the several years prior to reauthorization, Senator Sam Nunn, chair of the Permanent Subcommittee on Investigations, held a series of hearings focused on abuses in the federal student loan program. The subcommittee's 1991 report included a number of statutory, regulatory, and administrative recommendations to improve the integrity of the program, most of which were addressed by both the House and Senate education committees and included in the 1992 HEA Amendments. The administration was generally supportive of the subcommittee's efforts and welcomed the additional authorities and tools provided in the 1992 amendments to address program abuses.

But the 1992 amendments included other, less visible (but no less important) policy changes driven by the Department. The run-up to the 1992 amendments was one of just two instances I can recall where the administration submitted a comprehensive, fully formed legislative proposal to Congress, complete with a transmittal letter addressed to the Speaker of the House of Representatives and President *pro tempore* of the Senate.[11] Then Secretary Lauro Cavazos, rumored inside the Department to have been embarrassed that the Department sat out the previous reauthorization in 1986, decreed to staff—and the higher education community—that the Department would be the first to submit a reauthorization proposal in advance of its expiration in 1991.

Secretary Cavazos asked Deputy Education Secretary Ted Sanders to lead the Department's efforts. In true corporate fashion, Sanders established a hierarchy of thirteen "working groups" that would advise the Reauthorization Task Force, comprised of political officers and the most senior career staff. The working groups were made up of personnel from the Department's higher education program and staff offices. Each of the thirteen working groups was assigned a particular topic to explore, using their findings to recommend policy alternatives to the task force, which in turn would recommend policy positions to top-level administration officials. Over a period of several months the working groups were free to consult with external experts, conduct research as appropriate, and periodically report their progress to the task force.

I was asked to cochair the working group charged with examining the statutory need-analysis formulas. At the time, there were two formulas for each student: the Pell Grant Index, which determined eligibility for and size of the grant, and the Expected Family Contribution, which determined eligibility for Stafford loans and the three campus-based aid programs.[12] By 1991, in an early expression of the now-perennial desire to simplify the Title IV programs, the higher education community was coming around to the idea that two measures of ability to pay for federal student aid eligibility purposes was one too many.

In reauthorizing the HEA, Congress accepted the notion that a single need analysis for federal purposes was indeed desirable and feasible, and it established a single formula in the statute. While the enacted formula was not identical to that developed by the working group and included in the Department's legislative proposal, it was very similar. More importantly, supporters of the single-formula approach indicated to the Department that

Congress would likely not have acted had the Department not proposed and strongly advocated for it. At least in this instance, the Department seized a leadership role and actively advanced its policy position through the legislative process.

The single need-analysis formula, along with several additional provisions, were policy "wins" for the Department in the 1992 HEA reauthorization. The single formula provided the essential framework for future efforts to further simplify the student aid programs and application processes. The wins reflected a concerted effort to shape policy on the part of the agency charged with implementing those policies. The Department's 1991–1992 HEA reauthorization effort was an agency-wide effort that resulted in a comprehensive legislative proposal. And by so doing, the Department established itself as a policy development partner rather than simply the implementer of Congress's policies.

Intra-agency Divisions

This is not to say that all within the Department speak with one voice on student aid. Each time there is a change in presidential administration a new crop of political appointees comes in to work with the career staff. Differences on policy inevitably emerge. Even in 1991–1992, when the Department was engaged in an agency-wide policy development process, there were important divisions among the staff. For instance, I can say without reservation that one topic—merit aid—consumed the bulk of the task force discussions. My cynical view: because there was no existing merit-based program authorized by the HEA, any particular task force member need not be bound by any facts or prior experience in vigorously discussing the benefits (naturally there were many) and drawbacks (of course there were few) of merit aid. There was scarcely any input from the career staff on merit aid proposals inasmuch as there was no existing program from which to draw experiences. Career staff, for the most part, simply observed the task force develop its merit aid proposal, albeit with some small sense of bemusement and aware of its likely fate in Congress.

Even though Representative William Ford, chairman of the House Education and Labor Committee, repeatedly and vigorously stated his opposition to merit aid at the federal level until all need-based aid programs were fully funded, the task force insisted that the Department's reauthorization bill include a proposal for Presidential Merit Scholarships. In response, Congress did include a somewhat similar program that featured a financial need component for recipients—Presidential Access Scholarships. However, the program was never funded. The incoming Clinton administration was far more concerned with the persistent Pell Grant funding shortfall it inherited. A few years later, Congress repealed the program's authority.

POLICY MAKING VIA THE BUDGET PROCESS: STUDENT AID REFORM IN AN ERA OF FEDERAL DEFICITS

As student aid programs have grown in size and their footprint has expanded, they now make up an increasingly large chunk of the federal budget. And as the politics of the federal deficit have heated up, the budget has become a particularly powerful policy-making tool. Policy makers have come to rely on the budget process—both budget proposals from the administration and budget reconciliation bills in Congress—to advance policy preferences.

Prior to the Reagan administration, the annual program budget development process seemed more traditional in approach: each agency indicated its priorities—proposed funding levels—within the framework of existing programs. The Reagan administration took a new stance: instead of simply requesting funding for current authorities, it would use the annual program budget process not only to demonstrate its priorities (funding requests) but also to advance new policy proposals that required amending the authorizing legislation.[13]

This Reagan-era innovation was a sign of things to come. Political turnover, an increasingly polarized two-party system, and a growing budget deficit have led leaders to adopt a dollars-and-cents approach to policy—one focused on how much programs cost and how changes could reduce costs or pay for the expansion of other programs—rather than more fundamental questions of policy design and reform. Indeed, the political turnover of the 1990s and the first decade of the 2000s led to a loss of institutional memory in Congress, with members steeped in policy details and used to working across the aisle replaced by polarized, less well versed freshmen. These legislators, in turn, would rise to positions of power on the committees. As a result, I think, focus shifted to the price tags for particular policy options. After all, a bottom-line, dollars-and-cents approach is far easier to grasp than trying to understand how to make programs more effective or how program participants might respond to a specific policy change.

For most of the first decade of the 2000s a routine HEA reauthorization became less of a sure thing, leading policy makers to find other avenues for influencing student aid policy. In 2003 the HEA expired, and its automatic one-year extension came and went. The House Education and the Workforce Committee did manage to report a bill in 2005 (H.R. 609), but it was never brought up for debate on the House floor. During this time the Senate did nothing, though I do not know the reason. Perhaps it was a sign of increasing polarization between the parties. Or possibly it was the fact that a reconciliation bill—with several HEA program amendments—was already in the legislative pipeline. At any rate, prior to August 14, 2008, when the president signed the Higher Education Opportunity Act reauthorizing the HEA, there had been sixteen separate statutory extensions of the HEA authority.

The extensions were simply that—temporary extensions of the general HEA program authorities. However, there were several instances of legislation, typically budget reconciliation acts, that changed student aid policy, established new programs, modified requirements for existing programs, reduced subsidies to certain federal program participants, or changed eligibility requirements for program beneficiaries. In effect, these efforts—the Taxpayer-Teacher Protection Act of 2004, the Higher Education Reconciliation Act of 2005, and the College Cost Reduction and Access Act of 2007— were "mini-reauthorizations" that were used to implement policy priorities of the administration and Congress. The Senate's limited debate and simple up-or-down vote for budget reconciliation bills have made this legislative vehicle the preferred way to change student aid policy.

Similarly, the Obama administration pushed its student aid policy priorities using the stimulus package along with the budget reconciliation process. The American Recovery and Reinvestment Act provided significant funding for Pell Grants—sufficient to retire yet another shortfall and provide a $5,350 maximum grant. The following year, savings generated from moving to direct lending (as mandated by the Health Care and Education Reconciliation Act of 2010) provided additional funding for the Pell Grant program.

It is worth noting that advancing new policies and programs via reconciliation did little to change the design or delivery of existing programs like Pell Grants or Stafford loans. Instead, they either added resources to those programs or layered new programs on top of existing ones.

With the permanent elimination of the subsidies to private lenders, expanding future Pell Grant benefits will have to be paid for by new revenues or redirecting resources from other program areas. Policy makers still raid the student loan program to fill Pell shortfalls, but now student borrowers are being asked to forgo long-standing benefits, including interest-free grace periods. Even Pell Grant recipients have been asked to shoulder some of the load; they now face lifetime limits on the amount of Pell Grants they can receive.

CONCLUSION

Over the thirty-plus years I was involved in the student aid policy-making process, I participated in a number of notable student aid reform efforts, several of which I have shared in this chapter. I learned that while windows of opportunity seemingly opened serendipitously, it was really a confluence of events that policy makers recognized and exploited. Direct lending picked up speed in an environment characterized by political desire (expand community service opportunities), political imperative (reverse deficit spending), and technical change (pricing federal credit programs). Similarly, the Hope Scholarship and Lifetime Learning tax credits emerged from a general political desire to provide tax relief to families, but presidential leadership challenged the prevailing tax policy preferences and successfully pushed for a program of targeted tax relief. In both instances, leadership positioned these reform efforts as responsive to contemporary political interests.

I further learned that it is important to ensure that a particular policy is sustainable. This did not occur in the initial expansion of direct lending, when the political environment changed before the policy was fully implemented. However, when such sustainability is ensured, other issues may arise that are difficult to address. For example, any effort to modify the higher education tax credits would likely result in claims of tax increases if all current beneficiaries are not held harmless for any change to the tax policy.

The Department's 1992 HEA reauthorization effort arose from what I would characterize as an institutional desire to regain lost prestige and become a must-be-reckoned-with participant in the policy development process. Early in the process of "getting back in the game," the Department positioned itself as a principal "change driver" for the reauthorization effort. It tapped its broad, internal programmatic expertise and understanding of the interests of its various constituencies. And the nature and significance of the results it achieved—spanning the entirety of the HEA—demonstrated that it deserved that standing.

In recent years, as the preferred legislative approach for addressing policy concerns has shifted to the budget process, it has become easier to layer new aid programs on top of old ones than to consider reforming foundational programs like Pell and student loans. Part of this is likely due to the decentralized nature of higher education in this country, and its diversity and varied interests. But it is also certainly due to increasing fractiousness within Congress. In general, HEA reauthorizations have tended to be models of consensus; these bills typically passed each chamber with very large majorities. But consensus implies a coalition, which is difficult to forge within an increasingly polarized group like the current Congress. So we become more inclined to a least-common-denominator approach, like the Pell Grant maximum or student loan interest rate, which makes it even more difficult for reform-minded members of Congress to accomplish fundamental change.

As Mr. Warner's waterman might say, "And that's about the smart of it."

3

The Promise of "Promise" Programs

Rodney J. Andrews

INTRODUCTION

In November of 2005, anonymous donors committed to pay all mandatory fees and up to full tuition at any public college or university in Michigan for high school graduates who both resided in the Kalamazoo Public School District and were enrolled continuously in Kalamazoo public schools for a minimum of four years. Known as the Kalamazoo Promise, this extraordinary act of philanthropy has garnered national attention.[1]

In the years following the introduction of the Kalamazoo Promise, a number of Promise Programs—essentially place-based scholarships offering access to postsecondary education—have emerged. This chapter attempts to assess the potential of Promise Programs to become a significant innovation in financial aid. However, despite the popularity of these programs, there is little published evidence of their efficacy as a means of encouraging postsecondary education. Therefore, I also examine research on scholarship programs similar to the Promise Programs, with the aim of carefully extrapolating from those results to garner insight on the potential impact of the actual Promise Programs. For example, I consider lessons from state merit aid programs—such as Georgia's Helping Outstanding Pupils Educationally (HOPE) Scholarship—which offer funding to students from particular states who meet a set of academic performance criteria, and the DC Tuition Assistance Grant (TAG) program, which offers assistance to qualified residents from the District of Columbia.

The chapter begins by defining Promise Programs, drawing on distinctions that have developed over time and focusing in particular on the programs that are locally implemented, as these community-based endeavors have generated the most interest. The following section describes the mechanisms by which Promise and similar scholarship programs affect postsecondary outcomes, namely access, retention, and completion. Issues related to both the scalability and sustainability of the Promise Programs are discussed in the third section, followed by a general conclusion.

WHAT IS A PROMISE PROGRAM?

Like state merit aid programs, Promise Programs offer funding to qualified residents of a particular area. However, Promise Programs serve areas that are smaller than a state, and the qualifications they impose are generally less restrictive than merit-based scholarships. It should be noted that the presence of "Promise" as part of the name is not sufficient to establish the taxonomy for Promise Programs. For example, the state of West Virginia has a program called the West Virginia Promise; however, it is a merit-based program with minimum cutoffs for both GPA and the SAT or ACT.[2] Therefore, for the sake of coherent discussion, I define a Promise Program as a local place-based scholarship program that offers near-universal access to funding for postsecondary education. Information about this funding reaches potential recipients well in advance of the decision to acquire postsecondary education. The Upjohn Institute maintains a list of programs that meet these criteria.[3]

Newer Promise Programs have clearly been influenced by the Kalamazoo Promise. PromiseNet is a network of communities that invest in education and economic development through place-based scholarship programs.[4] In 2008, soon after the establishment of the Kalamazoo Promise, PromiseNet convened its first annual conference, bringing together communities that had already established Promise Programs with others that were interested in doing so. As a sign of how inspirational the Kalamazoo Promise has proved, the conference was held in the city of Kalamazoo. The newer Promise Programs share some of the features of the Kalamazoo Promise but possess a considerable array of differences. The following subsections summarize the key elements that constitute Promise Programs and also describe some of the differences in these elements across the various programs.

Locations of Promise Programs

The areas that Promise Programs serve are restricted to a particular set of schools. Typically the schools whose students are eligible for funding are located in either the same school district or else the same city or county. The canonical example is, of course, the Kalamazoo Promise, which defines the set of potentially eligible students as those who both reside in and attend schools that are part of the Kalamazoo Public School District for a minimum of four years. The Pittsburgh Promise, the Detroit College Promise, and the El Dorado Promise and Leopard Challenge programs (both located in Arkansas) are examples of Promise Programs that, like Kalamazoo, serve particular school districts.[5]

There are several Promise Programs serving schools that are located in the same county. For example, the Jackson Legacy Program is potentially available to students who graduate from high schools in Jackson County, Michigan. Students in Pinal County, Arizona, are potentially eligible for the benefits of the Promise for the Future Scholarship Program.[6]

The Peoria Promise—in Peoria, Illinois—and the College Bound Scholarship Program—in Hammond, Indiana—are examples of Promise Programs that are available to students who graduate from high schools located in those respective cities. The Peoria Promise lists as one of the eligibility requirements that students come from a residence that pays property taxes to the city of Peoria.[7]

There is a significant range in the geographical and demographic characteristics across the areas that Promise Programs serve. Norphlet, Arkansas—home of the Leopard Challenge—is a rural area that has fewer than one thousand individuals, with more than 90 percent of the residents being classified as white. In contrast, Pittsburgh—home of the Pittsburgh Promise—is among the thirty largest cities in the country, with approximately 66 percent of the population classified as white and 27 percent as black.[8]

Promise Programs are not uniformly distributed across the country. Michigan is home to seven Promise Programs. Many of the Promise Programs are located in communities in Midwestern states or in states that are fairly close to the Midwest. This is unsurprising given both the influence and location of the Kalamazoo Promise.

Types of Postsecondary Institutions That Are Subsidized

Most Promise Programs follow the Kalamazoo Promise and offer access to funding for public postsecondary institutions that are close to the locations served by the programs. For example, the Leopard Challenge subsidizes tuition for eligible students to attend any public college or university in Arkansas. In some cases, such as the Pittsburgh Promise, eligible students may also attend a private college or university located in the relevant state.

While Promise Programs tend to subsidize the tuition cost of postsecondary institutions that are close to the locations they serve, there are interesting differences across programs in the set of institutions they are willing to subsidize. Some Promise Programs offer to subsidize the tuition cost for a more restrictive set of postsecondary institutions, which in certain cases may be limited to a single institution. For example, the Peoria Promise subsidizes the cost of attending Illinois Central College; the Great River Promise only applies to Phillips Community College, in eastern Arkansas; and the Promise for the Future program only applies to Central Arizona College.[9] Still other Promise Programs direct their funding toward a limited selection of postsecondary institutions. Examples include the Jackson Legacy Program that provides scholarships for eligible students who attend Jackson Community College, Spring Arbor University, or Baker College of Jackson, and the Bay Area Commitment Fund that offers funding to eligible students who attend either Saginaw Valley State University or Delta College.

Finally, there is a subset of Promise Programs that place few, if any, restrictions on the set of eligible postsecondary institutions. The El Dorado Promise allows students to use the funds at any four-year college or university that is accredited by one of six regional accrediting organizations. The Arkadelphia Promise allows recipients to use the funds at any college or university in the United States.[10] The Sparkman Scholarship Foundation—located in Sparkman, Arkansas—provides scholarships for students that defray tuition costs and mandatory fees at any accredited two-year or four-year public or private college, university, or trade school in the United States.[11] It should be noted that Promise Programs that allow the scholarship to be used anywhere in the United States serve areas with small numbers of students.

Promise Programs seek to increase the level of human capital in the communities they serve, making the communities more attractive to employers by providing them with an adequate supply of skilled and able workers. This pathway, however, relies on recipients of the scholarships remaining in the area after completing their education. This is an issue. College-educated individuals are more mobile.[12] Increasing education could possibly decrease the likelihood that individuals remain in the community. I assert that one of the primary reasons that Promise Programs subsidize tuition for colleges that are close to the areas they serve is the belief that being educated "locally" increases the likelihood that the resident will remain in the area upon graduation. Extant research, however, does not provide clear support for this notion.

State merit aid programs offer a similar rationale—that having state residents complete their educations in-state increases the probability that they will remain in-state after completing their education—to justify subsidizing in-state postsecondary institutions. However, research that examines a number of state merit aid programs suggests that where students go to school has a relatively small effect on where they locate after graduation.[13] Further, some research estimates that for every hundred students that are induced by state merit aid programs to remain in-state (rather than pursue their education out of state), only ten will remain in the state ten to fifteen years later.[14] Taken together, this suggests that Promise Programs should be conservative with respect to the expectation that providing funding for postsecondary education at local institutions will have a large impact on local labor markets.

Eligibility Criteria and Funding Determination

The primary criterion to qualify for funding from Promise Programs is that students possess a substantial connection with a community and with its associated schools. The substantial connection usually consists of enrollment in the designated set of schools in the community as well as residence in the community. Promise Programs require that students both continuously attend the schools within a community for a minimum amount of time and graduate from designated high schools in the community. The magnitude of the benefits that students receive from the Promise Programs is generally a function of the amount of time that a student is continuously enrolled in schools affiliated with a Promise Program. Below, I provide examples of how various Promise Programs determine funding as a function of continuous enrollment.

Graduates of Kalamazoo public schools who both lived in the district and attended Kalamazoo public schools continuously for at least four years are eligible for funding. Eligible graduates who have been continuously enrolled since kindergarten receive 100 percent of the tuition to any public college or university in Michigan. Eligible graduates of Kalamazoo public schools who have been continuously enrolled since the first, second, or third grade will have 95 percent of their tuition subsidized. Eligible graduates whose continuous enrollment begins at grades four through nine will receive a subsidy where the percentage of tuition obeys the following formula:

$$0.95 - 0.05(G - 3)$$

where G is the grade the student began continuously attending Kalamazoo public schools. Students whose period of continuous enrollment begins after the ninth grade receive no funding.

Other Promise Programs use subsidy schedules that follow the Kalamazoo Promise in making the subsidy a declining function of continuous enrollment. The Arkadelphia Promise, the El Dorado Promise, and the Leopard Challenge use the same subsidy schedule as the Kalamazoo Promise. The Northport Promise offers full tuition for students who attend Northport, Michigan, public schools for twelve or thirteen years. The percentage of tuition subsidized then declines by 5 percent per year of decreased continuous attendance for ten, nine, eight, seven, and six years; five and four years of continuous attendance result in a 50 percent subsidy. The Pittsburgh Promise, on the other hand, imposes a simple continuous enrollment requirement that requires students to both attend and graduate from either a high school in the Pittsburgh Public School District or an approved charter school since the ninth grade. The Legacy Scholars Program in Battle Creek, Michigan, provides up to sixty-two hours of credit at Kellogg Community College for students who have been continuously enrolled in either the Battle Creek or Lakeview Public School District since the eighth grade until graduation. Students who begin their continuous enrollment in the ninth and tenth grades qualify for 46.5 credit hours and 31 credit hours, respectively.

Promise Programs generally require that students reside within the community served by the Promise Program. Again, this requirement originates from the Kalamazoo Promise. The Kalamazoo Promise provides the educational subsidy to innervate development in Kalamazoo. The benefits of the Promise Programs can be substantial. For example, if a student eligible for the Pittsburgh Promise was accepted at the University of Pennsylvania, an ivy league school, the Pittsburgh Promise would pay more than one-fourth of the $39,000 yearly tuition (during the 2012–2013 academic year).[15] The residency requirement secures these benefits for the community. However, the residency requirement is not universal across Promise Programs. Beginning with the graduating class of May 2013, the El Dorado Promise no longer requires scholarship recipients to reside in the El Dorado Public School

District. Transfers from neighboring districts that meet the other requirements will now be eligible, too.[16]

Promise Programs impose minimal academic criteria at the high school
level. The Pittsburgh Promise, Sparkman Promise, and Arkadelphia Promise
require a 2.5 grade point average. The extent of the academic requirement
at the high school level for most Promise Programs is simply that students
graduate from the appropriate high schools.

At the postsecondary level, Promise Programs generally require that
students maintain a full course load—at least twelve credit hours—and
make reasonable progress toward a degree or certificate. A minimum grade
point average of 2.0 is generally required; however, there are exceptions. For
example, the Arkadelphia Promise requires that recipients also qualify for
the Arkansas Challenge Scholarship, a merit program funded by proceeds
from the Arkansas lottery. Since a student must maintain a 2.5 cumulative
grade point average in order to remain eligible for the Arkansas Challenge
Scholarship, the Arkadelphia Promise in effect requires a 2.5 cumulative
grade point average as well.

Generally, Promise Programs require students to complete a Free Application for Federal Student Aid (FAFSA) form. This requirement is intended
to reduce the cost of maintaining a Promise Program. This issue is addressed
in more detail later in the chapter.

The criteria discussed so far in this section are common to most Promise Programs, but many such programs also specify nonstandard eligibility
criteria. For example, the Jackson Legacy Scholarship requires students to
perform twenty hours of community service per year. The Northport Promise requires scholarship recipients to earn twenty points per year where the
points are awarded for raising funds for the Northport Promise.[17] The Peoria Promise requires students to write and send a thank-you letter by the
first of July or the student loses her funding.

The College Bound Program is a particularly interesting case. It requires
that students perform forty hours of documented community service per
year. In addition, this particular Promise Program only grants funding to
students from families that own homes in Hammond, Indiana. An explicit
goal of the College Bound Promise is to increase home ownership and thus
strengthen the community.[18]

Promise Programs are designed to benefit the community. Both the
common and the uncommon eligibility criteria are designed to explicitly
make the individual benefit—the funding for postsecondary education—a

function of a substantial connection to the community and increase the likelihood that the community benefits from the investment.

HOW ARE PROMISE PROGRAMS FINANCED?

One of the factors that make the story of the Kalamazoo Promise a compelling one is the funding by a group of generous anonymous donors. The magnitude of the gift—as of 2012, the Kalamazoo Promise has paid out approximately $35 million for approximately 2,500 students—is noteworthy.[19] Promise Programs are so appealing because many are funded via donations. Donations are gifts, and gifts are a source of funding for education that is not as contentious as, say, tax revenues.

Sources of Funding

Promise Programs differ in the amount of funding they offer, with the Kalamazoo, El Dorado, and Pittsburgh programs being among the most generous. For example, the El Dorado Promise—which was established by the Murphy Oil Corporation in January 2007 with a $50 million investment—will pay up to the highest annual resident tuition at an Arkansas public university toward tuition and mandatory fees for students to attend any accredited two-year or four-year institution in the United States. The Pittsburgh Promise will pay up to $10,000 annually, with the total to not exceed $40,000, for eligible students to attend any accredited postsecondary institution in Pennsylvania.

The Pittsburgh Promise was established in 2006. The program gained momentum in December of 2007 when the University of Pittsburgh Medical Center gave the Pittsburgh Promise $10 million directly for the 2007–2008 academic year and also offered a nine-year, $90 million challenge grant. To leverage the first $10 million of the challenge grant, the Pittsburgh Promise had to raise $15 million by June 30, 2009.[20] They raised more than $15 million after seventeen foundations donated $13 million and thirty-one corporations and organizations donated $2 million. More than 500 individuals also donated approximately $200,000. The Pittsburgh Promise set a goal to raise $250 million over ten years; after four years they had already raised $160 million.[21] This ability to attract funding explains why the benefits offered by the Pittsburgh Promise have grown from $5,000 per year to $10,000 per year. Promise Programs that secure large initial endowments are the most generous and the most stable.

It is interesting to consider why corporations might want to fund Promise Programs. There are two primary reasons. First, corporations require skilled workers. If Promise Programs increase the education level of local workers, then it is less costly for firms to acquire skilled labor, as a local supply of viable workers is readily available. Second, this type of investment enhances the public image of a corporation and generates goodwill.

Not every Promise Program is so lucky as to begin operation with a huge initial investment. In what follows, I describe some Promise Programs whose funding sources are not so reliable and whose benefits are often curtailed as a result. For example, consider this description of the Detroit College Promise:

> The Detroit College Promise is a grassroots version of the Kalamazoo Promise for Detroit and Detroit Public Schools. We began in spring 2008 and differ from the Kalamazoo Promise because we serve many more students, we have a more challenged school district, and we need to raise the money ourselves for scholarships and administration.[22]

The Detroit College Promise offers funding for eligible students to attend any public college or university in Michigan. Eligible members of the class of 2013 receive a maximum of $600 for one semester only.[23] The Detroit College Promise is funded through donations. It has not been as successful at raising donations as some of the Promise Programs mentioned earlier. As of April 25, 2013, only one donor had donated at least $50,000 to the Detroit College Promise.

The Peoria Promise Foundation is a 501(c)(3) public charity and is funded by donations. The Peoria Promise requires $1 million per year to continue its efforts; the goal of the foundation is to establish an endowment to secure the future stability of the program. A Promise Program that cannot attract adequate donations risks being unable, in the future, to honor the promises that they make today.

Funding instability is not limited to Promise Programs that rely on donations. The College Bound Scholarship, which offers scholarships to eligible students of homeowners in Hammond, Indiana, is funded via gaming tax revenues received from the Horseshoe Casino. The program was established in 2006. The College Bound Scholarship is slated for a ten-year run and will be evaluated at the end of that period. Due to the vicissitudes of the gaming revenues, Hammond's city officials are currently searching for a more stable source of funding that will carry the program forward.[24]

For comparative purposes, table 3.1 summarizes information on some of the more noteworthy Promise Programs.

TABLE 3.1   Noteworthy Promise Programs

Program name	Eligibility	Funding amount	Funding source
Kalamazoo Promise	Reside in Kalamazoo Public School District; ≥ 4 years of Kalamazoo Public Schools; graduate from high school in Kalamazoo Public School District	Percent of tuition paid is a function of length of attendance in Kalamazoo Public School District	Anonymous donors
Arkadelphia Promise	≥ 4 years of continuous enrollment in Arkadelphia Public Schools; graduate from Arkadelphia High School; receive an Arkansas Lottery Scholarship; maintain Arkansas Lottery Scholarship eligibility throughout college	Percent of tuition paid is a function of length of attendance in Arkadelphia Public School District; based on highest public tuition in Arkansas	Ross Foundation and Southern Bancorp
El Dorado Promise	Minimum of 4 years enrollment in El Dorado Public Schools	Percent of tuition paid is a function of length of attendance in El Dorado Public Schools; maximum amount payable is up to highest resident tuition at an Arkansas public university	Murphy Oil Company
Pittsburgh Promise	Reside in Pittsburgh Public School District; graduate from designated high school in Pittsburgh Public School District; 90% attendance rate; minimum 2.5 GPA	Up to $10,000 per year, no more than $40,000 total	Corporations and foundations in and around Pittsburgh—e.g., University of Pittsburgh Medical Center and the Heinz Endowments
Detroit College Promise	Live in Detroit in grades 9–12; attend and graduate from Detroit Public Schools. For 2011–2014 classes grades 9–12 must have registered by 12/3/2010; class of 2015 and beyond must register by 12/1 of 9th grade	As of 2013, minimum is $150 and maximum is $600; one semester only	Corporations, foundations, and individuals—e.g., PathologyOutlines.com, Inc. and Hermelin Family Support Foundation

Last-Dollar Programs

The Kalamazoo Promise is a first-dollar program; that is, funds from the Kalamazoo Promise are applied before other sources of aid are considered. In this regard, the Kalamazoo Promise is the exception rather than the rule among Promise Programs, which are mainly last-dollar programs. This means that after all other sources of aid have been utilized, the funding from the Promise Programs will be applied to the remaining balance. Last-dollar Promise Programs require students to complete the FAFSA form. These programs want students to exhaust all other sources of funding before they use funding from the Promise Programs. This is a means of both reducing the burden on the Promise Programs and permitting them to "stretch their dollars." The Arkadelphia Promise advances the idea of "last dollar" a bit further. It specifies that a student must qualify for the Arkansas Challenge Scholarship before the Promise funds can be applied. This requirement potentially reduces the financial burden on the Arkadelphia Promise both by ensuring that there is an additional source of funding in place and by limiting access to the Promise funds due to academic requirements associated of the Arkansas Challenge Scholarship.

HOW DO PROMISE PROGRAMS IMPACT POSTSECONDARY OUTCOMES?

One of the primary goals of the Promise Programs is to increase postsecondary access, retention, and completion for the students from the places that the programs serve. Promise Programs are relatively new; therefore, there is little direct research on their impact on postsecondary outcomes. Indeed, the Degree Project, the first randomized controlled trial that attempted to assess the effects of a Promise Program on educational outcomes, was launched on a single cohort of Milwaukee public school ninth graders in November 2011.[25] This evaluation examines the effect of the intervention on postsecondary outcomes and provides letters to recipients to keep them informed of the necessary steps to allow a smooth transition to postsecondary education. The Promise Programs considered in this chapter, however, intend to provide funding for multiple cohorts within the same community; therefore, the findings from the the Degree Project may not generalize to the Promise Programs discussed above. Still, research on scholarships similar to the Promise Programs, with appropriate consideration of salient differences, can provide insight on how the Promise Programs may affect postsecondary outcomes.

Access

Postsecondary education is costly and becoming more expensive every year. The average of the sum of published tuition and fees for public four-year and two-year colleges has increased by 31 percent and 18 percent, respectively, beyond the rate of inflation during the five-year period from 2007–2008 to 2012–2013. The salient feature of the Promise Programs is that they provide funding for students to attend a designated set of post-secondary institutions. Reducing the cost of attendance for a particular set of schools should increase the likelihood that potential attendees consider these schools. Quasi-experimental estimates suggest that students from the Kalamazoo Public School District are more likely to consider public colleges and universities in Michigan after the introduction of the Kalamazoo Promise.[26] In addition to impacting *where* eligible students go to college, Promise Programs may increase the likelihood of attending an institution of higher education more generally. The elimination of the Social Security Student Benefit Program suggests that an additional $1,000 in grant aid increases the likelihood of attending college by 4 percentage points.[27] This in turn suggests that Promise Programs, which offer near-universal access to funding that need not be repaid, can impact attendance.

The informational content of Promise Programs provides a mechanism via which college attendance is increased. The presence of a Promise Program in a community brings additional attention to postsecondary education and promises that there will be a source of funding for it well in advance of when it is needed. There is evidence that early notification increases the likelihood that a student will engage in postsecondary educational activities.[28] Research suggests that skills and attitudes develop dynamically over the life cycle—that is, engaging in certain behaviors early in life is strongly associated with similar behaviors later in life.[29] This implies that early interventions that positively impact attitudes toward college early in the life cycle tend to produce behaviors that make college attendance more likely. Soft skills—which include goals and motivations—that are developed early in life have been shown to contribute causally to success later in life.[30] Promise Programs provide early notification to both students and families that postsecondary education is a viable option. The promise of funding for post-secondary education expands a student's feasible set of options, which in turn can motivate the pursuit of loftier educational goals and promote the development of behaviors necessary to achieve those goals. Promise Programs can thus impact college attendance by serving as an informational catalyst that initiates this dynamic process.

Some of the more convincing evidence of the potential of Promise Programs to impact postsecondary attendance comes from considering popular merit aid programs—for example, Georgia's Helping Outstanding Pupils Educationally (HOPE) grant. The merit aid programs considered here have characteristics that are similar enough to those of the Promise Programs to warrant a comparison between the two. First, the merit aid programs have both a geographical and residential component. Eligible students must reside in the state and graduate from a high school in the state to qualify for the funding. And second, the funding from the merit aid programs applies to a specific set of schools; generally, these are public universities that are located within the state.

Quasi-experimental estimates suggest that Georgia's HOPE scholarship increased the attendance of eighteen- and nineteen-year-old students in Georgia by 7 to 8 percentage points.[31] A more comprehensive analysis of a number of merit aid programs suggests that they increase the probability of college attendance among college-age youths by 5 to 7 percentage points.[32] These findings suggest that the Promise Programs may impact the likelihood of attendance; however, the applicability of these findings to Promise recipients should be viewed with caution because the merit aid programs tend to have higher academic requirements at the high school level. This means that the recipients of funding from Promise Programs and merit aid programs may differ in academic ability—a factor that directly impacts college attendance.

Retention

How would the Promise Programs impact retention? A potentially important channel for the Promise Programs is time, or more accurately, the allocation of time across activities. The Gates Millennium Scholars Program is a national scholarship program that is designed to improve access to and success in higher education for low-income, high achieving minority students by providing them with full tuition scholarships and nonmonetary support. Quasi-experimental estimates of the program's effects show that it reduces the number of hours that college students work per week.[33] Working while enrolled in college has an adverse impact on first semester academic performance and reduces retention.[34] The amount of time spent studying increases academic performance.[35]

Taken together, this research suggests that a factor that allows a student to reduce the amount of time working and increase the amount of time spent studying could increase both academic performance in college and the likelihood of being retained. Promise Programs reduce the cost of post-secondary education, which may reduce the need to work. The first-year retention rates of the 2008 and 2009 cohorts of Pittsburgh Promise recipients is higher than the first-year retention rate among students in the 2008 and 2009 ACT national samples.[36] An independent study of the El Dorado Promise finds that 91 percent of El Dorado freshman complete at least one year of college.[37] These findings are consistent with the proposed mechanism outlined above.

Completion

The ultimate goal of the Promise Programs is to increase the number of local students who complete a degree. Unfortunately, the Promise Programs, on the whole, haven't been in place for a sufficient amount of time to properly assess their impact on college completion. A common metric of college completion is the six-year graduation rate. The earliest Promise Program started in 2005. There are an insufficient number of cohorts of Promise Program recipients to estimate the effects of these Programs on completion. However, Promise Programs provide recipients with resources, and the same mechanisms that suggest that the Promise Programs enhance retention also suggest that the programs may enhance completion.

The evidence on the impact of other financial aid programs on college completion is mixed. A study that examines the 1982 elimination of the Social Security Student Benefit program provides evidence that a decline in funding decreased the years of completed education; this finding is particularly compelling as the benefits from this program were directed to students of low socioeconomic status.[38] West Virginia's merit aid program has been shown to increase the likelihood of finishing college.[39] An empirical analysis of the impact of merit aid scholarship programs introduced in Arkansas and Georgia in the early 1990s finds that these programs increase the share of young people with a college degree by 3 percentage points from a base of 27 percent.[40] However, a subsequent study that investigates merit programs in those same states but uses a larger sample and appropriately adjusts the standard errors, produces estimates that are substantially smaller in magnitude and statistically insignificant.[41] Research examining the Adams Scholarship—a merit scholarship in Massachusetts—finds that the offer of funding reduces completion rates for students who just qualify for the funding, and posits that the reduction in completion rates for these students is due to the scholarship inducing students to attend colleges of lower quality. That the evidence on the impact of the programs discussed above is mixed suggests that other factors besides the availability of funding influence the likelihood of completion.

ARE THESE PROGRAMS SUSTAINABLE AND SCALABLE?

Sustainability

The cost of postsecondary education is increasing and the amount of postsecondary aid provided by states is decreasing.[42] If a Promise Program serves an area with a changing population, then it is difficult to forecast the demand for funding. This confluence of factors in conjunction with a potentially fragile funding base suggests that Promise Programs are not sustainable.

This problem is mitigated in locations with a relatively stable population and a strong funding base—for example, El Dorado, Arkansas, and the Murphy Oil Corporation—or in a location with a population that is changing but has access to an adequate supply of donors who are willing to give large sums of money. The nature of the Promise Programs places the risk on the programs. The Pittsburgh Promise, which has proven to be successful, had to raise $15 million from other donors to access the funds from the challenge grant offered by the University of Pittsburgh Medical Center. It requires resources to raise resources. It is not clear that the types of communities that are interested in the Promise Programs possess the infrastructure necessary to generate sufficient donations to secure the promise of funding for postsecondary education.

The State of Michigan implemented an innovative program that adopts some of the elements of the Promise Programs while not relying solely on the beneficence of donors. On January 31, 2009, then Governor of Michigan Jennifer Granholm signed legislation that led to the creation of ten Promise Zones in high-poverty areas.[43] The legislation provides scholarships to students who live in a designated Promise Zone and graduate from any of its public, charter, private, or parochial high schools. Students are required to fill out the FAFSA form. The Promise Zone program relies on three sources of funding to cover tuition and mandatory fees: a Pell Grant or other need-based aid, private contributions, and revenue from the state tax increment financing mechanism.

Tax increment financing establishes the Promise Zone as the tax district; all property subject to the State Education Tax—which includes residential, commercial, and industrial property within the zone's borders—is part of the district's tax base. Once a base year is established, half of the growth in the State Education Tax that occurs from that year forward is allocated to fund the scholarship. If the value of the taxable property increases, it leads to growth in State Education Tax revenue; a portion of the revenue is then captured by the Promise Scholarship. Relative to traditional Promise Programs, the Promise Zone model offers an additional source of funding. All else being equal, diversifying the funding sources enhances the sustainability of the Promise Zones relative to Promise Programs that rely solely on contributions.

Scalability

The same issues that make it difficult to sustain Promise Programs also make these programs difficult to scale. Increasing the number of students served by a Promise Program while holding benefit levels constant requires additional funding. The financial structure adopted by most Promise Programs—namely, dependence on a willing pool of donors—precludes the programs from being scalable. Without additional funding, if a Promise Program endeavors to scale up, it must reduce the amount each recipient receives. This introduces a choice: is it better to offer reduced funding to a larger number of recipients or a more substantial aid package to a smaller number of recipients? To offer insight, I examine how Georgia—the first state to implement a merit aid program—dealt with these issues.

Georgia's HOPE scholarship began in 1993 and is fully funded from lottery receipts. The requirements were fairly straightforward: any Georgia resident with a 3.0 grade point average from an accredited Georgia high school qualified for the funding. A student had to maintain a cumulative GPA of 3.0 to continue receiving the scholarship. The student's cumulative GPA was checked at regular intervals—30, 60, 90, and 120 attempted credit hours. Students who graduated from high school before 1993 were not eligible for the scholarship. Initially the HOPE scholarship was for two years, did not make allowances for books and mandatory fees, and was unavailable to families with at least $100,000 in income per year. Within five years of the program's inception, however, changes were implemented that increased its costs: the amount of funding was increased, the scholarship was expanded to cover books and mandatory fees, the income cap was lifted, and home-schooled students who met the residential requirements as well as residents who graduated before 1993 became eligible for funding if they maintained a 3.0 average in college after the first year.

The number of HOPE recipients grew rapidly. For the fiscal year 1993–1994, there were 42,796 recipients who used $21.4 million in scholarship funds. In the 2010–2011 fiscal year, there were 256,938 recipients who used $747.7 million in funds. Officials in Georgia recognized that the growth in scholarship outlays threatened to outstrip the lottery revenues. In response, several steps were taken to stem the growth in scholarship expenditures.

In 2004, the state of Georgia passed legislation designed to ensure the solvency of the HOPE program. House Bill 1325 tightened the GPA requirements at the high school level, transferred the responsibility of computing the high school GPA to determine initial HOPE eligibility to Georgia's state finance commission, implemented an additional GPA check after the spring semester, and added a provision that allowed the amount of the book coverage to decrease if lottery revenues declined.[44] In May 2007, the new HOPE high school GPA calculation and transcript exchange project was implemented. The downturn in the economy—which affected lottery revenues—prompted further changes to the scholarship, and it was estimated that the program would be insolvent by 2013.

In 2011, Georgia's legislators passed House Bill 326, further overhauling the HOPE scholarship. The changes were twofold. First, while the traditional scholarship and its requirements were kept intact, the scholarship amount was reduced and only covers up to 90 percent of tuition. Second, the Zell Miller Scholarship, which requires a high school GPA of 3.7 and either an SAT score of at least 1200 or an ACT score of 26, was created. The Zell Miller scholarship covers full tuition, but requires that the student maintain a cumulative GPA of 3.3.[45] Mandatory fees and books are no longer covered. For the fiscal year 2012–2013, the number of scholarship recipients was 178,742 and the scholarship expenditures totaled $409.2 million, steep declines relative to 2010–2011 fiscal year.

The HOPE scholarship began modestly, increased in generosity, and relaxed the eligibility criteria. There was huge growth in demand, and the scholarship attempted to accommodate the additional students. The revenues that fund the HOPE scholarship derive from an activity that is sensitive to economic conditions. Solvency concerns prompted lawmakers in

Georgia to both adopt tougher standards and reduce scholarship benefits. Furthermore, Georgia created a scholarship that offers a larger reward for academically exceptional students. These experiences are relevant because Promise Programs face these same issues. For many Promise Programs, the source of funding is subject to uncertainty and the changes in demand for funding are difficult to anticipate. In addition, Promise Programs lack the resources and expertise of an entire state to commit to solving these issues. Georgia's experience with the HOPE scholarship point to some of the issues and difficult choices that the Promise Programs may face.

Operating at a larger scale—without additional resources—means that benefit levels must decline. There are tradeoffs. Is it preferable to offer less so that you can support more students? How does a Promise Program decide to allocate the burden of extending benefits? Must it impose higher academic requirements to temper usage? If so, then does this not abrogate the promise of near-universal access to postsecondary funding? There is evidence that the Promise Programs are aware of this issue. The Northport Promise states explicitly that, should enrollment in its schools exceed 250 students, it reserves the right to impose a more stringent geographical requirement to ration funding.

CONCLUSION

There are social returns to education. A one percentage point increase in the supply of college graduates raises high school dropouts' wages by 1.9 percent and increases high school graduates' wages by 1.6 percent.[46] Education increases both civic participation and engagement.[47] The returns to education are economically significant.[48] The difference in monetary returns for those with postsecondary education relative to those who lack postsecondary education has increased over time.[49] Education benefits both society and the individual, and the penalty for lacking education is growing. Given the benefits of postsecondary education, the salient question is this: what can we do to make postsecondary education more accessible? Decades of research and many papers have shown that funding affects educational attainment, but money alone is not enough. The Kalamazoo Promise makes me cautiously excited because I think that the Kalamazoo community understands. In Kalamazoo, it appears that they have managed to galvanize the community and coordinate the efforts of multiple actors—for example, local churches and schools—around the idea of putting students in a position to take advantage of the opportunity that the Kalamazoo Promise affords.[50] Educators in Kalamazoo believe that the school climate has changed positively as a result of this program.[51] The Kalamazoo Promise and the efforts of local organizations on its behalf have given the residents of Kalamazoo a greater awareness of the value of education, and a community that values the education of its residents is more likely to increase program success.[52]

The Kalamazoo Promise is transparent and simple: graduate from high school and you get money for college. A transparent financial aid process increases the likelihood that the individuals who need it most—the poor, minorities, and the less educated—will access the funds.[53] The Kalamazoo Promise demonstrates that coupling accessible scholarship funding and significant community involvement makes it possible to deliver a program that enhances the educational trajectories of those who need it most.

The difficulty is that it is not clear that one can count on this level of community engagement in all locales. Is this level of community involvement unique to Kalamazoo? Is community engagement a function of the magnitude of the initial outlay? Is there a set of initial conditions that make a Promise Program a particularly effective strategy for communities? We do not know the answers to these questions, but as the various Promise Programs move forward, I am hopeful that we will learn them.

The Promise Programs are a bold attempt to marshal local resources to defray the costs of postsecondary education. Given the funding structures adopted by many Promise Programs, however, I conclude that they do not yet offer a replicable and sustainable path to postsecondary education. Still, they do provide examples of elements that should influence financial aid innovation going forward. Transparency is important; families and students should understand how to access funding that is available. The source of funding must be stable. The Promise Programs that have stable sources of funding are in a position to honor the promise of postsecondary education, alter the expectations that surround it, and incentivize a community to provide the complementary services that are necessary to put students in a position to take advantage of the opportunity.

Cost is not the only barrier to a postsecondary education, but it is the barrier that is most easily recognized. The Promise Programs are a clarion call exhorting policy makers to acknowledge that the effectiveness of financial aid may be inextricable from the local context.

4

From FAFSA to Facebook

The Role of Technology in Navigating
the Financial Aid Process

Regina Deil-Amen and Cecilia Rios-Aguilar

INTRODUCTION

The evidence is clear: a college education is key to promoting economic mobility.[1] Yet, despite decades of financial aid policy, substantial gaps in college access by income level and race remain.[2] It is well known that a major impediment to increasing college enrollment among underrepresented and low-income students is the lack of information about actual college tuition levels, financial aid opportunities, and how to navigate the admission process.[3]

While research and policy have begun to address the need to streamline the financial aid application process, critical gaps in our knowledge about how the current financial aid regime affects students (and their families) remain, particularly those in community colleges. We know, from the work of researchers at MDRC, that low-income community college students are at particular risk of not persisting to earn a certificate or degree, often because of competing priorities, financial pressures, and inadequate academic preparation for college.[4]

What we do *not* know is the role technology plays in the financial aid process, or what role it could play if leveraged effectively to address the concerns above. Various Web sites, Web-based desktop tools, and Web-based and smartphone apps have recently emerged to connect students and their families with financial aid tools. Similarly, colleges and universities with limited resources are utilizing various technologies to reach as many students as possible. While these entrepreneurial efforts are a welcome sign, much less is known about how they are implemented within specific institutional contexts and how they impact students' ability to access and navigate the financial aid process.

The goal of this chapter is twofold. First, we discuss the role of technology in the process of accessing financial aid. We profile and discuss evolving efforts that use various technologies to enhance opportunities for community college students to communicate about and navigate the financial aid process. Second, we identify a specific social media intervention—Schools App—and analyze data to examine if and how it can effectively serve the needs of disadvantaged students.

Our chapter explores the ways technologies like social media, apps, and Web-based resources can be effective, yet challenges assumptions about their "power" as successful tools in financial aid reform. More specifically, we argue that reformers interested in leveraging technology to improve the financial aid process must ground those efforts in a clear understanding of students' (and their families') life circumstances and how these intersect with institutional contexts. Technology can play a role in improving access to financial aid, but it is no substitute for solving some of the structural issues that limit the effectiveness of aid programs, including the failure of application procedures and program requirements to reflect the needs of nontraditional students. As we argue below, technology-enhanced solutions are meant to supplement well-designed federal and state policies, not replace other needed meaningful reforms that can ease and improve existing processes.

HOW MIGHT TECHNOLOGY MATTER?

Higher education leaders, policy makers, and entrepreneurs have increasingly used technology to disseminate and deliver information to prospective and current students. From the reliance on institutional Web sites to the digitization of the FAFSA to new innovations in social media and mobile technology, more information about college-going, including financial aid, is flowing to students through these technologies.

In particular, social media has reshaped the way college students communicate generally and within their college community. Martínez-Alemán and Wartman describe how, beyond just transmitting information, college students use social media to connect with each other, to generate and consume content, and thus to experience college in both real and virtual communities.[5] Also, the 2009 Community College Survey of Student Engagement found that the more students use social networking tools to communicate with other students, instructors, and college staff regarding coursework and other academic purposes, the higher their levels of engagement.[6]

Simultaneously, as documented in a recent survey, colleges have begun to embrace various technologies to communicate with students, potential students, alumni, and broader communities.[7] But while both students and institutions utilize various forms of technology more and more, we know less about how these new technologies affect student access and success, particularly for community colleges. For instance, very little is known about how community colleges find and allocate resources to develop coherent institutional strategies around social media, about how community colleges train staff and faculty to use these tools, and about the value and impact of social media on institutional processes and student outcomes (e.g., providing financial aid information, marketing, academic success, retention, and graduation).[8]

IS TECHNOLOGY THE SOLUTION?

Embracing technology as a solution to access and completion problems is built on fundamental assumptions that the technology

- may reduce the need to interact face-to-face;
- is a cost-effective tool;
- requires minimal resources from colleges to maintain it;
- provides accurate and accessible information to all; and
- will have willing students that are equally savvy users.

As technology has increasingly taken hold in higher education, researchers have had opportunities to unpack these assumptions. And although the literature on technology-enhanced solutions is scant, the idea of using technology to address the challenges of the financial aid process is not new. Kristan Venegas studied how policy makers, researchers, and practitioners were eager to use the Internet as a resource for financial aid processes.[9] It was expected the Internet would allow students to connect with financial aid and admission offices in a more proactive way. Similarly, EDUCAUSE described how federal and state governments also began to transition toward Web-based registration and application processes.[10]

In line with this early thinking, observers often assumed college Web sites presented a low-cost opportunity to effectively and efficiently provide thousands of students with essential information about colleges, programs, and financial aid. Moreover, evidence suggests that community college students want and expect college Web sites to provide such information.[11] However, the usability of community college Web sites remains a serious issue. Recent evidence suggests that community college students had a difficult time using the Web site to calculate cost of attendance; only one in ten students knew the approximate cost of full-time attendance.[12] Furthermore, although students could find standard information about tuition and programs offered, they often were unable to use this information to answer questions about program duration and how much college would actually cost.[13]

These usability problems are particularly troubling in light of how much students appear to rely on Web sites for information about financial aid. Data from a survey of 13,000 current college students and recent graduates of two- and four-year programs who received financial aid show that the majority of these students receive information about financial aid primarily from college financial aid offices and Web sites.[14] Web sites that are poorly designed but widely used may cause students to miscalculate the duration and cost of college, which in turn may lead them to make inappropriate financial plans or erroneously decide that being a full-time student is not feasible.

Luckily, students today have more avenues to access information than institutional Web sites. Consequently, choosing an effective pathway to distribute financial aid information is essential to ensuring that it reaches today's college students.[15] But despite the attention paid to social media, new evidence suggests that only a small proportion of college students (16 percent) would prefer to receive financial aid information via social media. Actually, students showed interest in obtaining financial aid information through other technologies such as e-mail, grant/loan specific databases, and grant/loan specific Web sites.[16]

The financial aid access problem is more convoluted and multifaceted than current initiatives have acknowledged and has more layers than technological solutions alone can address. Serious efforts have been made to streamline the financial aid process. Though Bettinger and his colleagues find that some of these initiatives have shown some success,[17] the most successful efforts seem to involve *face-to-face* support for low-income individuals filling out their taxes and FAFSA form. Such evidence contradicts the assumption that technology alone presents a feasible solution.

Furthermore, technological solutions will likely prove inadequate to overcome structural problems in the financial aid process. There is a need to move beyond simplifying the FAFSA and reducing the time it takes to apply for and receive aid and enroll in college. Specifically, current and future efforts need to address several facets of the financial aid process that intersect with specific features of postsecondary institutions and policy, including limited and overworked advisors designated to guide students through the steps and to process the applications; the link between academic performance/progress and aid qualification; and the prioritizing of particular family forms embedded in financial aid criteria.

Though social media is certainly not a silver bullet, particularly in the absence of other reforms, it does differ from previous efforts to leverage technology: the interactional component of social media facilitates person-to-person contact and communication in ways that other technologies are not able to accomplish. Can the dynamic nature of social media, paired with policy/institutional reforms, better address some of these more interactional aspects of the financial aid "problem" discussed above? We think so, but caution that technology alone cannot compensate for the difficulties students face in navigating the financial aid process as a whole, especially if policies are not well designed. However, an often unrealized benefit of using social media is that it provides an opportunity to observe, or make visible, student interactions that reveal their struggles, which is an important tool to aid reform.

PROFILE OF TECHNOLOGICAL SOLUTIONS RELEVANT TO FINANCIAL AID

Fortunately, over the past four years, entrepreneurs have been actively building new technology-enhanced tools to help students navigate the college-going process, many of which focus specifically on the financial aid process. Tables 4.1 to 4.3 present information on various technologies—Web sites, Web-based desktop tools, games, and Web, mobile, and Facebook apps—that address, either directly or indirectly, some component of the financial aid process. More specifically, some solutions were built to provide various types of *users* (e.g., students, families, high school counselors) with concrete information on the cost of attending specific colleges. Such social media solutions are described in table 4.1. The solutions featured in table 4.2 are some that provide students (mainly targeting under-resourced and

TABLE 4.1   Technological solutions for financial aid/college funding

Name	My College Dollars	FAFSA Community*	College Abacus*	Raise*	Studentaid.ed.gov
Type of technology	App/Web tool	Web site	Web site	Web app	Web site
Description	Facebook app and desktop tool designed to help match students' interests with available scholarships	Resource to improve the accessibility of federal financial aid to low-income and first-generation college students	Web-based tool that combines net-price calculators from more than 4,000 institutions into one easy-to-use system	Designed to help students (as early as 9th graders) to get scholarships to pursue higher education	Provides information to make it easier to acquire money for higher education
Founded/Designed by	Get Schooled Foundation/College Board/MTV	NerdScholar	Whitney Haring-Smith and Abigail Seldin	Preston Silverman	U.S. Department of Education
Purpose	To make it easier to help students find money for college	To help students achieve their college goals by improving financial literacy, providing FAFSA tutorials, and offering guidance for students with special family circumstances and dependency overrides To provide an online community for parents and students to obtain support and information on the FAFSA, paying for college, student loans, and managing money	To help students and families learn about how much financial aid to expect from different schools, based on individual student circumstances, before students apply or any financial aid determination is made	To rethink and expand the way students earn scholarships for higher education through the provision of microscholarships based on achievements such as: perfect attendance, high engagement, community service, doing well on STEM courses, etc.	To provide information to make it easier to get money for higher education
Target user(s)	Students	Students, parents, and counselors	Students, families, and counselors	Students, families, and counselors	Students and families
Cost	Free	Free	Free	Free	Free

*Winner of the College Knowledge Challenge contest launched by the Bill and Melinda Gates Foundation and College Summit.

first-generation college students) with guidance in getting to college—to prepare and plan for college and to improve their college search and choice. Solutions featured in table 4.3 promote positive college-going and college persistence behaviors (e.g., rigorous coursework, high grades, engagement). Most of the tools in tables 4.2 and 4.3 incorporate financial aid aspects into their platforms. Below we discuss some of the advantages and challenges of these technologies.

Advantages of the Technological Solutions

First, most of these solutions target students, though some require or encourage parent or counselor participation (e.g., Raise Labs, FAFSA Community, College Abacus, Tractus Insight). Second, nearly all solutions are free to students and families, with costs absorbed by colleges or high schools (e.g., MyCoach, College Abacus, and Schools App). Third, these apps exploit different aspects of students' existing networks—for example, most were built either as Facebook apps or to enable login through Facebook or other social media, allowing students to share their activities with friends/peers and create ties of support (with counselors, teachers, and college advisors) that may help them acquire information and accomplish their goals.[18] Without access to counselors or other sources of high-quality financial aid information, poor students are less likely to apply for college or submit the FAFSA.[19] FAFSA Community, College Abacus, Raise Labs, Schools App, MyCoach, Tractus Insight, and Logrado have intentionally built a role for mentors/advisors/counselors into the technology.

Some of these solutions go beyond passive information dissemination to encourage and reward success behaviors. For instance, some apps (MyCoach, Raise Labs, GradGuru) include a system of incentives, known as badges, that reward behaviors like completing certain tasks on time and attending classes regularly—behaviors known to improve college enrollment and success. For example, through Raise Labs, high school students can set up an account and have opportunities to earn weekly microscholarships totaling anywhere from $1,000 to $15,000 over the course of their high school careers. These features provide incentives for students to engage in actual college preparation and planning behaviors.

Challenges of the Technological Solutions

First, all of these solutions require students (and, in some instances, their families) to have Internet access and, in some cases, Facebook accounts,

TABLE 4.2 Technological solutions to inform college preparation, planning, search, fit, and choice

Name	College Board	ConnectEDU: ConnectI College and Career Planning Portal	CollegeGO*	PossibilityU*	Applyful*	Tractus Insight*
Type of technology	Web site	Web site + Webinars	Mobile app	Mobile/Web app	Web app	Web app
Description	Provides information about college testing, planning, and readiness, including how to "get help paying for college"	Allows educators, parents, and students to collaborate in developing an academic, financial, and future career plan that aligns with student aspirations	Interactive interface that presents 25 steps for lower-income, first-generation students to take in order to find, apply to, and attend the right college for them using game, video, and search features to help students plan their college journey	Designed to help students find the college that fits—academically, socially, and financially, including creation of a financial strategy	Designed for college applicants to collect and share information with one another on the road to choosing a college	Guides students through process of building strong college application lists; provides data about individual colleges such as need- and merit-based aid awards, average net price by income bracket, and convenient links to net price calculators
Founded/Designed by	College Board	ConnectEDU	College Board	Cambium Enterprises	Mikala Streeter and Tony Zanders	Lori McGlone and Mike McGlone

Purpose	To ensure that every student has the opportunity to prepare for, enroll in, and graduate from college	To provide interactive Web tools for users to access cost calculators and understand key components of the college financial aid process. To provide users with a budget plan tool that offers indebtedness scenarios for families to examine based on career choices after completion of a postsecondary degree	To improve college access for underserved students and connect students to college opportunity and success	To personalize each student's search, to visualize important trade-offs in the process, and to persuade them to stay on time/on track	To manage research during the application process, encourage informed decision-making, and develop peer groups	To provide innovative features that help students discover colleges that are a strong fit and keep them engaged in the college search
Target user(s)	Students and families	Students, families, educators	Students and families	Students, parents, counselors	Students	Students, families, and college advisors
Cost	Free	Free	Free	Free starter kit, then family or schools pay	Free	Free 30 days, then $9.99/month; free to needy students

*Winner of the College Knowledge Challenge contest launched by the Bill and Melinda Gates Foundation and College Summit.

TABLE 4.3   Technological solutions to motivate college-going behaviors and persistence

Name	Collegeology: Mission Admission	Zombie College*	MyCoach*	Logrado*	GradGuru*	Schools App
Type of technology	Facebook app	Mobile/Web app	App	Mobile/Web app	Mobile app	Mobile/Web app
Description	Game designed to teach underserved students the process of getting into college and help them navigate the complex process of applying for college and financial aid	Game designed to help students "internalize" the steps needed to go to college, including requirements for course selection, attendance, standardized tests, financial planning, and more	Provides college students with automated alerts on their mobile devices and Facebook accounts to help them track deadlines; they are rewarded with badges for completion and mastery of tasks and skills, and are able to share progress with their support network	Provides a guidance system supporting students in accessing, persisting in, and completing college; uses interactive missions that guide students through critical steps in preparing for college	Provides reminders to guide, motivate students to complete college; sends relevant, timely campus, transfer, state, and federal financial aid deadlines; sends college-knowledge tips and to-dos. Those who reach key milestones are issued badges and cash rewards.	Creates a private community for college students that allows them to meet their classmates, ask questions, and share interests
Founded/Designed by	University of Southern California	Get Schooled Foundation	Beyond 12	Brian Co	Catalina Ruiz-Healy	Uversity (formerly Inigral)

Purpose	To develop, operate, and evaluate a set of fun, inspiring, and educational games that will increase the number of low-income youth preparing for, applying to, and finding success in the nation's four-year college programs	To engage and motivate students through an interactive game that takes students through the key steps involved in going to college while incorporating the media, technology, and popular culture	To bridge the "information gap" and to help students master the activities, behaviors, and habits that increase their success in college and beyond	To enable schools and college access programs to improve the quality and scale of guidance, communication, and individualized support for low-income and first-generation students	To give the right kind of information at the right time so students can make the right decisions to reduce drop-out rates and accelerate college completion	To improve enrollment and retention through the creation of a private social network that increases student engagement and sense of belonging to the college
Target user(s)	Students	Students	Students and counselors	Students, families, and counselors	Community college students	Students, staff, and faculty
Cost	Free	Free	Free, but students have to be members of a Beyond 12 partner organization	Free for students; colleges/universities pay	Free for students; subscription service for colleges	Colleges and universities pay

*Winner of the College Knowledge Challenge contest launched by the Bill and Melinda Gates Foundation and College Summit.

which some of them may not be utilizing. In addition, many low-income communities still have inadequate Internet service (especially American Indian communities). Second, we think adoption of the technology is a major roadblock for these technological solutions, which require users (students, families, counselors, and/or professional staff) to know about the product, understand its value, and know how to use it. In other instances, the solutions require educational institutions to buy the services, thus limiting access to the apps.

Third, despite the proliferation of new social media and other technologies, no research has yet been published on how students experience or navigate the financial aid process using these resources. The only available existing research relates Facebook use with multiple outcomes, such as increased social capital, student engagement, and college persistence. Some preliminary results indicate these new solutions are "working," but what that means exactly is up for debate. How many students are being served with these technologies? Who is being served? How effective are these tools? How is success defined, and do those definitions of success include financial aid access in particular institutional contexts? These questions raise important issues that have not yet been addressed.

To fill in these gaps, we need rigorous research that examines both the impact and limitations of these technologies. The good news is plenty of data will emerge from the use of these technological platforms. But data availability is only part of the equation; we also need to update our theoretical understanding of how financial aid works in light of new students and new technologies. In fact, we know little about the mechanisms contributing to the impact of financial aid on student success as it is, let alone how rapidly advancing developments in technology might affect these mechanisms.[20] We should examine in more depth the role various forms of technology play in the financial aid process for both students (and their families) and educational institutions. We should also examine in more depth the creation, meaning, and value of online ties. Students (and families) engage in multiple networks (both on- and offline) and we need better conceptual and methodological tools to examine how these networks function in the financial aid process.

In the following section we identify a specific social media–based technological intervention—Schools App—and analyze data to examine if and how it can effectively serve the needs of disadvantaged students. Specifically, we explore the ways Schools App can be effective, yet we challenge assumptions about the "power" of social media as a successful tool in financial aid reform.

SCHOOLS APP: A CASE STUDY OF COMMUNITY COLLEGES AND SOCIAL MEDIA

Our case study relies on multiple sources of data from Getting Connected, a three-year study of the role of social media in the success of community college students.[21] Beginning in fall 2011, nine community colleges (see table 4.4) were selected to adopt a closed, Facebook-based application for use by invited students, staff, faculty, and administrators. Schools App, developed by Uversity, is purposefully designed to host, manage, and facilitate *social* engagement for newly admitted students.[22] Schools App creates a private proprietary community for students attending a specific college, inviting

TABLE 4.4   Main characteristics of community colleges in Getting Connected study

Institution	Enrollment	Location	Enrollment by student race/ethnicity
CC #1, California	15,734	City Large	6% White, 52% Hispanic, 27% African American
CC #2, Arkansas	8,365	City Small	77% White, 11% Hispanic, 2% African American
CC #3, Ohio	31,250	City Large	54% White, 4% Hispanic, 33% African American
CC #4, Arizona	13,000	City Large	33% White, 33% Hispanic, 11% African American
CC #5, Arizona	12,296	Suburban Large	60% White, 18% Hispanic, 4% African American
CC #6, New York	11,783	Suburban Large	73% White, 3% Hispanic, 10% African American
CC #7, Texas	28,549	City Large	38% White, 41% Hispanic, 10% African American
CC #8, Wisconsin	5,573	Rural Medium	89% White, 1% Hispanic, 2% African American
CC #9, Wyoming	4,905	Rural Medium	83% White, 7% Hispanic, 3% African American

Source: Based on information from IPEDS and the Carnegie Classification 2010.

them to join via e-mail invitation, then allowing them to make friends, ask questions, share interests, seek advice and information, create their own self-defined "communities," and get involved by organizing "meet-ups" for social or other activities offline. The goal is to connect students to a virtual campus community, providing a space for the social, academic, and socio-academic integration identified by many scholars to be so valuable in prior models of college persistence.[23] For commuting, predominantly nontradi-tional-age, working, lower-SES and/or part-time students attending community colleges, Schools App aims to function as a virtual social media alternative to more traditional opportunities for student engagement known to benefit residential students.

Data we present in this chapter come from two primary sources: text data collected from the "school feed" of Schools App at eight of the community colleges, interview data from 372 interviews and 24 focus groups, and field notes from 9 site visits conducted during the spring 2012 semester.[24] In total, we had access to app data from 18,826 college students who joined the social media application since launch. Social media analysis used text mining techniques to reveal complex patterns and trends hidden in the posts.[25] The data were preprocessed by removing numbers, punctuation, and common "stopwords." Once precleaned, we quantified the frequency of words per college as they appeared in the text, allowing us to generate the final graphic word-cloud representations.[26] Figure 4.1 provides the wordcloud for the California college. Note the prominence—indicated by size and centrality—of the words "financial," "aid," "money," "office," and "check" (circled). After word-clouds were produced, posts were loaded into Nvivo—a qualitative research tool—and then coded and analyzed for content. Specifically, we examined the topics of "conversations" within which these frequent words appeared and the purpose of these posts and comments. Interview and focus group data were also coded and analyzed using Nvivo.

FINANCIAL AID FINDINGS FROM TEXT ANALYSES AND INTERVIEWS

Although Schools App is marketed primarily as a social space and is not specifically designed to address the financial aid process, at the community colleges in the study, financial aid content emerged as a prominent topic in students' posts and in the interviews.

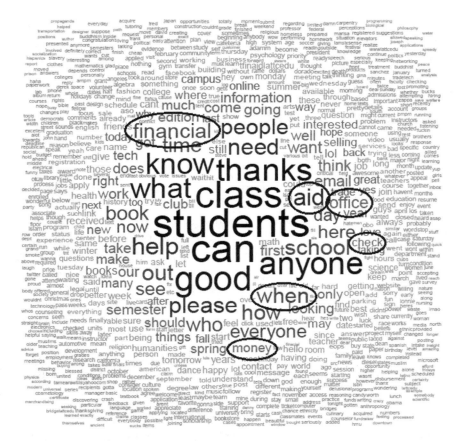

FIGURE 4.1   California community college wordcloud

Successful Features of Schools App Relevant to Financial Aid

In our analysis, the most frequently posted comments focused on "procedural" matters, things like academic and class-related issues, enrollment and course-taking, and financial aid. The most frequent topics in financial aid exchanges fell into several categories. The first involved students attempting to clarify financial aid disbursement timelines and distribution guidelines. For example, "Does anyone know how long it takes to receive financial aid once it shows in the student information system?" and "When does our excess financial aid usually get refunded?" The high frequency of the word "when" in our analyses was embedded in these types of inquiries.

The second category included attempts to clarify income and academic stipulations for qualifying for, maintaining, or losing aid. The following post is a good example:

> Can someone help explain this to me? I got the Pell Grant for school. I get an e-mail tonight saying that there had been financial aid activity on my account. I go online and the Pell Grant reward had been taken off so I now owe a balance? I have all A's, have been to all my classes, and have no "red flags" on my account . . . my income hasn't changed and I already did my FAFSA (which didn't change) for next year . . . what's going on? I am FREAKING OUT . . .

Schools App provided opportunities to discuss these topics, and it was heartening to see so many students (and staff) willing to use the space in an effort to offer help, assistance, and advice. Many students were confused or anxious about receiving their financial aid refunds or disbursements, and others offered their knowledge or experience on the topic. This interaction was typical:

> *Esteban:* Anyone know when financial aid is coming out?
> *Carla:* No later than the 30th, but I'd check everyday starting Monday if I were you :) last semester they were disbursed about a week earlier than the date they estimated.

Another recurrent concern was the loss of aid due to dropping classes. For instance, a staff member at the Texas college jumped into a student exchange about the impact of dropping classes on financial aid:

> You can still drop a class, but it could affect your financial aid depending on how many hours are required for your aid. Please talk to a financial aid advisor before dropping the class.

The ability of school staff to use Schools App to systematically respond to student requests for financial aid information was particularly impressive, especially the efforts of the college with the highest rates of student poverty (the California college). Here, the director of financial aid responded actively to student questions, and eventually the financial aid office created a "profile" for the entire office so any particular financial aid advisor could receive e-mail alerts whenever words pertaining to financial aid were posted, allowing any of several staff members attached to that profile to respond quickly on the school feed to student questions, offer advice, or disseminate information about procedures or deadlines. For example, one student posted his confusion regarding why he was ineligible for aid, providing enough detail for a financial aid advisor to post this reply:

> You need to log onto the SIS portal and change your goal. Go to online forms
> . . . update your educational goal . . . select [name of college] as your school
> . . . click where it says "Click here to confirm and/or update your educational
> goal." You will need to pick a goal that is financial aid eligible and submit it.

If more specific information was needed to contend with a student's individual case, then an advisor replied to the student's post by providing a phone number and e-mail to contact the office directly. Such interactions resulted in an increase in e-mail exchanges (from about twenty to over two hundred per term), reduced lines at the financial aid office, a decrease in the time it took to resolve individual financial aid problems, and significantly less frustration.

Components of Successful Implementation

Our observations of each college's attempt to implement Schools App led us to three aspects of successful implementation that were underdeveloped: exposure to the technology, awareness of its value, and routine engagement.

Student Exposure to the Technology

The impact of the Schools App was restricted by gaps in students' exposure to it. Many who had not joined the app admitted in interviews that they were not even aware it existed. We observed all colleges make efforts to increase the number of app members. However, given the low persistence and high stop-out rates at community colleges, the students actually enrolled could change drastically each semester. This necessitates a more pervasive and continuous digital promotion. Digitally, in print, and physically on campus, Schools App was not consistently visible in more than one or two obscure places. There were not enough ways for students to become aware of how to become members. The primary means through which students are made aware is an e-mail invitation to their college e-mail account. This is problematic because many students, having not been warned they would receive it or informed of what Schools App was for, regarded the invitation as spam or irrelevant. Some schools provided a link to the app from their school's Facebook page, but the link was not evident on the mobile version of the page. These seemingly minor issues constrained the spread of Schools App.

Student Awareness of the Technology's Value

Uversity describes its technology as a "private Facebook community" that is "exclusive to students" at the particular college. This might be appealing, even exciting, for traditional-aged students attending residential colleges. However, for nontraditional college-goers, the social component may not seem as attractive. Yet, while some students were excited to join and participate, others failed to recognize its purpose and value.

Neither Uversity nor the colleges had the foresight to define the multiple purposes the app could serve to meet various community college needs, such as the potential to create a socio-academic, financial, and procedural help-seeking community that students needed and desired—essentially a community to acquire "campus capital," as defined by Ana Martínez-Alemán and her colleagues.[27] Since this was not a thrust of the marketing campaign, many students we spoke with failed to understand how this tool could serve them. Based on their personal experiences with Facebook, they assumed Schools App was a space to socialize with other students, and thought, "It didn't pertain to me." As one Ohio student stated, and many others echoed in their interviews, "I need to have a reason to go to it." In interviews and focus groups, students noted they would be excited to join if it provided a space to engage with others across similar classes or program/career trajectories, in ways that differ from traditional course management systems, which function more like listservers than spaces to interact with classmates individually.

Consistent, Routine Engagement

We found that ensuring ongoing levels of engagement is another key component of successful implementation. In some of the colleges, the relatively low proportion of active users limited the routine engagement of the other students. Interviewed students said, "I don't think people are using it." Schools App relies heavily on the social component of social media; in order for a single user to reap benefits, other college users must be present for social interactions to occur. It relies to a greater degree on widespread use by an entire school, college, or community.

The colleges in our study managed a relatively high adoption rate. On average, 35 percent of enrolled students have joined the app since implementation started. Moreover, adoption rates range from a low 5 percent to half of all students. Colleges offered incentives to join—often a chance to win giveaways, such as college bookstore gift cards, iPads, and so forth.

However, student willingness to engage after joining seems to depend in part on the extent and frequency of engagement of other students within the college.

The importance of the level of engagement extends into another aspect of implementation to consider: not all users have to be active users. This is perhaps a benefit specific to *social* media, which allows for two-way engagement observable by other users who are involved but not actively communicating, just watching. Indeed, we found that both active users (i.e., members who spent time on the app commenting/posting) and passive users (members who spent time only observing others comments/posts) were significantly more likely to re-enroll to college (28 percent and 35 percent, respectively) compared to nonmembers.

Addressing Needs Within Limits

Studying the attempt to implement a specific technology within the context of community colleges brings to light not just the benefits but also the challenges of such efforts. In this section, we consider how Schools App provides some inroads toward addressing contextual realities, but also consider how simply layering technology on top of existing structural issues is extremely limited in its ability to offer comprehensive solutions.

Limited and Overworked Staff/Advisors to Guide Students and Process Applications

Student after student discussed long and arduous attempts to secure staff help with the often nontransparent financial aid process, particularly in the post-application stage, or in the reapplication stage that needs to occur year after year. Students' frustrations reflect a combination of the overwhelming complexity of the decentralized, bureaucratically segmented system paired with the lack of directed guidance from a single source. As Thomas described, "Financial aid is a very frustrating process, and there's not enough people . . . to take care of the number of students. I sat for three hours in line a week before school." Wanda, a returning adult student, summed it up succinctly: "I would make six trips to financial aid . . . Pulling my hair out." Wanda is a straight-A student; she is a work-study Student Ambassador and works at the college's newly formed one-stop enrollment center. "Before we had this one-stop center, it was go here, go there . . . and if you didn't know and weren't assertive enough to ask questions or think about it, not so good, wasn't so good."

Schools App provides students like Wanda the opportunity to help other students quickly and on a massive scale. Her activity on the app includes continual procedural and financial aid information, routinely offering posts like this one:

> HEY STEM students—registration for Fall 2013 opened TODAY. Register for classes ASAP! Why? To get the best teachers and times. MORE importantly it helps your financial aid (book advance) get paid BEFORE you need it!! REGISTER PRONTO!!!

Systematizing such posts routinely as a small part of the responsibilities of multiple staff or work-study positions like Wanda's would be optimal if embedded in more streamlined financial aid services integrated with registration and enrollment services. Two other colleges now have such one-stop services all in one place for students—Wyoming and New York—and we came across fewer frustrated and confused students at these two colleges.

Understaffing relates not only to the access students have to guidance and assistance but also to the processing of paperwork and awards. At the Ohio college, a staff of five processes aid applications for the more than 30,000 students who enroll each year. The Texas college has six staff processing nearly 30,000 students. The lack of assistance with applying for aid combined with processing delays inevitably leads to an even longer wait time for students. Social media, particularly Schools App, makes students' financial aid frustrations evident and available on the school feed. Colleges can use this as a mechanism for troubleshooting and making decisions about where to allocate resources.

Accuracy of information was also an issue. In interviews, students were often frustrated at being given incorrect or changing information. Schools App posts mirrored this same frustration, presenting yet another opportunity for institutions to use such "data" to identify areas for improvement:

> I called financial aid today . . . I had a class that was a late start . . . started feb 20th. She told me I'd get my refund late . . . like another 2 weeks she thinks . . . and classes that start in march will get refund mid april . . . she thinks. I don't know if they even know. Ridiculous.

*   *   *

> I am in the same boat as you. I still have yet to get my money, patiently waiting and all they can say is "It's coming" They have absolutely no clue

what they are doing down there and it is very frustrating. I cannot even register for summer classes or see my midterm grades because I have a financial hold on my record . . . its just so aggrevatingggg

A final important point is that financial aid and other student services staff generally resisted turning to social media as a tool. In our interviews they revealed several reasons for this. One of them was precisely that they were limited and overworked—they did not have enough time to add one more thing to their list of tasks, ruling out spending time responding to student questions on a social media platform. Yes, the California college engaged enthusiastically, but they were an exception to the rule in their responsiveness, and the direct involvement of upper-level administrators was necessary to get staff fully engaged.

The Link Between Academic Performance/Progress and Aid Qualification

The "Satisfactory Academic Progress" standard is a federal requirement that dogs community college students. Under its rules there are several ways students can lose their aid and end up having to repay part or all of the aid that has already been disbursed, or lose their access to financial aid for the following semester. They could be in this situation if they withdraw from classes after the official withdrawal deadline and therefore receive F grades, if they fall below a C average, or if they fail to complete at least 67 percent of their credits attempted.

Unfortunately, community college students are among those most likely to be dealing with poverty, financial instability, and related life crises—all of which can, at any point, threaten their academic performance or ability to continue in college. They are also more likely to be academically underprepared, further exacerbating the threat of financial aid loss. Many students we interviewed lived in fear or had suffered from loss of aid due to academic struggles. Schools App posts were riddled with student concerns about this and their attempts to avoid loss of their financial aid:

Has anyone ever had to appeal a financial aid exclusion? My completion rate will only be 50% and I was placed on warning at the beginning of the semester. Just curious how lenient they are because I can't pay for college without it.

* * *

So I had started this semester with 12 units but I had to drop two classes due to my work schedule, do I get penalized from financial aid for doing that or what?

Furthermore, some students recognized the intersection of these requirements with time limits, in which students are denied any further aid if they do not complete their degree or certificate by the time they reach credits equal to 150 percent of the number of credits required for their primary degree program. Therefore, students feared not only losing their aid because of a drop in their academic performance, but also "running out" of aid if they did not pursue an efficient enough path through postsecondary education. Many were not aware of these policies and potential complications when they first enrolled. The posting of information—and student experiences—regarding these issues on Schools App could inform and warn other students to prevent such vagaries.

The Prioritizing of Particular Family Forms Embedded in Financial Aid Criteria

After spending a year observing activity on Schools App and talking with hundreds of community college students, one thing became abundantly clear: the traditional family form with a young adult enrolled full-time while being supported by, or financially dependent upon, her or his parents is *not* the norm. Yet the current system of federal financial aid is biased. It privileges families in which children are financially dependent through the age of twenty-four by providing them with tax breaks. However, most community college students in their early twenties are adults who are independent of their parents, yet they must go to lengths to prove they are not dependents. This is sometimes very difficult, especially when their parents are not in contact or do not cooperate because they do not want to lose the tax benefits.

Community college students' normative divergence from federally-defined "dependent/independent" criteria puts them at a disadvantage. Students can request a change from dependent to independent status only if they can document extreme, unique, or unusual family circumstances such as abuse, neglect, or parental desertion. In other words, the burden of proof is on the students to document that their family form is "abnormal" in order to receive needed aid. Consequently, busy aid advisors are overburdened by cases with special circumstances that must be considered on an individual basis. This further stretches an already limited staff and further complicates the financial aid process for already financially struggling students. Students used Schools App to help clarify these requirements to other students who appeared substantially overwhelmed by them:

> I live on my own, pay my own tuition, and opted in fafsa not to include my family's income. Talk to financial aid (I did . . .) and they will fix it for you. You just have to have a bill (utility or rent) showing that you do in fact live by yourself.

SCHOOLS APP AS A SOLUTION?

Schools App exposes one of the greatest flaws in the current financial aid process for community college students—namely, that it is a procedural nightmare. Despite efforts to simplify the FAFSA and application process, the complexity of rules and policies for receiving, sustaining, and maintaining aid post-application present ongoing challenges, particularly for community college students whose institutional context, life circumstances, academic vulnerability, and financial instability tend to lack conformity with the family form and college-going norms privileged by current financial aid policies. In fact, one could argue that these students are unduly penalized by such policies and consequent institutional practices.

To some extent, however, Schools App provides small-scale solutions. It exposes problems, making them visible. Students were initially given the opportunity to use Schools App as they saw fit, with little staff or administrator involvement. In that sense, analyzing the postings provided a window into what students needed in a college community. The message came through loud and clear that students want and need help navigating college-going procedures, particularly financial aid.

The app also proved helpful to enhance opportunities for peer mentoring. Victor is on the app every day and describes how he uses it to guide other students:

> I like to comment back when a student has a question. You get students that have simple questions like Financial Aid. If you attend an orientation you find out what the protocol is of Financial Aid—what deadline dates are. I like to inform students of what scholarships are going on at the moment especially if it pertains to them, just talk to them about whatever . . . or if they have questions . . . When it comes from a student's perspective they're more able to relate to that.

Students like Tina remarked on the value of a student-based site to provide guidance on "core questions" about financial aid to provide "some way that students can navigate the system a whole lot easier." We encountered this behavior disproportionately among older returning adult students, who took on parent-like roles in guiding younger students by responding to their posted financial aid questions and confusions.

Schools App also reduced the need to repetitively address one-on-one common financial aid mistakes, confusions, and false assumptions by allowing advisors to communicate with multiple students simultaneously. A student posted, "Do FAFSAs need to be done each semester? Or just once a year?" A financial aid representative replied, "Hi Blanca. These need to be done just once a year."

We found Schools App also provides opportunities to reduce unnecessary waiting. Tyrone, a California student, explains how he avoided going to the financial aid office to have his questions about financial aid answered, "because I know it's a long line and it's practically a half a day wait just to get an answer." Then he posted his question on the app, "and one of the workers . . . told me, 'E-mail us in the office. Just write your name, your student I.D., and what your question is, and we'll answer you.'" And so that's what Tyrone did, and he received his answer within an hour.

Finally, we found Schools App provides a space to implement preventive measures regarding financial aid. For example, students could avoid long wait times if they know not to seek help during "peak" times. Some colleges use Schools App to "announce" reminders to students during slower times to get their financial aid processed before the busier rush periods at the start of each term. Due to their open access structure, community colleges do not have the luxury to begin processing the financial aid applications of their incoming and returning students at least a whole semester ahead of time. Community college students are more transient, often registering and applying for aid just before or just as the term begins, constricting processing times into just a few weeks. For institutions like the Ohio college, with a financial aid staff of five, this is a nearly impossible task.

In order for community colleges to benefit in the ways described above, efforts need to extend beyond students to administrators and staff who should focus on carefully defining and marketing the social media space as a place for financial aid and related exchanges. They should detail exactly how social media can translate not just as an informational tool and convenience to students, but also as a time-saver for student services staff, perhaps by showcasing colleges that have successfully implemented the technology.

DISCUSSION AND IMPLICATIONS

Lately there have been quite visible efforts to improve the transparency of college information. The White House recently released a College Score-card that would summarize several key measures of college affordability and value.[28] These include net cost, graduation rates, job prospects, and earnings potential. In 2012, the Department of Education expanded its online College Affordability and Transparency Center to support comparisons of costs among similar institutions.[29]

However, such scorecards are built on the assumption that the lack of transparency in cost relative to value is the major obstacle. For community college students, the cost is relatively low, but the complex and ever-changing processes involved in acquiring and retaining their aid seem to provide a much larger hurdle. Federal policy criteria set with traditional student and traditional college-going norms in mind fail to reflect the majority of students at community colleges. These students would benefit from greater transparency around financial aid procedures and rules, as well as friendlier, less punitive policies.

Financial aid regulations are also archaic in other respects. For instance, income requirements for Pell Grants are dropping, disadvantaging much of the working poor earning more than $23,000 annually.[30] Furthermore, existing approaches to award aid are designed around traditional semester-length courses, thus jeopardizing some of the most promising institutional and statewide innovations (led by Achieving the Dream, Developmental Education Initiative, Completion by Design, and Jobs for the Future) that aim to experiment with the time and structure of course delivery, using dual enrollment and modular courses to accelerate student progress through developmental education and to contextualize basic skills instruction.[31]

Financial aid rules and regulations also benefit particular family structures while disadvantaging other family structures and norms. Community colleges tend to enroll students from a greater diversity of family forms, making the process of financial aid application and receipt more complex and potentially time-consuming. Additionally, the risk of changes in and loss of financial aid are more common since changes in family circumstances are more pervasive in the lives of community college students. Instability in academic performance as a result of changes in life circumstances also puts such students at greater risk of unexpected changes in college financial aid or loss of aid.

With these larger dynamics in mind, the use of social media holds particular promise. It can create small-scale efficiencies to enhance communication, information dissemination, and guidance efforts by supplementing or sidestepping inefficient systems. Yet social media, and the related technological solutions we featured earlier, are limited in their ability to address larger institutional structures. No, such technologies cannot change these structures directly, but their use and the data they generate can illuminate areas of weakness and gaps that exist in the assistance institutions attempt to provide students in their application, acquisition, and use of financial aid. By providing a view of financial aid from lower-income, community college students' perspective in their attempts to navigate the system, we hope to have provided clues about where the system is flawed. We also hope to have illuminated the ways in which research is misguided, with its over-focus on individualistic rational choice emphases that downplay institutional context and the ways policies and procedures impact college-going processes for students in under-resourced college contexts.

5

Incentivizing Success

Lessons from Experimenting with Incentive-Based Grants

Lashawn Richburg-Hayes

INTRODUCTION

Financial aid has long been the tool of choice to increase access to higher education. In fact, one of the original purposes of student financial aid was to ensure more equitable access to postsecondary education for those traditionally underrepresented and those least able to afford it.[1] However, the current financial aid system serves far more students than originally envisioned by the legislation and for purposes beyond an inability to pay. Almost two-thirds of all undergraduates receive some form of financial aid, and many institutions are using financial aid for other reasons, such as enrollment management to attract competitive students to attend their institutions over others.[2]

As a result of both the size of the financial aid system ($226 billion) and the widespread use of financial aid for various purposes, financial aid must be thought of as another tool that can be leveraged to improve academic success and postsecondary completion.[3] Yet little is known about whether financial aid causes an increase in access and an improvement in academic success. Previous research suggests that financial aid is positively correlated with both increased enrollment in postsecondary education[4] and increased persistence, but correlations do not imply causation.[5] There have been a few studies of the effect of financial aid on other student outcomes, such as the type of institution chosen by students (two-year versus four-year institutions), the composition of the financial aid package (grants versus loans), course-taking patterns, and completion, but the few findings that do exist are correlational and mixed.[6]

This chapter focuses primarily on interventions that use financial aid as an incentive to improve academic success, and the discussion is limited to programs evaluated through the use of random assignment.[7] Since it is not ethical to eliminate need-based aid and experiment with randomly providing aid to students, the studies covered in this chapter focus on randomly providing additional aid.[8] The nine studies summarized here demonstrate that incentive-based grants—an innovation on traditional financial aid—result in a larger proportion of students meeting academic benchmarks, a greater number of credits earned, and modest effects on Grade Point Average (GPA) in the first year.

The remainder of the chapter provides an overview of the theory behind the use of incentives, describes various incentive-based financial aid interventions, and reviews the evidence on their effectiveness. After setting forth some possible explanations for these results, the chapter concludes with lessons learned about implementing financial aid interventions and the implications of these findings for federal and state policy as well as philanthropic giving.

THE PROMISE OF INCENTIVES

Economic theory posits that rational consumers will respond predictably to prices. A subfield, incentive theory, posits a more complex response when the actors involved in a transaction do not have access to the same information.[9] An example of this occurs in any relationship in which a principal (say, a manager) wants an agent (say, a worker) to perform a task, but the principal cannot perfectly monitor whether the required level of effort went into the production. In this situation there is a need to align desires, and such alignment may be achieved through the use of incentives. Empirical research across a number of fields provides evidence that incentives do work in aligning actual behavior with desired behavior, with positive relationships found between monetary incentives and a number of behaviors such as welfare exits, crime reduction, and smoking cessation.[10] Perhaps as a result of this, there has been a recent explosion of work applying incentive schemes in the field of secondary education to encourage students to increase reading time, test scores, course performance, and matriculation.[11]

While the findings from these studies have been mixed, the underlying theory is potentially powerful: with the correct incentive scheme, it may be possible to induce a change in behavior to produce desired educational outcomes without costly monitoring, which will benefit both students and society in the long run. However, there are also potential downsides in that incentive schemes may induce undesirable behaviors such as cheating.[12] There is a considerable body of literature in the field of psychology that suggests that monetary incentives could result in *decreases* in the desired behavior as a result of the destruction of intrinsic motivation.[13] As a result, the design and implementation of incentives must be done carefully. The best evaluation approach to disentangle alternative explanations is a Randomized Controlled Trial (RCT).

IMPROVING ACADEMIC SUCCESS THROUGH INCENTIVE-BASED GRANTS

Several recent studies have been conducted—all employing rigorous experimental designs—to evaluate the efficacy of a particular type of incentive scheme, known as incentive-based grants, on academic progress. In this chapter, incentive-based grants are defined as *additional* financial aid to students that is *contingent* on academic performance. These grants are in addition to aid that students would typically receive based on their institutions' provision of financial aid and therefore represent a net increase. In some instances the incentive grants—which do not need to be repaid— are geared to provide students with supplemental resources while simultaneously incentivizing them to meet performance benchmarks. In other instances the grants have a pure incentive focus to motivate students to be more academically productive. In contrast, pure need-based aid provides students with resources to attend college while requiring that they meet minimal performance benchmarks.[14]

The theory of change underlying incentive grants is that conditioning additional financial aid on achieving certain benchmarks and/or completion of activities will lead students to increase their effort toward their studies, which, in turn, will lead them to perform better in their classes in the short term and progress through their degree requirements at a quicker rate in the medium term. That is, providing the opportunity to earn a contingent grant (a financial motivation) along with making this opportunity

salient to students (perhaps through reminders about the opportunity and/
or requiring other services) will result in a number of students meeting the
performance criteria, earning the incentive grant, and performing better in
their studies, which may increase the likelihood of their graduation from
college in the future.

Methodology Employed in This Chapter

This chapter employs an integrative research approach that examines the
average effect of incentive grants on student-level outcomes. However, this
review is *not* a systematic meta-analysis, as the studies examined were not
intended to be exhaustive and no attempt was made to locate research that
may not be in the published domain. Rather, studies were chosen on the
basis of their focus on incentive grants applied in postsecondary settings that
were evaluated through RCTs, and the analysis is intended to be a descriptive look at some of the most commonly cited studies meeting these criteria.

The Randomized Control Trials of Incentive-Based Grants

Over the last twelve years there have been at least nine RCTs of incentive-
based grants, each attempting to evaluate the impact of the grants on postsecondary student outcomes such as credits earned, GPA, and persistence.
Table 5.1 presents a summary of the intervention design in each of the studies. While the studies vary in the targeted student populations, most evaluate outcomes for traditionally aged students and have incentives that last for
at least two semesters. The maximum total incentive grant amount ranges
from a low of $215 to a high of $7,000. The GPA performance requirement is
often lower than what is typically required of grants targeted to high achieving students, so it is inaccurate to consider these incentive-based grants to
be similar to merit-based grants.[15] Collectively, the studies represent over
16,200 randomly assigned students.[16]

Project STAR offered student services (specifically, peer advising), an
incentive, or a combination of both to entering college freshmen of a large
Canadian university. Incentives were paid based on high school quartiles
such that students would receive the highest pay relative to the stretch they
would need to make above their high school performance. In other words,
students who did not perform well in high school were eligible for the largest incentive amount if they managed to become a top student in college.[17]

Opportunity Knocks was implemented at a large commuter college
in Canada. The program aimed to incentivize students to earn higher

TABLE 5.1 Description of experimental interventions of financial incentives

Study	Eligible population	Need-based	Number of sites	Treatment groups	Incentive duration	Maximum incentive amount	Academic benchmarks	Additional service criteria	Analysis sample
Project STAR (Canada) 2005–2006	Full-time, 1st-year college students High school GPA in 1st to 3rd quartile[a]	No	1	3	2 semesters	$5,000	Meet GPA benchmark depending on high school quartile Register for 2nd year	Peer advising[g]	1,571 (P:619; C:952)
Opportunity Knocks (Canada) 2008–2009	1st- and 2nd-year college students Applied for financial aid HS GPA on file Enrolled for half of a full load	No	1	1	2 semesters	$7,000[e]	Attain minimum grade of 70 (benchmark by course)	Peer advising	1,271 (P:400; C:871)
University of Amsterdam (Netherlands) 2001–2002	1st-year college students in economics and business	No	1	2	3 terms	$215 or $644[f]	Complete all 1st-year requirements by start of next term	None	249 (P:167; C:82)
Foundations for Success (Canada) 2007–2009	Full-time enrollment Canadian citizen Identified as at-risk based on Accuplacer and FastTrack survey	No	3	2	3 semesters	$2,250	Meet 2.0 GPA benchmark Eligible to continue at institution	12 hours of activity	3,110 (P:2,056; C:1,054)

(continues)

TABLE 5.1 Description of experimental interventions of financial incentives *(Cont.)*

Study	Eligible population	Need-based	Number of sites	Treatment groups	Incentive duration	Maximum incentive amount	Academic benchmarks	Additional service criteria	Analysis sample
OD Louisiana (United States) 2004–2005	Age 18 to 34 Parent Family income below 200% of poverty level	Yes	2	1	2 semesters	$2,000	Complete 6 or more credits with a C average or better	Meet with adviser	537 (P: 264; C: 273)
PBS California (United States) 2009–2012	Age 16 to 19 High school seniors applying for financial aid Below Cal Grant A/C Income Threshold[b]	Yes	Portable	5	1 term to 2 years	$1,000 to $4,000	Complete 6 or more credits with a C average or better	None	4,642[h] (P: 1,361; C: 3,281)
PBS New Mexico (United States) 2008–2011	Age 17 to 20 Freshmen Pell-eligible	Yes	1	1	4 semesters	$4,000	Complete 12 or more credits (1st semester) or 15 credits (subsequent semesters) with a C average or better	Meet with adviser	1,081 (P: 536; C: 545)

PBS New York (United States) 2008–2010	Age 22 to 35 Live away from parents In need of developmental education Pell-eligible	Yes	2	2	2 full semesters and 1 summer semester[d]	$2,600 or $3,900	Complete 6 or more credits with C or better in each	None	1,502 (P: 754; C: 748)
PBS Ohio (United States) 2008-2010	Age 18+ Parent Zero EFC[c]	Yes	3	1	2 semesters or 3 quarters	$1,800	Part-time: Complete 6 to 11 credits with C or better in each Full-time: Complete 12 or more credits with C or better in each	None	2,285 (P: 1,359; C: 926)

Sources: Angrist, Lang, and Oreopoulos (2009); Angrist, Oreopoulos, and Williams (2010); Leuven, Oosterbeek, and van der Klaauw (2010); MacDonald et al. (2009); and MDRC Opening Doors Louisiana and Performance-Based Scholarships Demonstration studies.

[a]Academic benchmark was conditional on high school grade quartiles. See text for description.

[b]Cal Grant is a financial aid program funded by the state of California. The awards do not have to be paid back, but to qualify, students must fall below certain income and asset ceilings.

[c]EFC, or Expected Family Contribution, is the amount of money a student is expected to either pay out of pocket or procure in loans to cover the costs associated with postsecondary attendance. All else equal, a lower EFC is associated with higher levels of need-based aid.

[d]The study in New York randomly assigned program group members to one of two scholarship types. One type was offered over two semesters only; the other was offered over two semesters plus one summer semester.

[e]The incentive grant is $100 per course plus an additional $20 per percentage point. A full course load consists of 10 credits per year.

[f]The low-reward group was offered 227 euros ($215 in 2002 dollars); the high reward group was offered 681 euros ($644 in 2002 dollars).

[g]There were three treatment groups: the Student Support Program (SSP) group was eligible for peer-advising, the Student Fellowship Program (SFP) group was eligible for incentive grants, and the SFSP group was eligible for both peer-advising and the incentive grant. SFSP students did not need to participate in peer-advising in order to earn the incentive grant.

[h]The PBS California program group consists of performance-based scholarships only (Scholarship Types 2 through 6).

grades through a partially linear payout scheme that provided $100 for each class in which a grade of 70 was earned and $20 for each percentage point above 70 percent.[18] In addition to the incentive, peer advising was provided.

The University of Amsterdam program sought to incentivize college students in economics and business to pass their first-year classes. The incentive, paid at the end of the year, was provided in a high amount (around $644) and low amount (around $215) and randomly assigned to two separate program groups.[19]

The Foundations for Success project was targeted to incoming freshman at three Canadian colleges. The program randomly assigned participants to two program groups: the Service Group that provided case management where students were required to complete twelve hours of approved activities that could include tutoring and assessments such as the Myers-Briggs Type Indicator; and the Service Plus group where students were required to complete the same case management objectives, but were also eligible for a fellowship after completion of the twelve-hour requirement. The fellowship, worth $750 per semester (or $2,250 total), was paid at the start of the following semester for three semesters.[20]

The remaining studies are part of the Louisiana study within the Opening Doors Demonstration (OD Louisiana) or the Performance-Based Scholarship (PBS) Demonstration.[21] The incentive grants in these studies are called "performance-based scholarships" and are need-based, contingent grants geared toward helping reduce the financial burdens of low-income college students while incentivizing good academic progress. The scholarships are paid directly to students, allowing them to use the funds for their most pressing needs (books, child care, or other financial obligations that might disrupt studies) and are generally paid at multiple points during the semester if the student earns a certain number of credits with a C or better grade.

Selected characteristics of the sample in each of the nine studies are presented in table 5.2, which shows that women comprise the majority of sample members across the studies. Slightly more than half of the studies focus on traditionally aged students, while several studies of performance-based scholarships focus on students in their mid-to-late twenties. Other common demographic measures are not available for the studies, but the presented entries show that a diverse set of students are represented.

TABLE 5.2 Selected characteristics of incentive study sample members at baseline, by report

Characteristic	Project STAR	Opportunity Knocks	University of Amsterdam	Foundations for Success	OD Louisiana	PBS California	PBS New Mexico	PBS New York	PBS Ohio
Female (%)	57.7	65.0	—	58.6	93.1	60.2	60.8	69.1	86.4
Age (years)[a]	18.3	18.7	—	—	25.5	17.6	18.0	26.5	29.9
Race/Ethnicity[b] (%)									
Hispanic	—	—	—	—	2.9	60.7	60.6	44.3	8.6
White	—	—	—	—	9.5	20.3	21.8	6.1	54.6
Black	—	—	—	—	85.7	3.8	2.7	37.2	31.4
Other	—	—	—	—	1.9	15.1	14.9	12.5	5.4
Sample size	1,571	1,271	249	3,110	537	4,642	1,081	1,502	2,285

Source: MDRC calculations using baseline demographic data from Angrist, Lang, & Oreopoulos (2009); Angrist, Oreopoulos, & Williams (2010); Leuven, Oosterbeek, and van der Klaauw (2010); MacDonald et al. (2009); and MDRC Baseline Infomation Form (BIF) data.

Note: "—" = data not available because question was not asked at baseline for this site, or was not listed as a characteristic for this report. Only the first two cohorts are shown for OD Louisiana. The PBS California program group consists of performance-based scholarships only (Scholarship Types 2 through 6). Calculations for this table used all available data.

[a]Average age was not provide for the University of Amsterdam report. While the average age was not reported for the Foundations for Success report, nearly 73% of the sample was 22 or younger.

[b]Respondents who said they are Hispanic and chose a race are included only in the Hispanic category. Respondents who said they are not Hispanic and chose a race are included in the "Other" category, which also includes those who said they were American Indian, Alaskan Native, or another race/ethnicity.

Do Incentive-Based Grants Help Improve Student Performance?

The combined results from the nine studies discussed above show that incentive-based grant aid can improve students' success on key academic outcomes. Table 5.3 reports means for the program group and the control group, the impact estimate (column 4), a measure of variability of the impact estimate (column 5), the percent change, effect size, and standardized impacts (that is, differences generated per $1,000 in funds offered in column 8), to show how these programs have affected matriculation, benchmarks met in the first year, credits earned, GPA, persistence, and degree attainment. By using random assignment, the observed "impact" of the program represents the causal effect of the intervention on the outcome in question.

Findings on Matriculation

The first panel of table 5.3 presents findings on matriculation. Of all of the studies, only the California PBS program is able to measure matriculation effects as a result of the incentive-based grant being randomized during the summer after students' senior year in high school. The California PBS program resulted in a 4.9 percentage point increase in matriculation (for a 5.8 percent increase). The average eligible scholarship amount across the five performance-based scholarships offered in this study is about $1,400. This translates into an increase of 3.7 percentage points per $1,000. Effect sizes (column 7) are shown on the table to facilitate comparisons between the studies.[22] The effect size of the estimate is 0.14, which may be considered modest in postsecondary education.[23]

Since the California PBS program is among one of the few random assignment evaluations to affect matriculation in the literature, it is useful to draw upon other—nonrandom assignment—work to assess the magnitude of the reported effects. A quasi-experimental study of matriculation is reported by Susan Dynarski, who uses changes in the provision of a generous Social Security benefit for college students to explore the effect of aid on matriculation.[24] Dynarski's preferred specification, which controls for covariates and adjusts for classification error, results in an impact estimate of 3.6 percentage points per $1,000 in grant aid (for an effect size of 0.04 standard deviation units).[25] In earlier work, Larry Leslie and Paul Brinkman report that a $1,000 decrease in net price is associated with a 3 to 5 percentage point increase in attendance.[26] Further, Thomas Kane, using a quasi-experimental

TABLE 5.3   Postsecondary outcomes across prior research on financial incentives

Outcome	Sample Size (1)	Program Group (2)	Control Group (3)	Diff (4)	Standard Error (5)	Percent Change (6)	Effect Size (7)	Diff per $1,000 (8)
Matriculation (%)								
PBS California								
Enrolled in any college	4,642	89.3	84.4	4.9***	1.1	5.8	0.14	3.7
Enrolled in any 2-year college	4,642	47.9	43.2	4.7***	1.6	10.9	0.09	3.5
Enrolled in any 4-year college	4,642	42.8	42.8	0.0	1.6	0.1	0.00	0.0
Met academic benchmark in second term of first year (%)[a]								
OD Louisiana	537	32.5	17.3	15.2***	3.6	87.8	0.35	6.8
PBS California[b]	4,642	25.9	23.8	2.1	1.4	8.7	0.05	1.6
PBS New Mexico	1,081	49.8	32.3	17.6***	2.9	54.4	0.36	9.1
PBS New York	1,502	57.4	56.8	0.6	2.5	1.1	0.01	0.2
PBS Ohio	2,285	28.8	18.3	10.5***	1.8	57.5	0.24	5.7
Average credits earned in first year								
Project STAR[c]								
Student Support Program (SSP)	1,418	2.4	2.4	0.1	1.0	2.3	0.00	—
Student Fellowship Program (SFP)	1,418	2.4	2.4	0.0	1.0	-0.5	0.00	0.0
Combined Program (SFSP)	1,418	2.5	2.4	0.1	1.0	3.9	0.00	0.0

(continues)

TABLE 5.3 Postsecondary outcomes across prior research on financial incentives (Cont.)

Outcome	Sample Size (1)	Program Group (2)	Control Group (3)	Diff (4)	Standard Error (5)	Percent Change (6)	Effect Size (7)	Diff per $1,000 (8)
University of Amsterdam								
Low incentive	166	31.6	33.2	-1.5	3.5	-4.6	-0.07	-2.0
High incentive	165	32.7	33.2	-0.4	3.5	-1.3	-0.02	-1.7
OD Louisiana	537	11.0	7.7	3.3***	0.8	43.7	0.32	1.5
PBS California[b]	4,642	8.9	7.9	1.0***	0.4	12.9	0.09	0.8
PBS New Mexico	1,081	25.7	24.8	0.9	0.6	3.7	0.10	0.5
PBS New York	1,502	16.3	15.5	0.9*	0.5	5.6	0.09	0.3
PBS Ohio	2,285	15.6	13.9	1.7***	0.4	12.1	0.16	0.9
Average GPA in first year[d]								
Project STAR[c]								
Student Support Program (SSP)	1,399	1.8	1.8	0.0	0.1	0.6	0.01	—
Student Fellowship Program (SFP)	1,399	1.8	1.8	0.0	0.1	-2.2	-0.04	0.0
Combined Program (SFSP)	1,399	2.0	1.8	0.2*	0.1	9.4	0.10	0.0
Opportunity Knocks	1,203	2.5	2.5	0.0	0.0	0.8	0.03	0.0

Foundations for Success[e]

Service group	2,078	1.9	1.9	0.0	NA	1.1	0.00	—
Service Plus group	2,086	2.0	1.9	0.1*	NA	6.4	0.08	0.1
OD Louisiana	391	2.1	1.8	0.3***	0.1	16.8	0.25	0.1
PBS California[b]	2,324	2.3	2.3	0.0	0.0	1.8	0.04	0.0
PBS New Mexico	1,050	2.8	2.7	0.0	0.1	1.2	0.04	0.0
PBS New York	1,390	2.6	2.6	0.0	0.1	0.2	0.00	0.0

Second year persistence (%)[f]

Foundations for Success

Service group	2,078	62.9	61.0	1.9	NA	3.1	0.03	—
Service Plus group	2,086	66.3	61.0	5.3**	NA	8.7	0.11	2.3
OD Louisiana	537	30.1	22.9	7.2**	3.6	31.6	0.16	3.2
PBS California	4,642	81.4	79.0	2.4*	1.3	3.0	0.06	1.8
PBS New Mexico	1,081	77.6	78.5	-0.9	2.5	-1.2	-0.02	-0.5
PBS New York	1,502	61.9	60.7	1.2	2.5	2.0	0.03	0.4
PBS Ohio	2,285	60.5	59.2	1.3	2.1	2.2	0.03	0.7

(continues)

TABLE 5.3 Postsecondary outcomes across prior research on financial incentives *(Cont.)*

Outcome	Sample Size (1)	Program Group (2)	Control Group (3)	Diff (4)	Standard Error (5)	Percent Change (6)	Effect Size (7)	Diff per $1,000 (8)
Average credits earned in second year[9]								
University of Amsterdam								
Low incentive	166	23.9	26.1	-2.2	3.6	-8.4	-0.10	-2.9
High incentive	165	25.0	26.1	-1.1	3.7	-4.2	-0.05	-4.3
OD Louisiana	537	13.7	10.0	3.7***	1.2	36.9	0.26	1.7
PBS New Mexico	1,081	46.5	44.3	2.2*	1.3	5.1	0.11	1.1
PBS New York	1,502	26.7	25.6	1.1	0.9	4.3	0.06	0.3
PBS Ohio	2,285	24.8	22.4	2.4***	0.8	10.6	0.13	1.3
Earned any degree or certificate as of end of second year (%)								
PBS Ohio	2,285	20.5	16.9	3.6**	1.7	21.3	0.09	2.0
Earned any degree or certificate as of end of third year (%)								
PBS Ohio	2,285	26.9	23.3	3.5*	1.8	15.1	0.08	1.9

Source: MDRC calculations using credits earned and GPA data from Angrist, Lang, and Oreopoulos (2009); GPA data from Angrist, Oreopoulos, and Williams (2010); credits earned data from Leuven, Oosterbeek, and van der Klaauw (2010); GPA and enrollment data from MacDonald et al. (2009); National Student Clearinghouse data; and transcript data from Delgado Community College, Louisiana Technical College, the California Community College Chancellor's Office, the University of New Mexico, Borough of Manhattan Community College, Hostos Community College, and the Ohio Board of Regents.

Note: Statistical significance levels are indicated as: *** = 1 percent; ** = 5 percent; * = 10 percent. Rounding may cause slight discrepancies in sums and differences. MDRC estimates are adjusted by research cohort and campus. Only the first two cohorts are shown for OD Louisiana. The PBS California program group consists of performance-based scholarships only (Scholarship Types 2 through 6). For the Foundations for Success report, only students in the Service Plus group were eligible for the incentive grant. All standard errors and effect sizes are derived from p-values provided in text.

[a]Due to the timing of scholarship-eligible terms and data limitations, some of these measures are proxies. For Louisiana, this represents the proportion of students who earned 6 or more credits with a C or better overall in their second term (depending on the cohort, this could be a fall, spring, or summer term). For California, this represents the proportion of students who earned 6 or more credits with a C or better overall in their second term (a spring term), and does not include students who earned the award over the summer. For New Mexico, this represents the proportion of students who earned 15 or more credits with a C or better overall in their second term (a spring term), and does not include students who earned the award over the summer. For New York, this represents the proportion of students who earned 6 or more credits with a C or better in their second term (depending on the cohort, this could be a fall or spring term). For Ohio, this represents the proportion of students who earned 12 or more credits in their second term (depending on the cohort, this could be a fall, winter, or spring term).

[b]Credits earned and GPA are based on intent-to-treat averages using data for California community colleges.

[c]Estimates are taken from Table 6 for the full sample. SSP is a student service program only, without a financial incentive component. Estimates represent coefficients from a single regression that estimates the effects of both treatment groups relative to the control group. The SFSP program combined student services with a financial incentive. Differences were detected by gender, with impacts being significant for women in the combined group. If these impacts are used, the difference per $1,000 is 5.4 percentage points. Sample size represents the analysis sample used to analyze treatment effects on second year outcomes. See Table 6 in Angrist et al.

[d]GPA calculations do not include students who did not enroll or did not receive a GPA as a result of taking all non-graded courses. Foundations for Success does not report the standard error of the impact estimate, but does report p-values. The effect size was derived by converting the p-value to a t-statistic and calculating Cohen's d as detailed in endnote 22 in the text.

[e]GPA shown is for the second semester of the first year only. Estimates for missing GPA scores are imputed.

[f]Persistence is defined as registration in the third semester or fall-to-fall persistence.

[g]Figures for the University of Amsterdam represent credits earned in the second year, while the remaining entries reflect cumulative credits over the first two years.

design, finds that a $1,000 drop in tuition results in a 3.7 percentage point increase in attendance (as reported by Dynarski, 2003).[27]

Overall, the California PBS findings seem similar to those reported previously. This indicates that relatively small incentive-based grant amounts could be effective in increasing matriculation among students.

Findings on Meeting the Academic Benchmarks

The second panel of table 5.3 shows the effect of the different performance-based scholarship studies on students' meeting the academic benchmarks in the second term of the first year (these requirements are listed in table 5.1). Although the academic benchmarks were set at levels nearly equivalent to Satisfactory Academic Progress (SAP), students' ability to reach and surpass the benchmarks was fairly low. For example, in Opening Doors Louisiana, only 17.3 percent of control group students attained a grade of C over at least 6 credits. Figure 5.1 graphically depicts the variation in the effect size estimates across the studies. The average effect size for meeting the academic benchmark across these studies is 0.20—which may be considered a large change in postsecondary education—and the 95 percent confidence interval for the average effect size ranges from 0.06 to 0.35. This is compelling evidence that lends reassurance that the effects are real and these programs seem to work in getting students to meet the academic benchmarks.

Despite the movement in meeting the benchmark, figure 5.2 shows that across all sites for which data are available, program group students only received between 43 and 77 percent of the maximum grant amount available to them in the first year of the incentive grant. That is, since the payment of the grants is conditional on performance, some students will not receive the entire amount as they fail to meet the requirements. The figure shows the difference in the maximum eligible amount and the average amounts of incentive grant actually earned or the remaining incentive grant money "left on the table" by students failing to meet the benchmarks. Whether this is a negative outcome or a positive outcome depends on one's values: if the goal is to induce behavioral change with the smallest necessary expenditure, then figure 5.2 suggests that these incentive programs may accomplish that task at a cost lower than the "sticker" price.[28] Alternatively, if the goal is to increase the resources available to students, then figure 5.2 suggests that the incentive structure may need to be tweaked in

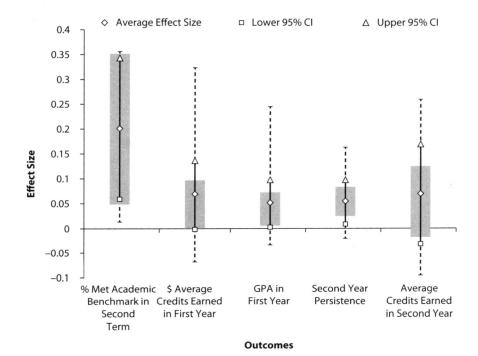

FIGURE 5.1   Effect sizes across prior research on financial incentives

Source: MDRC calculations using credits earned and GPA data from Angrist, Lang, and Oreopoulos (2009); GPA data from Angrist, Oreopoulos, and Williams (2010); credits earned data from Leuven, Oosterbeek, and van der Klaauw (2010); GPA and enrollment data from MacDonald et al. (2009); National Student Clearinghouse data; and transcript data from Delgado Community College, Louisiana Technical College, the California Community College Chancellor's Office, the University of New Mexico, Borough of Manhattan Community College, Hostos Community College, and the Ohio Board of Regents.

Note: Shading shows effect sizes between the 25th and 75th percentiles (the interquartile range).

ways to ensure a larger proportion of actual recipients while continuing to induce behavioral change.

Findings on Credit Accumulation After One Year

The third panel of table 5.3 examines credits earned in the first year of college. The first set of rows report findings from Project STAR and University of Amsterdam, both of which had little effect on credit accumulation. The next set of entries shows findings from the Opening Doors Louisiana study and a number of studies that are part of the PBS Demonstration. The

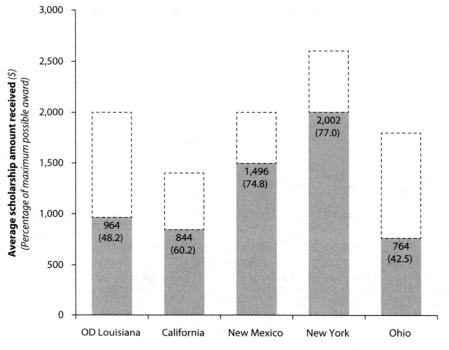

FIGURE 5.2   Average amount received among program group members in the PBS Demonstration in the first two terms

Source: MDRC calculations using scholarship payment data from Delgado Community College, Louisiana Technical College, the California Student Aid Commission, Lorain County Community College, Owens Community College, Sinclair Community College, the University of New Mexico, Borough of Manhattan Community College, and Hostos Community College.

Note: Dotted lines above the bars represent the maximum amount of money for which students were eligible over the first year of the program. Only the first two cohorts are shown for OD Louisiana. The PBS California program group consists of performance-based scholarships only (Scholarship Types 2 through 6). The dotted line representing the maximum amount available is the average scholarship amount that students were eligible for across all scholarship types, excluding Scholarship Type 1.

entries show that all of the programs (with the exception of New Mexico's) resulted in increases in credits earned in the first year (ranging from 6 percent to 44 percent).

Figure 5.1 shows that the average effect size for credits earned in the first year is 0.07 standard deviation units, with a 95 percent confidence interval ranging from slightly below zero to 0.14.[29] Given that the confidence interval spans zero, this suggests that there is not an effect on credits earned across these studies at the 5 percent significance level.

GPA in First-Year and Second-Year Persistence

The next panel of table 5.3 reports on GPA in the first year. Overall, the interventions have not been able to induce large changes in GPA. This may not be surprising, as GPA represents the cumulative experience of students and their decisions, which may be difficult to alter with modest interventions. The combined incentive program in Project STAR and the OD Louisiana performance-based scholarship program induced the largest changes in GPA of 0.10 standard deviations and 0.25 standard deviations, respectively. However, the assumptions made to handle dropouts and stop-outs across half of the studies are unclear, so the findings for this outcome should be interpreted cautiously.

Persistence and Average Credits Earned in the Second Year Along with Degree Attainment

The next four panels of table 5.3 examine second-year persistence, or persistence in the third term; credits earned in the second year; and degree attainment in years two and three. Only the Foundations for Success, Opening Doors Louisiana, and PBS California programs affected second-year persistence, with the Opening Doors Louisiana program increasing persistence by 3.2 percentage points per $1,000.

Second-year credit accumulation appears mixed, with statistically significant increases among the Opening Doors Louisiana, PBS New Mexico, and PBS Ohio sites, but no impacts among the other studies.

The last two panels show degree attainment rates for PBS Ohio, the site with the longest follow-up data. Performance-based scholarships increase the proportion of students earning a degree two years after random assignment by 3.6 percentage points (an increase of 21 percent). This impact continues into the third year of follow-up (a 3.5 percentage point impact, for an increase of 15 percent). Given that this is the only study included in this analysis with degree outcomes, it is unclear whether incentive grants will generally yield this finding or whether the finding is being driven by factors specific to the study.

Figure 5.1 shows similar effect sizes for two of these three academic outcomes. The average effect size for second-year persistence is 0.05 and the 95 percent confidence interval is 0.01 to 0.10. This may be considered modest. The effect size for the average number of credits earned in the second year is 0.07 and the confidence interval is –0.03 to 0.17. Since this range spans zero, the current evidence suggests that incentive grants may not be effective in increasing credits earned in the second year (a period when most grants are no longer available).

WHAT DRIVES THESE RESULTS?

Together, these studies suggest that innovations in financial aid are possible to implement and evaluate in a rigorous manner, indicating the possibility for others to execute similar innovations in this area. Further, the studies suggest that the innovations may not cause harm to students based on the lack of negative impacts on the primary outcomes of interest reported in table 5.3. While students could be responding in other reasonable but undesirable ways (such as taking easier courses or choosing "easier" majors), the analyses reported to date do not indicate any such patterns.[30]

In general, impacts for the performance-based scholarship programs seem to drive the modestly positive results reported above.[31] More specifically, the impacts on first-year credit accumulation for the performance-based scholarship programs are toward the middle to higher end of the range of impacts in other random assignment studies of financial incentives for postsecondary students. And while the impacts are modest, the findings from Ohio suggest that these incremental improvements could potentially lead to impacts on graduation down the road.

The positive impacts shown in table 5.3 may reflect the deliberate targeting of programs; on average, students in the PBS Demonstration have one or more at-risk factors for not completing college, such as being low-income, older, or a parent, which may contribute to the larger effect of the contingent grant on academic outcomes. This also suggests that larger impacts from these types of designs may not result from larger infusions of money (table 5.1 shows that the amounts in the PBS Demonstration studies are not the largest), but rather from better targeting of students who may be responsive to incentives and the careful shaping of the incentive program itself.

INSIGHTS GAINED FROM EXPERIMENTATION WITH INCENTIVES IN FINANCIAL AID

Taken together, the above projects provide five useful lessons on how to implement changes to financial aid to help low-income students succeed in college. Many of these lessons mirror those provided by John A. List on how to successfully launch a RCT.[32]

1. Identifying the target group for a program may be the most important first step. Colleges need to examine institutional or organizational priorities before deciding on a population to target for an intervention. Which populations are currently targeted under different programs and efforts at the college? Which students are most at risk of stopping out? Which students are most in need of financial aid to help them succeed in college?

Identifying an appropriate target group could be essential for the program to add value (that is, show an impact). It is possible that students closest to the margin of meeting the academic benchmark feel more induced to change their behavior than others. This seems reasonable conceptually; high performing students would not need to do anything differently, as the benchmarks are not binding for a student routinely earning grades of, say, B or a 3.0 GPA. In contrast, very low performing students may have deeper needs that cannot be easily met through an incentive scheme. For example, such students may struggle with time management, or display help-seeking behaviors (such as visiting a tutor) at much lower rates than other students, or they may simply not know what to do to be successful despite having the desire to achieve.

Targeted programs—by definition—create more programs, and this attempt at greater "precision" in identifying students may come at the cost of simplicity. However, it seems problematic to continue as public policy has done, which is to treat financial aid as a blunt instrument that impacts all students equally when there is a growing body of evidence that suggests there are segments of students who are likely to benefit much more than others.[33]

2. It is also important to consider the details and logic model for the program and to develop realistic outcomes and goals. For the PBS Demonstration, this meant considering what benchmarks to incentivize and considering how students were reasonably expected to respond to these incentives. In order to facilitate this systematic intervention development process, colleges need to look at the levels of success that different target populations had in meeting academic benchmarks in the past.

For incentive-based grants, selecting the benchmark also has cost implications. All else being equal, selecting a benchmark that students are less likely to meet (that is, a benchmark that is "harder" to achieve) will result in a lower aid amount paid per student. With a set amount of money available, setting a higher benchmark can allow the institution or organization to *offer more students* the opportunity to earn the scholarship, while maximizing the potential behavior change. For example, the designers of Project STAR set the $1,000 incentive target in expectation that 20 to 25 percent of students would qualify in the absence of a treatment effect. Assuming a generous impact of 10 percentage points, this means that the baseline expected direct cost of the program is $300 to $350 per student, not $1,000. In contrast, offering $1,000 to all students independent of targeting could result in expected per-student costs of, say, $600, if the take-up rate is 60 percent—the additional cost being driven by students who would have met the benchmarks without the incentive. In this sense, such students would receive a "reward" for their behavior, not an incentive.

3. Line staff buy-in should be secured as well as higher-level leadership support. In all of the performance-based scholarship studies reported in this chapter, MDRC worked closely with various levels of administration within college campuses in order to move the efforts forward. While this can be tedious, especially at the outset of the program, its importance cannot be overstated—doing so at the beginning of an intervention can avoid obstacles down the road. Different stakeholders should be incorporated into the planning and implementation of any financial aid reform, and one also has to consider how their ongoing support will be maintained.

For example, it is important to work closely with the financial aid office to determine how incentives will be integrated into financial aid packages and with the bursar to determine how grants will be distributed. Generally speaking, financial aid packaging begins with need-based grants and work-study and then moves to outside scholarships, institutional aid, and loans, with institutional aid and outside scholarships often competing to be the "last dollar" aid in the package (likely as a way to preserve resources). In the PBS Demonstration, it was important to assure that the incentive grants would be regarded as last-dollar aid, such that their institution did not replace other aid that would have been in the package in the absence of the intervention (a practice called displacement). Since most scholarship providers and institutions also want this cherished position, the tension could result in decisions that undermine the incentive. That is, it is possible for an incentive not to have the desired effect because it does not represent a net increase in aid.[34]

4. The intervention must be integrated with other efforts. Incorporating reform with other efforts on-campus can help ensure that the reform has a "home" and staff to keep the project moving. For example, in the performance-based scholarship studies described here, each of the programs was housed in a specific area on campus (such as financial aid or student services). In this way, the program was incorporated into an already existing structure, making it easier to implement. In a few cases, the program was designed with existing campus resources such as advising and tutoring in mind and structured to help incentivize support services that the college felt were underutilized.

5. Communications with students and additional student services can enhance the program model. In the majority of the studies summarized in this chapter, communication was a critical component of the model. Communications with students were purposefully planned around certain dates in the academic school year; school leaders incorporated positive messages to encourage students and relayed important information about the program and what students needed to do in order to receive the incentive dollars (in accordance with the growing behavioral economics literature on the importance of reminders).[35]

At other sites, colleges incorporated services that were already offered at the college to be coupled with the scholarship—such as advising, tutoring, and academic workshops. Often the colleges felt that pairing the scholarships with other resources was an effective way to motivate students to use these often-underutilized resources. And last, the intervention could also be paired with new or targeted services at the college. For example, at one site in the PBS Demonstration, the program was paired with an interactive discussion (or forum) for students to discuss various topics.[36]

For communication with students, technological advances are occurring at such a rate that costs may not be a major factor in reaching students early and often through text messages, smartphone applications, and social media. Indeed, these conduits are already being used to provide reminders and other student services, such as advisement.[37]

IMPLICATIONS FOR POLICY

Given that incentive-based aid in general—and performance-based scholarships in particular—seem to improve outcomes for students, some may wonder whether the strategy of tying federal financial aid payments (such as the Pell Grant) more closely to achievement would achieve similar outcomes. There are several points to keep in mind with this strategy. The first is that the size of the programs is dramatically different; the Pell Grant program is far more generous than the performance-based scholarships reported in this chapter. In fact, the average Pell Grant received in the PBS Demonstration sites analyzed over one year ranged from $3,400 to $3,700 (33 to 45 percent of the total aid package), while the performance-based scholarship amounts received ranged from $765 to $2,050 (or 10 to 25 percent of the total aid package).[38] Since these dollars comprise the "foundation"—or "first dollar" in a package—to which other aid dollars are added, reducing the Pell Grant in any way could possibly have a larger effect on behavior than a similar reduction in last-dollar aid.[39] That is, Pell Grants are often considered to be an entitlement (though they are not) and are therefore expected to be received by some, unlike institutional and scholarship aid. Thus any uncertainty around receipt of Pell Grants could have greater behavioral responses as a result of this expectation.

Second, the Pell Grant is generally paid all at once, near the beginning of the semester. In this way it is used to pay for tuition and fees first, prior to other educational expenses. In contrast, the performance-based scholarships are paid in increments, and could help with other educational expenses such as room and board, books, and transportation. These expenses are important, but only secondarily, after the primary expense of tuition is covered at the outset of the semester.

Third, the academic criteria and penalties for failure to meet the requirements are different. To maintain eligibility for the Pell Grant most institutions require a GPA of 2.0 and some minimum course pass rate to meet SAP; those who violate the requirements are placed on academic probation. For those on probation, Title IV eligibility may be revoked in the year following the failure to meet SAP. While performance-based scholarships have a similar academic benchmark, they have a more immediate impact on students' financial aid packages: if students do not meet the benchmark in the given term, they do not receive a payment. Without great care, this could further contribute to already low college completion rates.

Finally, while major unintended consequences have not been observed in the study of performance-based scholarships, adding performance criteria and changing the disbursement policy for the Pell Grant program could have very different consequences. The potential for these unintended consequences is likely to be exacerbated by the scale of the program. As mentioned, the current Pell Grant program reduces uncertainty for students who are eligible. To some extent, students are able to plan to receive some amount of funding to help cover tuition and fees at the beginning of the year. Removing this certainty has the potential unintended consequence of fewer low-income students accessing the higher education system at all. For example, on average, the structure of performance-based scholarships were such that students were offered a quarter of their total scholarship near the beginning of the semester. If a student is receiving the maximum Pell Grant, and receives one-quarter of the Pell Grant at the beginning of the semester, she would only get $694. At most colleges, this would not be sufficient to cover her tuition and fees.[40]

In short, the question of whether the Pell Grant should be more performance-based is really a second-stage study. While adding additional performance criteria to an expansion of the Pell Grant program (such as to provide "bonuses" for earning additional credits) would be more in line with the research summarized in this chapter, such a policy change could still result in different outcomes as the public may not understand the distinction and change their behavior on the basis of misperception. These and other considerations would need to be carefully considered before informed decisions could be made around such a large change.

The question of whether state-based aid programs should be performance-based could be answered by states that are willing and able to experiment with these programs. States that are considering cuts to their programs might study the effect of randomly replacing some of the cuts with performance-based aid. Similarly, states with high levels of merit-based aid could consider reallocating some of that aid to be need-based aid with performance benchmarks. And lastly, when the economy recovers and states begin to have budget surpluses again, they can experiment with adding performance-based scholarships at the state level. Many of the above cautions apply to these considerations as well.

The findings in this chapter also have implications for private and employer grants, which account for $11 billion in financial aid for students across the country.[41] These grants are provided to students using criteria that may or may not include financial need, and some of these grants are administered somewhat randomly.[42] They often do not have a specific goal or, similar to merit-based scholarships, they go to students with an already high chance of academic success. The potential of incentive grants are that they can be tailored to meet a broad range of goals, including the goals of scholarship providers and community foundations looking to make existing scholarship dollars more effective. Incentive grants, when used thoughtfully and structured well, can help multiple stakeholders meet specific goals.

CONCLUSION

The national trends in degree completion are daunting. It is unlikely that any single intervention will close the chasm between the numbers of students matriculating and re-enrolling each fall and the dismal number attaining degrees. It is more likely that these trends reflect a complex intersection of barriers and that a compilation of solutions are needed (which may be complex when considered in totality).

While financial aid innovations alone will not solve the problem of low college completion rates, there is widespread acknowledgment that the financial aid system can be improved. Many students still have substantial unmet need after receiving financial aid. In addition, trends in student aid have shifted from need-based aid toward loans and merit aid. This is evident in the increasing number of states operating merit scholarship programs.

While the intents of merit aid—keeping the "best and brightest" students within their home states and helping middle-income families with the rising cost of college—are admirable, there are two possibly deleterious effects from its implementation. First, merit scholarships do not equalize access. Because they are based on high school records or standardized test scores, such scholarships may reward students with more privileged backgrounds and higher socioeconomic status, since these characteristics are associated with better schools and better academic preparation.[43]

Second, merit scholarships may crowd out state-level, need-based aid. Trends in state financial aid show large declines in the percentage of need-based aid awarded over the last decade in states that have increased merit aid awards.[44] Further, the financial aid process is too complicated, financial aid is targeted too broadly, and the current system is not structured to incentivize academic success and completion. The programs described in this chapter show that changes can be made, and that more innovation is needed to improve the return on investment that many students and their parents are making in the pursuit of the "American Dream."

6

Reforming Repayment

Using Income-Related Loans to Reduce Default

Nicholas W. Hillman

INTRODUCTION

More than half of all bachelor's degree recipients in the United States take out federal student loans to help finance their college educations. This is due in large part to the rising price tag of attending college in conjunction with shrinking median family income levels, making it increasingly difficult for individuals to pay for college without accumulating debt. While access to credit may help expand college opportunities, a growing share of borrowers are having a difficult time repaying their student loans.[1] Today, one in six borrowers are at least ninety days delinquent on their debts; another one in five default on their loan at some point in their lifetime.[2] Over the past decade, the number of student loan defaults has doubled, despite federal policy efforts designed to help students make on-time loan payments.[3] These are not the intended policy goals of the federal student loan system, nor are they sustainable outcomes for students and taxpayers alike.

As a result, federal policy makers are exploring alternative ways to make student loan debts more manageable for borrowers and more cost-effective for taxpayers. One possible way to work toward these goals is by indexing all federal student loan payments according to the borrower's earnings. Under an "income-related repayment" model, borrowers' monthly student loan bills would not exceed a certain percent of their personal income, and their payments could automatically be deferred during periods of unemployment or economic hardship. In theory, this repayment model should reduce (and possibly eliminate) student loan default and delinquency which, in turn, should also reduce the federal government's administrative costs associated with collecting student loan debts. In practice, however, there are several concerns and unknown questions regarding the expansion of income-related repayment plans.

Drawing from historical policy contexts, international examples, and existing research on income-related repayment schemes, this chapter weighs the merits of linking all federal student loans to students' future earnings. It begins with an overview of the goals of income-related repayment, followed by a discussion of the need for reforming loan repayment options. The latter half of the chapter examines the impacts of income-related repayment models in other countries and discusses the feasibility of implementing this reform in America.

GOALS OF INCOME-RELATED REPAYMENT

The idea of tying college financial assistance to students' future earnings is not new; in fact, the general concept has been proposed for several decades and has yet to take hold in America.[4] In 1967, President Johnson's task force on higher education proposed a federal Educational Opportunity Bank that would have required college graduates to repay a share of their future earnings into the bank.[5] This graduate tax was never adopted, though it was again proposed at the state level in Ohio during the early 1970s.[6] In 1968 the Carnegie Commission on the Future of Higher Education also recommended linking student loans with students' income levels, where "a federal contingent loan program [should] be created for which all students regardless of need would be eligible."[7] Although federal loans would eventually be expanded to students regardless of financial need, repayments were not contingent upon students' future earnings.

At the institutional level, Yale University experimented with the nation's first (and short-lived) campus-based income-related loan model in 1971, while the 1986 Higher Education Act authorized a ten-campus pilot program to scale up income-related loans (more on the Yale experiment in the discussion of income-based loans below).[8] The slow evolution toward income-related repayment was punctuated in 1993 when the federal government introduced the nation's first income-related repayment plan, which was eventually expanded in 2007 and 2012.[9]

This brief history illustrates the slow, halting progress toward the idea of income-related loan repayment in the United States. It also shows that policy entrepreneurs were promoting this financing model long before today's problems related to delinquency and default. These early proponents were trying to perfect the market for human capital, and they viewed income-related repayments as a preferred policy instrument to that end.[10] Despite decades of interest in connecting student loans to future incomes, this funding model has never fully taken root in America. Today, the federal government operates four small income-related repayment plans, serving approximately 1.5 million of the nation's 38 million federal student loan borrowers.[11] While the adoption and expansion of income-related repayment has been inconsistent, the literature provides a relatively consistent message regarding the potential goals behind this concept. Many of these lessons are drawn from international examples, as Australia (1989), New Zealand (1992), and Great Britain (1998) adopted income-related loans when they first began charging college tuition in the late 1980s and early 1990s.

For individual borrowers, income-related repayments should reduce if not eliminate student loan default. Borrowers below a certain income threshold (e.g., 150 percent of federal poverty guidelines) would not be required to make payments on their loans, resulting in lower default rates. Considering that one in ten borrowers now default within three years of entering repayment, income-related loans provide a potential pathway for helping students make on-time payments.[12] In addition to default protection, income-related loans provide consumption smoothing that is unavailable with traditional fixed repayment models. Consumption smoothing allows loan payments to rise and fall according to the borrower's income levels, thus insuring them against risks associated with unemployment or other labor market shocks.[13] These two criteria (default protection and consumption smoothing) are the hallmarks of proposals that link student loan repayments to incomes. It is also plausible, although not often discussed in the literature, that income-related repayment schemes can improve consumer information about the costs of college. Considering ongoing efforts to simplify the student aid process, it is feasible that students who are preparing for college could easily understand that their loans would be repaid according to a share of their future earnings. This back-end reform may dovetail nicely with front-end reforms associated with raising awareness and helping prospective students prepare for financing a college education.

The benefits of income-related loans are not limited to the individual borrowers, as the reduction in default rates should result in significant savings in terms of student loan collection costs. This is one of the primary goals of income-related loans, and a number of countries have reported collecting more debts at lower administrative costs as a result of adopting this repayment scheme.[14] Additionally, public policy makers believe this new repayment model could encourage individuals to not underinvest in human capital, as is currently the case with many talented students who "undermatch" or opt out of college altogether because of financial barriers. By tying debts to incomes, students from lower socioeconomic groups are expected to participate at greater rates, though this assumption has yet to be tested in America. Evidence from Australia's program suggests their repayment model has not substantially impacted (negatively or positively) low-income students, though further research is necessary.[15]

Considering the potential positive benefits of adopting income-related loans, yet the reluctance to embrace this model in America, many questions remain. These questions will be revisited at the end of the chapter; meanwhile, they provide a guiding framework for considering the implications associated with this funding model.

First, if one of the primary goals is to reduce student loan default rates, is income-related repayment the only (or most preferred) option for achieving this goal? Second, despite the claims that income-related repayment can achieve the aforementioned goals, what empirical evidence supports (or is missing from) these policy discussions? And third, despite how fragmented America's current student loan system is, how might income-related repayment exacerbate or ameliorate existing repayment challenges? There are no easy answers to these questions, yet they play a role in the ongoing conversations about student aid reform—particularly as they relate to using income-related loans as a solution to the student loan default problem.

THE NEED FOR REFORM

Today, approximately 13.5 percent of federal student loan borrowers default on their loans within three years of entering repayment.[16] It is widely noted that the majority of default occurs within the proprietary sector, which tends to enroll traditionally underrepresented students (e.g., low-income, adults, military veterans, ethnic minorities) who accumulate higher debt burdens than students attending public or nonprofit institutions.[17] Additionally, research has consistently found that unemployment is one of the strongest predictors of student loan default, yet students attending proprietary institutions have the poorest employment outcomes when compared against

TABLE 6.1   National three-year cohort default rates (2009–2012), by sector

	Number of borrowers in default	Cohort default rate	Share of total defaults
Public four-year	99,885	8.00%	20.40%
Public two-year	94,945	18.30%	19.40%
Private four-year	59,740	7.30%	12.20%
Proprietary	229,315	22.80%	46.90%
Other sectors	5,155	14.10%	1.10%
Total	489,040	13.50%	100.00%

students participating in other sectors.[18] Of course, default is not isolated to the proprietary sector, but as shown in table 6.1, these institutions represent the largest share (46.9 percent) of the nation's total number of defaulters.[19]

In addition to these default trends, borrowers are having a difficult time staying on top of their monthly student loan bills. As shown in table 6.2, only 39 percent of federal student loan borrowers make on-time payments; the remaining 61 percent of borrowers are either deferring their loans, in forbearance, or have not made payments for at least ninety days.[20]

Despite trends that clearly indicate students are struggling with debt, the standard option more borrowers are placed into is the ten-year conventional repayment plan. Under this plan, borrowers make fixed payments for 120 months that cover the principal and interest of their loan. This standard repayment schedule can be extended to anywhere from twelve to thirty years for borrowers with higher debt levels and for those who consolidate loans into graduated repayment plans. Due to the time value of money and accrued interest, the longer a borrower takes to repay his or her loan, the more expensive the loan becomes over the long run. Standard repayment

TABLE 6.2   Repayment statuses of nondefaulted federal student loan borrowers (2012)

Repayment status	Percent of borrowers
On-time (standard) payments	39%
Deferment/forbearance	44%
Delinquent 90+ days	17%
Total	100%

plans also allow students the opportunity to defer their loan payments while enrolled in college. After leaving (i.e., graduating or enrolling less than half-time), they have a six-month grace period before making their first payment. For subsidized Stafford loans, which account for the majority of federal loans, the federal government covers the loan's interest while students are enrolled; unsubsidized Stafford loans accumulate interest while students are still enrolled.

Alternative Repayment Options

Due to misinformation about eligibility criteria and complexity in the application processes, very few borrowers take advantage of the existing income-related repayment plans.[21] Instead, borrowers find themselves in one of the four alternative repayment outcomes that do little to help make student loan debt more manageable: emergency protection, delinquency, default, or income-related repayment.

Emergency Protection

Once a borrower enters repayment, she may find it difficult to cover monthly loan bills, which is why emergency protections are available to individuals who face such economic hardships as unemployment or certain medical conditions. There are two types of emergency protections—deferment and forbearance—and both are designed as short-term relief plans for borrowers, where their payments are temporarily suspended to help them avoid default. Under deferment, borrowers can stop their repayments for no more than three years while the federal government pays the interest on their subsidized loans. Under forbearance, borrowers can have loans suspended for up to three years, but the federal government does not subsidize the accrued interest during this period. To illustrate, a borrower with $18,000 in debt who enters into forbearance for three years would repay approximately $5,000 extra over the life of the loan.[22] Under both emergency protection plans, the borrower still owes the principal, and while the short-term protections may offer some relief for borrowers, they are not designed as long-term debt management strategies.

Delinquency

Even with these protections, many borrowers get behind on their payments. In 2012, approximately one in six borrowers were at least ninety days delinquent on their loans, up by nearly 10 percent since 2004.[23] Delinquency is often the "untold story" of student loan reform, as the number of delinquencies is on the rise yet we know relatively little about the characteristics of those borrowers who get behind on their payments.[24] Interestingly, most delinquent borrowers enter into emergency protections to help get back on track with their loan payments. Although emergency protections are designed to *prevent* delinquency, it is clear these protections also *respond to* delinquency.[25]

Default

After 270 days of delinquency, borrowers enter into default. Once a borrower defaults on a student loan, the federal government implements a variety of collection mechanisms to ensure that he repays the debt. For example, the federal government can garnish the borrower's wages, seize tax refunds, impose additional collection costs, enter litigation, or restrict the borrower from receiving additional federal aid. As a result, borrowers' credit scores will drop, making it even more difficult to secure other lines of credit, which are necessary for purchasing homes and cars. Since there is no statute of limitations on student loan debt, these risks follow borrowers for the lifetime of their loans. Historically, student loans have had some of the highest default rates among all federal credit programs. But because the federal government has such strong collection mechanisms for student loans, they have some of the highest recovery rates of all federal credit programs.[26]

Income-Related Payment Plans

Currently, the federal government operates four programs designed to adjust loan repayments according to borrowers' incomes: Income-Based Repayment, Pay As You Earn, Income-Contingent Repayment, and Income-Sensitive Repayment. Income-Based Repayment (IBR) is designed to cap monthly student loan payments according to the borrower's family income level—in most cases payments end up being less than 10 percent of family income.[27] If a borrower took out a federal loan after September 30, 2007, and at least one more after September 30, 2011, she could then qualify for the new Pay As You Earn (PAYE) program, which is similar to IBR but with lower payment caps and targeted to Direct Loan borrowers.[28] For borrowers who do not qualify for IBR or PAYE, they may be eligible for Income-Contingent Repayment (ICR) or its alternative, Income-Sensitive Repayment (ISR).[29]

There are numerous problems with this complex approach. From the taxpayer's perspective, it may be inefficient to continue operating four separate income-related repayment plans. Additionally, some observers warn that the current IBR model benefits the wealthiest borrowers and does not fully address the needs of those who are most financially burdened by their loan debts.[30] Still others argue the inflexibilities in the existing loan repayment system (in conjunction with rising loan volume) are slowing down our nation's economic recovery.[31] For example, the average borrower has a debt-to-income ratio that is often too high to qualify for typical home mortgages, so today's college-educated youth are less likely to own homes and are delaying other socially desirable investments.[32]

From the borrower's perspective, the current repayment models introduce additional confusion around how to financially plan and prepare for college. Recent federal reforms have focused on ways to help more students get into college via simplifying financial aid information (e.g., FAFSA simplification, net price calculators), where the underlying assumption is that greater information about college costs will help prospective students decide which college is right for them. While federal reforms often aim at improving information about college costs on the front end of the college experience, it is possible that back-end reforms (i.e., income-related repayment plans) may also help students financially prepare for college. If, prior to attending college, students knew that a certain percent of their future earnings would go toward repaying student loan debt, then it is possible that they would make educational choices based on academics rather than finances. Too often, high achieving students from low-income families undermatch to poorly resourced colleges simply due to financial barriers and debt aversion.[33] This underinvestment in human capital is not a desirable public policy goal, nor does it help reverse educational inequalities that persist within postsecondary education.

In addition to these economic and information challenges, current laws do little to help prevent student loan default. With one in ten borrowers defaulting within three years of entering repayment and the federal government spending more than $1 billion annually collecting defaulted student loans, it is possible that reforms could help reverse these trends.[34] However, under current federal laws, defaulted student loans cannot be discharged in bankruptcy, and once a borrower defaults, the federal government implements a variety of collection mechanisms to ensure repayment. It can garnish the borrower's wages, seize tax refunds, impose additional collection costs, enter litigation, or restrict the borrower from receiving additional federal aid (for example, Social Security benefits, Pell Grants, etc.). Since there is no statute of limitations on student loan debt, these risks follow borrowers for the lifetime of their loans. It is possible for Congress to change this policy and allow default to be discharged in bankruptcy, but it is also possible that an income-related loan model could reduce the incidence of default since unemployment and income are strong predictors of default.[35]

POSSIBLE REFORM OPTIONS

When considering ways students can finance their educations, income-related reform efforts might take one of three general strategies: human capital contracts, graduate tax, or income-based loans. None of these approaches are *new* ideas; in fact, versions of these ideas have been proposed, piloted, and implemented with varying degrees of success over the past several decades. Even more interesting, very few of these proposals have used evidence to support or justify the adoption of their preferred policy solution; rather, the supporting literature tends to rely on theoretical arguments about how reforms "should" yield intended outcomes. Because of this, debates about income-related repayment tend to sound more like "solutions looking for problems"[36] than evidence-based alternatives. This section briefly explores these three different income-related repayment plans available to federal policy makers with an emphasis on the latter—income-based loans.

Human Capital Contracts

In 1955, Milton Friedman proposed human capital contracts as an economically efficient way to finance postsecondary education.[37] Under this model, private investors would identify promising students who, in exchange for a free college education, would pay the investor a negotiated share of their future earnings for a predetermined period of time. He argued that private contracts "are economically equivalent to the purchase of a share in an individual's earning capacity," and could be highly profitable to both lenders and borrowers. For example, take a student who needs $25,000 for financing her education. She could enter into a human capital contract with her investor (or investor group); the investor provides the money in exchange for a fixed percentage of her wages for a set period of time. In theory, this could be a very profitable business model for investors who are able to recruit applicants who are expected to earn high wages directly out of college. It could also reduce uncertainties for the student because she would know how much was expected of her in the future, and she would have the incentive to borrow as little as possible in order to minimize her repayment rate.[38] However, this strategy would benefit too narrow a profile of students and would likely result in underinvesting in human capital. Only those who had sponsors would attend college, and some sponsors might be unwilling to take a risk on students who had high financial need or those who pursued lower-paying professions.

Graduate Tax

The graduate tax model is similar to human capital contracts, but with a more universal scope that would include all students regardless of their wealth or selection by private investors. This is a conceptually straightforward financing model where all borrowers who attend college would be charged a tax for the amount of time they were enrolled. Although "graduate" is in the title, the tax could be applied to all students regardless of degree attainment. Again, this approach would likely improve consumer information and enhance the ability for students to repay debts on the back end of their educational experiences. Since students would know how much of their earnings would go to tax, they might be more aware and careful about accumulating large amounts of debt. However, it is possible that this would become a regressive tax that ends up hurting poor individuals who have credit constraints. Since lower-income students are more reliant on aid, they would accumulate the most debt and in turn would pay higher tax rates after leaving college. In 1967, President Johnson's task force on higher education finance proposed this financing scheme, which would have created the Educational Opportunity Bank to oversee the tax collections. Under this plan, students would pay one percent of their gross annual income (for thirty years) for each $3,000 of student loan debt into the Bank. The United Kingdom is actively pursuing this financing model, although to date no country has implemented the graduate tax approach.[39]

Income-Based Loans (IBL)

Income-based loans insure against the risks of default by scaling payments according to borrowers' income levels. In 1971, Yale University implemented a "risk pooling" IBL scheme where the college loaned money to students, who in turn were mutually responsible for covering the debt of their entire borrowing cohort. To make good on the payments, borrowers paid a fixed share of their future earnings up to 150 percent of what they borrowed, plus interest.

In the end, the program was short-lived and failed to produce the results originally expected. First, some students chose not to participate in the plan because they expected to earn high wages in the future and did not want to subsidize the education of lower earners. This is referred to as "adverse selection," where the plan provided an incentive for individuals to not participate based on their expectations of high future earnings. The second shortcoming of risk pooling is that it transfers the default risk (and costs) to borrowers who make on-time payments. When a borrower in the pool defaults, costs rise for all members of the pool. As a result, those who are making on-time payments end up paying even more money when cohort members default. Because of these challenges, Yale University eventually cancelled the entire cohort's debt in 2001—approximately twenty years after the cohort made its first loan payment.[40]

An alternative to risk pooling is "risk sharing." Risk sharing is the more common form of income-based loans, since it eliminates the perverse incentive of adverse selection. Here, borrowers' repayments are scaled according to the amount of debt they accumulate relative to their income levels. But unlike risk pooling, borrowers are not penalized (or rewarded) when other borrowers make smaller (or larger) payments on their loans. Research consistently finds that risk-sharing models are more efficient than fixed-payment schemes (the current U.S. model), and they introduce greater consumer protections by reducing risk aversion and uncertainty in educational investments.[41]

For example, Australia and New Zealand operate two of the longest-standing risk-sharing income-based loan schemes, where borrowers repay a share of their income according to how much debt they accumulated. There is a minimum income threshold, where borrowers earning less than a certain income level are automatically entered into emergency protection where they are not required to make payments. This risk-sharing mechanism reduces the costs of delinquency and default, since the government spends less on collection costs, but it also increases the possibility of repaying student loans in full, since payments are tied directly to incomes. Research on the Australian experience finds that the risk-sharing model is inexpensive to administer (2 percent of total revenue) and has consistently generated enough revenue to cover annual recurrent costs.[42] The United Kingdom also operates a risk-sharing IBL model, where 98 percent of borrowers were meeting their obligations in 2010–2011, and only 2 percent of borrowers were unaccounted for (presumably in default).[43] Hungary's model (adopted in 2001) yields similar results, where default rates range between 1 and 2 percent and administrative costs are approximately 1 percent of outstanding debt.[44] Table 6.3 displays the maximum percent of income that borrowers are expected to pay in existing income-related loan schemes abroad.[45]

It is important to note that these countries operate fundamentally different higher education systems from the United States. The U.S. system of higher education is quite large comparatively: the total enrollment of 21 million students in U.S. postsecondary institutions is larger than the *total population* of both Sweden and New Zealand, for example.[46] Similarly, these countries have different higher education markets, governance structures, and financial arrangements that make it difficult to make clear comparisons to the U.S. context. For example, in the United Kingdom and Australia, income-related loans were introduced around the exact same time the countries first began charging tuition fees. These countries did not have to consolidate or eliminate legacy systems like the United States would need to do if it were to introduce income-related loans as the standard repayment plan for all borrowers.

Other implementation challenges rest with the degree of centralization each country has over its higher education system, where some are able to align administrative records between education and income tax offices to make the income-related repayments plan operate more seamlessly (at least at face value) than would likely be the case in the United States.[47] These complications make it difficult to make direct comparisons to other countries, though the lessons learned from abroad can certainly inform policy deliberations and policy design strategies in the United States.

TABLE 6.3   Maximum share of income paid to student loans, by country

Country	Maximum share of income
Australia	4–8%
Chile	2–5%
Hungary	6–8%
New Zealand	10%
Sweden	4%
South Africa	3–8%
United Kingdom	6–9%

EXISTING INCOME-RELATED REPAYMENT EFFORTS IN THE UNITED STATES

In the United States, the first national income-related repayment plan dates back to the early 1990s when Congress and the Clinton Administration implemented an optional ICR plan linking borrowers' loans with incomes. In addition to scaling repayments by income, the plan promised to forgive remaining debt after twenty-five years of repayment. From the beginning, the program was not widely marketed and, by 1999, fewer than 10 percent of eligible borrowers participated in ICR.[48] In the program's current design, borrowers' loans are reduced to the lesser of (a) 20 percent of their discretionary income, or (b) the amount owed under a twelve-year repayment plan, multiplied by a complicated formula that accounts for income, family size, and cumulative debt.[49] Likely because of the confusing eligibility requirements, along with the limited knowledge and awareness of the program, many borrowers who are eligible for ICR do not participate in the program.

Instead of making improvements to the existing ICR model, Congress created (in 2007) the IBR plan as part of the College Cost Reduction and Access Act, though it did not become available to borrowers until 2009. Under IBR, borrowers' monthly loan payments are capped according to income and family size; most participants end up paying less than 10 percent of their incomes toward their loans. Any borrowers who take out qualified federal loans (e.g., Direct, Stafford, or certain PLUS loans) are eligible to apply if they meet certain income thresholds. To qualify for IBR, borrowers must also have "partial financial hardship," meaning that the monthly amount due under a standard ten-year repayment plan is higher than what is listed on the federal government's IBR calculator.[50] This calculator accounts for family size, federal student loan balance, adjusted gross income, federal income tax filing status, and state of residence. After twenty-five years of qualified repayments, the federal government forgives the remaining loan debt. Despite low participation rates in both ICR and IBR, the Obama administration (in 2012) introduced the PAYE plan targeted for borrowers who entered repayment during (or after) the Great Recession. This plan effectively scales up the IBR model for borrowers with Direct loans, where eligible borrowers pay up to 10 percent of their discretionary income on their student loans and the federal government will forgive the remaining balance after twenty years of payments.

In the United States, the federal government has not fully adopted or scaled up any of these alternative repayment plans. Instead, it designed (in 1972) and expanded (in 1978) a conventional loan model based on fixed amortization schedules without regard to a borrower's income level. In the earlier years, aid was targeted only to lower-income students, but aid eligibility was liberalized in the 1970s to support educational investments for middle- and even upper-income families.[51] Despite ongoing interest and effort in improving the way students repay their loan debts, these efforts are not reaching a broad cross-section of students, and even when they do, many students experience administrative hurdles and complications that discourage them from benefitting from the plans.[52]

MAKING INCOME-RELATED LOANS THE STANDARD REPAYMENT PLAN

With the ongoing conversation around reforming student aid, now is a propitious time to seriously consider income-related loans. The policy solution has interest across the political spectrum, where both conservatives and progressives have promoted the idea as a solution to the student loan default problem. While the window of opportunity for reform may be opening, it is important to note that the federal government does not currently have the data necessary for evaluating the efficacy of existing income-related repayment efforts (ICR, IBR, ISR, PAYE). We do not know basic information about current programs: who participates, where they attended college, their income and employment history, whether they avoided default. Without basic data on the profile of students currently participating in these programs, there is no way of knowing whether current efforts are "working." Scaling up untested programs will likely result in several unintended consequences that could have been avoided with more careful planning and evaluation prior to adopting policy reforms.

Even if the federal government moved forward without providing basic data and evaluations, transitioning from the current repayment model to an income-related model would have its fair share of challenges and critics. For example, critics may argue that income-related loans introduce moral hazards into the aid system by encouraging individuals to attend more expensive colleges since they know their loans will only be a fraction of their future earnings: a student who would have attended the local state college may enroll in the more expensive out-of-state college. This may not necessarily be an irrational investment, as many talented low-income students undermatch to less selective colleges simply due to financial constraints.[53] Income-contingency could introduce a degree of financial security whereby students select colleges according to fit and academic merits, rather than price. Existing efforts to help students make well-informed decisions about their educational choices would still play an important role on the front end of choosing colleges, and these back-end reforms might be a way to help in that process.

Taking the same issue in the opposite direction, critics may argue an income-related model encourages students to take low-paying jobs in order to pay as little debt as possible. But this seems unlikely given the literature on the returns to schooling and behavioral economics; that is, many college-educated individuals are unlikely to submit themselves to a life of poverty solely to avoid paying debts. A more likely moral hazard is its potential impact on the decision-making of wealthier graduates, who may find ways to shelter income in order to pay less into the system. Whichever direction one believes this moral hazard tilts toward, the key feature of an income-related model is that there will need to be some monitoring expenses to reduce fraud and abuse. The current aid system does a poor job of this, but a new model may actually improve these conditions if it is able to share data with Internal Revenue Services (IRS) records.

This leads us to the second key challenge, where the Department of Education (as the originator of all federal student loans) and IRS would become partners in the loan repayment process. The IRS may not view itself as an appropriate or viable principal in collecting student loans because its mission is to collect taxes and not serve as a bill collector.[54] However, states are not in the position to link these records, and one of the main reasons the Yale Plan failed was the lack of administrative capacity (i.e., being the loan originator and servicer). It would be highly inefficient to have each individual college keep these records, and states' administrative capacity varies considerably in terms of student aid and college enrollment data systems.

To make this program work, a collaboration between the IRS and the Education Department is an essential ingredient to the sustainability of a new aid model. The IRS has the data infrastructure available to link students' income records with Department of Education loan data to ensure that borrowers' debts are tied to current incomes. Without intra-governmental collaboration between these two agencies, it would be difficult to scale income-related loans up to the entire borrowing population. Existing income-related programs illustrate these administrative challenges, as borrowers must go through substantial hoops in order to participate (and continue) in income-related repayment plans. These hoops come at a cost, as Department of Education staff must monitor claims, consult students, and audit the program; alternatively, an automated process that links loan records with IRS data should introduce substantial economies of scale into the administrative process.

Assuming these two challenges can be overcome, borrowers' monthly student loan payments would automatically adjust according to their personal income levels. As income rises or declines, so too does a borrower's payment. This single system would require a standard interest rate for all loans, which some have advocated being set at 3 percent.[55] After determining the interest rate, policy makers would need to agree on an appropriate share of income that borrowers would be subject to paying each month: aid advocates have argued for capping monthly repayments at 8 percent of adjusted gross income.[56] If a borrower's family income drops below a certain income threshold (likely 150 percent of the poverty line), or if he faces a medical emergency or unemployment, his loan will automatically enter into emergency protection where the federal government temporarily suspends payments.

By implementing a new repayment model, consumers would have clearer information about the risks and rewards of their educational investments. Because all students would be automatically set into this plan, there would be no forms to fill out, no reapplication process to work through, and a streamlined process could ultimately reduce administrative costs. This also means there would no longer be billions of servicer transfers, while collection agencies (and the billions of dollars in subsidies paid to them) would become irrelevant. Plus, borrowers would have a degree of security on the back end of their loans since they know their repayment will be scaled according to their resources. The political and administrative challenges discussed above do not appear to outweigh the potential benefits of modernizing the aid repayment system. In addition to eliminating the need for paying collection agencies, an income-related loan model could save the federal government up to $40 billion over the next ten years.[57]

Beyond the economic and political considerations discussed above, this model could also encourage students to pursue their academic interests and ambitions. It is plausible that more students would make educational choices according to their academic interests, rather than according to their debt and finances. For example, a social worker currently pays 14 percent of her income on repaying debt since the career pays low and debt can often be quite high. Alternatively, a chemical engineer pays only 6 percent of his income on debt.[58] Under the new model, these borrowers would pay the same rate, so it is possible that more individuals would pursue their passions without being discouraged by low pay and high debt. Occupations such as small business owners, teachers, and social workers would likely benefit from such an arrangement.

Loan Forgiveness Options

This new model could scale up other features of existing programs, should there be the political will to follow these pursuits. For example, borrowers with large debts often require more time to repay their loans. If a borrower makes on-time payments for twenty years, yet still has not repaid her balance, then the federal government could forgive this debt. Current income-related programs do this as an incentive to encourage borrowers to make on-time payments and to protect students from excessive interest payments that significantly add up the longer one takes to repay their loan. Some observers may see loan forgiveness as a windfall for high-debt borrowers—a feature that (at worst) could introduce a perverse incentive for students to borrow large sums of debt that will eventually be forgiven. Meanwhile, lower-debt borrowers (who can repay their debts more quickly) are not rewarded for making on-time payments. Critics may argue on the grounds of fairness and moral hazard that loan forgiveness is not a desirable option under the income-related repayment model.

While this may be a fair concern, it should be taken with the following context in mind. The federal government currently spends over a billion dollars collecting defaulted loans—loans made to borrowers who failed to make good on their debt obligations. The irony of the current system is that it spends so much money on collecting defaulted loans, while doing very little to support borrowers who are making on-time payments. Borrowers who anticipate their debt will eventually be forgiven might have an incentive to make on-time payments in order to benefit from loan forgiveness.

If critics see loan forgiveness as a windfall to high-debt borrowers, then perhaps a more viable policy option is to cap the amount of interest that accrues on loans. For example, once a borrower pays interest that equates to 50 percent of the original loan balance, then federal subsidies could cover the remaining principal payments. This strategy would serve a similar function as loan forgiveness, since it offers relief for high-debt borrowers, and it would likely be less costly, since it does not forgive the principal on student loans. Both policies—loan forgiveness and interest caps—serve the purpose of preventing students from a lifetime of debt. Borrowers who are able to repay their debts in relatively short time periods are clearly ineligible to receive loan forgiveness or interest cap benefits; however, they benefit greatly by not having to continue to pay interest and by freeing up funds that no longer go toward student loan payments.

Cohort Default Rates

In addition to the challenges discussed above, expanding income-related repayment could actually take away one of the few federal policy levers for holding colleges accountable for their students' performance. Currently, the federal government measures Cohort Default Rates (CDRs) and sanctions institutions from participating in federal student aid programs if too many borrowers default on their loans within three years of repayment. As displayed in table 6.1, nearly 500,000 borrowers who started repayment in 2009 defaulted by 2012. Assuming this pattern holds, then we can expect another half million borrowers to default annually, with most defaults occurring among borrowers attending proprietary colleges.

If all borrowers repaid their loans via income-related repayment, it would likely reduce their chances of defaulting. While this would be a positive outcome for individual borrowers, it would create a perverse incentive for colleges to continue whatever poor practices led them to having high CDRs in the first place. Expanding income-related repayment would effectively make existing CDR policies useless, thus limiting one of the federal government's few institutional accountability mechanisms. If the federal government expands income-related repayment to all borrowers, then it will need to consider how this reform affects existing accountability measures such as CDR.

CONCLUSION

Income-related student loans hold promise as an effective way to encourage more individuals to invest in human capital. If a potential college student knows that 8 percent of his future earnings will be set aside automatically to cover his student loan debt, then he may have an incentive to make educational choices according to academic—rather than financial—considerations.

Of course, potential students should be well aware of the implications associated with borrowing money to pay for college, but having some certainty about "how much" money will be spent on repaying loans should introduce a degree of certainty and predictability that can help students make well-informed educational investments. Furthermore, by improving student loans on the back end of repayment, it can reduce (if not eliminate) default and delinquency, since borrowers will automatically have their payments adjusted according to their financial conditions.

The current repayment model is not sensitive to the awkward economics of higher education finance and human capital investment decisions. Since students have no collateral, and many have no credit history, student loans are often viewed as a risky investment, especially when compared to other forms of consumer credit such as auto loans, mortgages, and revolving credit. Additionally, recent college graduates are entering into very weak labor markets defined by constrained wages and persistently high unemployment. The current fixed payment model is not sensitive to these economic realities, so an income-related model could help recent college graduates navigate the labor market and plan for their financial futures. It may also help prevent delinquency and default, since payments would be automatically deducted from paychecks, and those who face economic hardships could receive automatically suspended payments for a temporary period.

Taken together, income-related loans have the potential to introduce simplicity and predictability into the aid system, which in turn may help improve consumer protections while also reducing administrative costs. However, income-related loans are no "silver bullet" for helping achieve these policy goals. College affordability and student loan debt present complex policy problems that cannot be resolved with any single reform, yet changing the way students repay their loans may be part of a broader policy agenda designed to simplify the aid process and streamline the way students finance their postsecondary educations.

This chapter cites evidence that a policy of income-related loans has helped some countries collect on their student loans, so it seems plausible that this solution could help the United States achieve similar outcomes. However, is income-related repayment the only (or most preferred) option for achieving this policy goal? Considering that the proprietary sector of higher education accounts for nearly half of the nation's student loan defaults, some advocates may argue that the best way to reduce default/delinquency is by introducing greater regulation into this sector to ensure students are able to find gainful employment that allows them to avoid defaulting on their loans. Since unemployment is so closely tied to defaults, some advocates may argue that borrowers who collect Unemployment Insurance should automatically be entered into existing emergency protection programs, which would likely reduce default/delinquency rates. Still others may believe that income-related loans are the best approach for reducing default. Clearly, there is no single policy solution to the default problem, but this chapter outlines some of the primary ways income-related loans could help borrowers repay their student loan debts.

A poorly designed income-related repayment policy has several pitfalls, and these too have been outlined here. Beyond the implementation and evaluation challenges noted above, it is important to consider how such a financing model might address (or ignore) current problems facing higher education in the United States. For example, a longstanding debate in higher education finance wrestles with the question about "who" should pay for college—students and their families, philanthropic organizations, or taxpayers? Ultimately, this is a shared responsibility between all three stakeholders, where no single group is burdened with paying the "full cost" of what it takes to deliver a college education. But under a system that indexes student loan repayment to individual earnings, this relationship could start to change. It is possible that colleges may actually have less incentive to keep tuition rates down, since debt would be more manageable. Interestingly, early proponents saw income-related repayment as a necessary first step in shifting financial responsibility toward individual students and away from taxpayers and philanthropy.[59] Questions about how this policy would impact the shared responsibility of higher education financing, and of college costs and affordability in particular, have been largely ignored in the current policy debate. In the absence of other reforms, income-related repayment may result in the unintended consequence of *less* institutional accountability while not necessarily fixing the underlying problems associated with financing today's higher education.

In light of these concerns, much more evidence is needed to fully understand whether and to what extent income-related loans might affect students and colleges. These issues are under-examined in the existing literature, since most of the research either compares how different countries design their loan schemes or develops theoretical arguments regarding the tradeoffs of linking repayments to students' incomes. There is surprisingly little rigorous research on how income-related loans affect students' borrowing, enrollment, and repayment behaviors. This is largely due to the lack of basic participation by—and of evaluation data from—the Department of Education, causing us to draw inferences from other countries that have richer data on their existing programs.

Even if we had good data on existing U.S. programs, it is necessary for us to have rigorous research designs that can point to causal relationships rather than simple correlations. Designing rigorous studies that test some of the conventional wisdom and unanswered questions about income-related loan models would be beneficial to the ongoing policy debates in the United States. This is a ripe area for further research, where policy-minded scholars could design experimental or quasi-experimental research studies to gain more information about how income-related repayment impacts students. Most importantly, a new repayment model should make students better off than they were without the new model, so careful consideration of the tradeoffs and unintended consequences will continue to play a central role in ongoing deliberations about income-related repayment schemes.

7

Rethinking Institutional Aid

Implications for Affordability, Access, and the Effectiveness of Federal Student Aid

Lesley J. Turner

INTRODUCTION

In each of the last three decades, increases in higher education prices outpaced inflation in the United States. According to data from the College Board's *Annual Survey of Colleges*, public four-year schools' tuition and fees increased by approximately 230 percent between the 1983–1984 and 2013–2014 academic years. The sticker price—that is, the published tuition and fees—of four-year nonprofit institutions followed a similar trend, increasing by over 150 percent.[1] Despite substantial growth in federal need-based grant aid, these trends raise concerns that many prospective students may no longer be able to afford college or may need to incur substantial debt to access higher education.

When considering postsecondary access and affordability, listed tuition and fees will not provide the full story. Within a given institution, many students pay substantially less than the sticker price due to the provision of institutional scholarships, grants, and tuition waivers. The growth in tuition and fees has been accompanied by an increase in institutional aid, with both the number of students receiving discounts and the amount of aid provided to recipients growing.

Institutional aid can target needy students with additional resources. Conversely, institutional aid may also be used by schools to "undo" the benefit of outside aid. Although institutional aid receives less attention than published tuition and other sources of financial aid, it matters for affordability and access to higher education, as well as for the effectiveness of federal and state need-based grant programs.

Implications for Affordability and Access

Prior to the expansion of the Pell Grant program in 2008, institutional grants made up the largest source of grant aid provided to undergraduate students.[2] In 2013, institutional grants counted for 19 percent of total expenditures on undergraduate student aid, with federal and state grant aid contributing 24 and 5 percent, respectively.[3]

Increases in published tuition overstate price increases, especially among nonprofit institutions. Higher tuition may allow schools to provide larger institutional grants to lower-income students. As long as prospective students can easily access information on their expected discounts, this "high-tuition/high-aid" strategy could increase postsecondary access for needy students. Implementing price controls may hurt low-income students if these individuals' discounts are subsidized by tuition paid by wealthier students.

However, prospective students—especially those from disadvantaged backgrounds—appear to systematically overestimate college costs.[4] The decoupling of the easily observable sticker price from an individual's specific net price likely affects students' college enrollment decisions. Prospective students who lack information on financial aid eligibility or who do not apply for aid due to the complexity of the application process may be deterred from enrolling in college.[5] Low-income, high ability students may be deterred from considering high-quality institutions with high sticker prices and may ultimately pay more to attend a less selective school.[6]

Most schools do not publish information on how institutional discounts are distributed across students with varying income, need, or other characteristics. The Department of Education requires all institutions that participate in federal student aid programs to report total expenditures on institutional grant aid and aid received by first-time, full-time, degree-seeking freshmen. Beginning in 2010, the Department also required schools to report the average grant aid (from all sources) received by students within specific income ranges. Unfortunately, this information doesn't distinguish between portable grant aid (from state and federal programs) and grants that are tied to a specific institution.

Implications for Equity and the Effectiveness of Federal and State Grant Aid

The provision of institutional aid affects the distribution of prices across students within a given school. Institutions may target low-income students with additional aid or use institutional grants to compete for high ability students. Past research indicates that selective nonprofit institutions direct a larger share of institutional aid to meet the needs of low-income students relative to more wealthy students.[7] Heller et al. (2010) examine differences in net prices by income quartile, college sector (nonprofit versus public), and selectivity, and show that with the exception of the most selective nonprofit schools, high-income students appear to receive a larger share of institutional grant aid than their lower-income counterparts.[8]

The increased use of institutional discounts has important implications for the effectiveness of federal and state need-based aid. Schools observe federal and state grant aid when choosing how much institutional aid to provide to a given student, raising concerns that schools may redistribute institutional aid in response to increases in the generosity of outside aid. Several recent studies provide evidence that institutional aid reductions crowd out federal and state grant aid.[9] The growth in the federal Pell Grant program underscores the need to understand whether institutional aid supplants other need-based grants and whether any policies can increase the effectiveness of these expenditures.

This chapter begins by describing trends in institutional aid and discusses whether institutional discounts have counteracted increases in higher education prices. For the purposes of this discussion, *net price* refers to the components of a specific student's price that are tied to a specific institution: listed tuition and fees minus institutional grant aid. I primarily focus on institutional discounts (including grants, scholarships, and tuition waivers) provided to undergraduate students.[10] The following sections discuss research on the impact of institutional discounts on student behavior, the interaction between institutional aid and federal and state aid programs, and the way in which current policy efforts may affect the distribution of institutional aid across students and discuss key considerations for future policy. A brief conclusion brings these threads together.

THE INCREASING IMPORTANCE OF INSTITUTIONAL GRANT AID

Between 1977 and 2013, inflation-adjusted tuition and fees at degree-granting postsecondary institutions participating in federal student aid programs increased by 177 percent on average, from approximately \$3,800 to \$10,500.[11] Total Pell Grant expenditures increased over this period, but the relative value of the average Pell Grant declined from 82 to 36 percent of average tuition and fees.[12]

Information on institutional discounts over this period is less reliable. The Integrated Postsecondary Education Data System (IPEDS), an annual survey of postsecondary institutions participating in federal student aid programs, collects information on aggregate expenditures on institutional aid and total revenue from tuition and fees. Combined with IPEDS data on student attendance, measures of gross and net tuition per full-time equivalent student (FTE) can be constructed.[13]

To test whether institutional grant aid has buffered students from increases in published tuition and fees, I calculate changes in gross and net tuition revenue per FTE between 2002 and 2011. Gross tuition revenue per FTE approximates published tuition (adjusted by the relative percentage of students paying in-state versus out-of-state rates for schools that charge tuition differentials). Net tuition revenue per FTE approximates the average net price paid by full-time students. The first four rows of table 7.1 display the average gross and net tuition per FTE in 2011 and the average increase in gross and net prices, broken down by sector of higher education.

Between 2002 and 2011, increases in institutional aid just kept pace with tuition increases in public schools. Students attending more selective public four-year institutions experienced an approximately 60 percent increase in both gross tuition and fees and institutional aid per FTE. In less selective public four-year institutions, gross and net tuition increased by 60 percent. Public two-year institutions provide lower levels of institutional grant aid; average gross and net tuition per FTE only differed by approximately \$240 in 2011, and gross and net tuition grew by 43 and 42 percent, respectively.

Conversely, institutional grant aid appears to have slowed rising costs at four-year nonprofit schools. Tuition and fees increased by 26 percent among more selective nonprofit schools, but due to increases in institutional aid, the net cost of attendance only increased by 16 percent. Trends for less selective nonprofit institutions are similar, with gross tuition increasing by

TABLE 7.1   Prices and institutional grant aid: 2002 and 2011

	1. Public 4-Year		2. Public 2-Year	3. Nonprofit 4-Year		4. Nonprofit 2-Year	5. For-Profit
	A. More selective	B. Less Selective		A. More selective	B. Less Selective		
Gross tuition and fees/FTE: 2011	$13,227	$9,285	$3,401	$32,795	$19,895	$11,721	$12,581
Percent increase 2002–2011	0.62	0.60	0.43	0.26	0.26	0.30	0.49
Net tuition and fees/FTE: 2011	$10,756	$7,967	$3,162	$21,708	$14,423	$10,111	$12,281
Percent increase 2002–2011	0.62	0.60	0.42	0.16	0.18	0.27	0.49
Institutional grants/FTE: 2011	$2,471	$1,318	$239	$11,088	$5,472	$1,609	$300
Percent increase 2002–2011	0.63	0.60	0.56	0.52	0.51	0.63	2.72
Number of institutions (2011)	114	440	1,429	330	818	374	3,127
Percent FTE Undergraduates: 2002	0.13	0.24	0.35	0.08	0.09	0.01	0.09
Percent FTE Undergraduates: 2011	0.11	0.22	0.36	0.07	0.08	0.01	0.15

Source: 2002–2011 IPEDS (institutional charactersitics, 12-month enrollment, and finance files) and Barron's Guide.

Note: All dollar amounts adjusted for inflation using the CPI-U (2013$). Unbalanced panel. Excludes schools missing enrollment or finance data. Gross tuition and fees is equal to tuition paid by all students plus student aid from all sources applied to tuition and fees. Net tuition and fees is equal to gross tuition and fees minus institutional grant aid. Full-time equivalent students (FTE) calculated using instructional activity (see IPEDS glossery for details). More selective schools are institutions that are classified as most selective, highly competitive, or very competitive by the Barron's Guide or, if missing from the Barron's guide, are institutions that admit 50 percent or fewer applicants. Less selective schools are institutions that are classified as competitive, less competitive, or non-competitive by the Barron's guide or, if missing from the Barron's guide, are institutions that admit over 50 percent of applicants. Two-year schools are institutions that offer any associate's degree programs and include schools that only offer non-degree programs. All for-profit institutions are less selective.

26 percent and net tuition growing by 18 percent. Institutional grants per FTE remained low within two-year nonprofit and for-profit institutions.

Although IPEDS has not yet released data on 2012 institutional expenditures, preliminary data from the College Board's *Annual Survey of Colleges* suggest that tuition increases outpaced increases in institutional grant aid between 2011 and 2012.[14] Among public schools in the top quartile of selectivity, institutional grant aid per FTE increased by 2.3 percent, while average published in-state tuition and fees increased by 5.1 percent. Likewise, the most selective four-year nonprofit institutions increased institutional grant aid per FTE by 0.4 percent between 2011 and 2012, while average sticker prices increased by 1.1 percent.

Institutional grant aid also affects the dispersion of prices across students within a given school. Increases in average institutional aid may represent an increase in the percentage of students receiving institutional aid, an increase in the amount of aid provided to recipients, or some combination of these outcomes. IPEDS can only provide information on the size of the pot of money being distributed to students.

Fortunately, the Department of Education also collects student-level data from a representative sample of IPEDS schools for the National Postsecondary Student Aid Study (NPSAS). The NPSAS contains a mix of administrative and survey data that provides detailed information on need and financial aid from all sources for a nationally representative cross-section of college students.

Table 7.2 presents information on the share of undergraduate students receiving institutional aid (Panel A) and average institutional aid conditional on receipt (Panel B) by school control and level using data from the 1996 through 2012 NPSAS.[15] Panel C displays the ratio of average institutional aid to the average cost of attendance.

Across all four-year public and nonprofit institutions, the percentage of students receiving institutional grants, the amount of institutional grant aid provided to recipients, and the ratio of institutional aid to the cost of attendance increased between 1996 and 2012. The share of undergraduates attending PhD-granting nonprofit institutions receiving institutional grant aid increased from 40 to 58 percent between 1996 and 2012. At the same time, the size of the average grant provided to recipients increased by 40 percent, from approximately $10,500 to $14,700.

The share of students receiving discounts also increased in the public two-year sector. In 2012, 13 percent of students attending public two-year

TABLE 7.2 Institutional grant aid receipt by sector and year

	1. Public 4-Year		2. Public 2-Year	3. Nonprofit		4. For-Profit	All Institutions
	A. Non-Doctoral	B. PhD-Granting		A. Non-Doctoral	B. PhD-Granting		
A. Percentage of students receiving institutional grant aid							
1996	0.11	0.15	0.07	0.40	0.40	0.06	0.14
2000	0.14	0.19	0.08	0.43	0.51	0.07	0.17
2004	0.16	0.24	0.07	0.46	0.54	0.07	0.18
2008	0.15	0.26	0.10	0.49	0.52	0.07	0.19
2012	0.13	0.25	0.13	0.55	0.58	0.03	0.20
B. Average amount of institutional grant aid (conditional on receipt)							
1996	$2,453	$3,830	$912	$6,369	$10,486	$1,389	$4,591
2000	$2,499	$3,952	$839	$7,820	$11,077	$1,547	$5,303
2004	$2,894	$3,976	$1,466	$7,911	$10,411	$2,959	$5,366
2008	$3,468	$4,305	$824	$9,642	$11,696	$1,805	$5,517
2012	$2,697	$4,695	$1,038	$12,354	$14,705	$2,347	$6,675
C. Ratio of average institutional grant aid (including zeros) to average cost of attendance[1]							
1996	0.02	0.04	0.01	0.13	0.15	0.01	0.06
2000	0.03	0.05	0.01	0.15	0.18	0.01	0.07
2004	0.03	0.06	0.01	0.15	0.17	0.01	0.07
2008	0.04	0.06	0.01	0.17	0.17	0.01	0.07
2012	—	—	—	—	—	—	—

(continues)

TABLE 7.2 Institutional grant aid receipt by sector and year (Cont.)

| | 1. Public 4-Year | | 2. Public 2-Year | 3. Nonprofit | | 4. For-Profit | All Institutions |
	A. Non-Doctoral	B. PhD-Granting		A. Non-Doctoral	B. PhD-Granting		
D. Number of Students (in millions)							
1996	2.05	3.00	7.46	1.81	0.76	0.89	16.68
2000	1.90	3.30	7.15	1.54	0.93	0.81	16.58
2004	2.06	3.65	7.87	1.73	0.96	1.47	19.05
2008	2.04	3.85	8.46	1.46	1.23	2.14	20.76
2012	2.24	4.29	8.87	1.35	1.42	2.97	23.06

Source: 1996, 2000, 2004, 2008, and 2012 NPSAS (via PowerStats).

Note: Outcomes for students attending multiple institutions not displayed (but are included in the calculations for all institutions). All dollar amounts adjusted for inflation using the CPI-U (2013$). Public two-year institutions include nondegree granting schools. Nonprofit nondoctoral institutions include nonprofit institutions offering two-year degrees and nondegree programs.

[1] Underlying sample limited to observations where cost of attendance nonmissing (N =16.45 in 1996, 15.51 in 2000, 17.72 in 2004, and 19.17 in 2008).

institutions received institutional grant aid, averaging approximately $1,000. Relative to the average cost of attendance, the purchasing power of institutional grant aid remained constant.

Students attending for-profit schools were the least likely to receive institutional aid in every period. In 1996, 6 percent of all for-profit students received institutional discounts, averaging approximately $1,400, while in 2012, only 3 percent received institutional aid, averaging $2,300. Average institutional aid represented just 1 percent of the average cost of attendance in the for-profit sector.

Who Benefits from Institutional Aid?

To understand how institutional aid is distributed across students with different levels of need, I use the 2008 NPSAS to calculate the percentage of all grant aid that is provided to students with no remaining need. As shown in figure 7.1, public institutions are the most likely to provide institutional aid to students with no remaining need.

However, these calculations are affected by the total cost of attendance within a sector. Even wealthy students may technically have remaining need when tuition is high. Additionally, schools have discretion over how institutional aid is distributed across students with remaining need. Schools that only provide institutional aid to students with remaining need may not be targeting the poorest students. Lower-income students receive more grant aid on average, and thus will have less unmet need. Pell Grant recipients may receive a smaller portion of the total pot of institutional aid because the school is not targeting these students or because they only require a small amount of additional aid to fully cover the cost of attendance. Any statistic that examines targeting should take into account how needy a particular group is after overall tuition and other grants have been accounted for.

To measure how well institutions target aid toward their neediest students, I use the 2008 NPSAS to calculate the ratio of total institutional grant aid to total unmet need for the set of students with remaining need. Table 7.3 displays these results, where I separately examine students who are eligible for the maximum Pell Grant award, students who are eligible for a Pell Grant less than the maximum award, and Pell-ineligible students.[16] Panel A contains information on students attending public two-year institutions. The neediest students—those eligible for the maximum Pell Grant—had approximately $6,600 in unmet need and received approximately $100 in institutional grant aid, on average. Furthermore, the unmet need of this group of

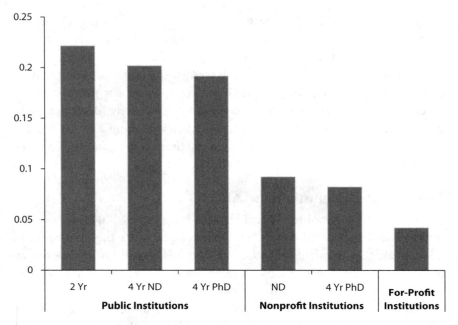

FIGURE 7.1   Share of institutional grant aid provided to students with no unmet need

Source: 2008 NPSAS (via PowerStats).

Note: Unmet need is equal to a student's total cost of attendance minus expected family contribution (EFC), state, and federal grant aid. For students with no unmet need, the sum of EFC and state/federal grant aid exceeds the total cost of attendance.

students represented 54 percent of all unmet need within this sector, while total institutional aid received by these students represented 34 percent of all institutional aid provided in this sector. The final column displays the ratio of the share of unmet need to the share of institutional aid, with the interpretation that a percentage point increase in the share of unmet need among students eligible for the maximum Pell Grant award is met with a 0.62 percentage point increase in the share of institutional grant aid.

Public and nonprofit institutions display similar patterns in their targeting of institutional aid to students with remaining need, although nonprofit students have greater unmet need and receive larger institutional grants. It is important to note that estimated differences in targeting across sectors do not necessarily represent within-institution differences in targeting since the publicly available NPSAS data does not identify individual institutions.[17]

TABLE 7.3   Institutional aid effectiveness and targeting by sector and Pell Grant eligibility, 2008

	Per Student Average			Percent of Total		
	Unmet need	Inst. grants	Ratio	Unmet need	Inst. grants	Ratio
A. Two-Year Public						
Max Pell Grant	$6,582	$107	0.02	0.54	0.34	0.62
Pell Grant < Max	$4,838	$104	0.02	0.33	0.26	0.81
No Pell Grant	$4,188	$157	0.04	0.13	0.18	1.42
B. Four-Year Public Non-doctoral						
Max Pell Grant	$10,067	$465	0.05	0.40	0.21	0.54
Pell Grant < Max	$8,637	$538	0.06	0.31	0.23	0.72
No Pell Grant	$6,745	$740	0.11	0.28	0.36	1.27
C. Four-Year Public PhD-granting						
Max Pell Grant	$13,235	$1,157	0.09	0.32	0.19	0.58
Pell Grant < Max	$11,998	$1,450	0.12	0.31	0.24	0.80
No Pell Grant	$8,485	$1,334	0.16	0.37	0.38	1.03
D. Non-doctoral Nonprofit						
Max Pell Grant	$18,510	$2,948	0.16	0.26	0.13	0.50
Pell Grant < Max	$19,625	$4,672	0.24	0.28	0.21	0.75
No Pell Grant	$16,933	$6,636	0.39	0.46	0.57	1.23
E. Four-Year Nonprofit PhD-granting						
Max Pell Grant	$23,833	$4,694	0.20	0.20	0.12	0.61
Pell Grant < Max	$24,997	$6,757	0.27	0.23	0.19	0.84
No Pell Grant	$21,472	$7,384	0.34	0.58	0.62	1.06
F. For-profit						
Max Pell Grant	$17,440	$108	0.01	0.50	0.39	0.77
Pell Grant < Max	$18,365	$167	0.01	0.27	0.31	1.14
No Pell Grant	$13,709	$128	0.01	0.23	0.26	1.17

Source: 2008 NPSAS (via PowerStats).
Note: All dollar amounts adjusted for inflation using CPI-U (2013$). Unmet need equals COA – EFC – federal and state grant aid.

Price Setting in Higher Education

Why do institutions provide institutional discounts, and why has this practice increased? The practice of price discrimination, or offering a schedule of prices that varies across consumers with different characteristics, has been documented in a variety of imperfectly competitive markets. Business travelers pay more for a last-minute plane ticket than individuals who purchase their ticket well in advance. Matinee movie tickets cost less than tickets for movies shown in the evening. In higher education, students pay different net prices for the same "product" within a given university.

In settings where price discrimination is possible, consumers who are more responsive to price increases (those with more elastic demand) generally pay less. In the case of plane and movie tickets, firms are able to infer consumers' responsiveness from their behavior (e.g., buying tickets in advance or willingness to attend a daytime movie) and adjust prices accordingly. Increases in competition generally lead to lower prices. Price discrimination has ambiguous impacts on overall welfare. In some cases, the inability of firms to vary prices across consumers may lead to the absence of markets for certain goods.

The market for higher education differs from this standard setting in many ways. Schools observe an extensive amount of information on most students' financial circumstances. Students who submit a federal financial aid application to college financial aid offices reveal information on family income and assets as well as outside financial aid.[18] Additionally, the market is served by public, nonprofit, and for-profit firms, which likely have different objectives. Some public universities lack control over tuition setting. And if peers matter, students serve as both consumers and inputs in the production of human capital.[19]

Economic models of college pricing suggest that the amount of institutional grant aid (or effective price) offered to students in a given group (defined by demographic or other characteristics) depends on how responsive their enrollment decision is to price changes and how much value the school places on enrolling students with these specific characteristics. This "weight" placed on students may depend on a combination of academic and nonacademic characteristics, such as high school achievement, contributions to diversity, and the variance of student quality within the group.[20]

Increased competition for high ability students by selective schools may have contributed to increases in institutional aid.[21] Declines in state funding for public institutions may also play a role in the increased use of student-specific discounts. Over time, selective public schools have faced more competition from elite private schools for high ability local students. Public schools may need to adopt the high-tuition/high-aid model of their non-profit competitors.[22]

IMPACTS OF INSTITUTIONAL AID ON COLLEGE ENROLLMENT AND EDUCATIONAL ATTAINMENT

Prior research suggests that a $1,000 decrease in price leads to an approximately 4 percent increase in the probability of college attendance.[23] Increases in grant aid should have the same impact on college attendance as decreases in tuition, as long as the application process is relatively easy for students to understand and complete. However, there is little evidence that Pell Grant aid increases the enrollment of traditional students. Students may have difficulty determining how much Pell Grant aid they are eligible for, and the federal financial aid application process is lengthy and complex.[24] Students do not learn about their financial aid package until after they have applied and been accepted to an institution.[25] The impact of institutional grant aid on college attendance should depend on the extent to which students can anticipate their institutional discounts when they are deciding whether to apply for college.

College and Major Choice

Lower-income students appear to underestimate their eligibility for need-based grant aid.[26] Hoxby and Avery (2012) show that many high ability, low-income students don't apply to schools that would maximize quality and minimize price, but rather end up paying more for lower-quality schools. Long (2004) finds a decrease in the importance of list prices on college enrollment between the 1970s and 1990s.[27]

Several studies examine the impact of institutional grant aid on the enrollment decisions of applicants to a specific institution. Van der Klauuw (2002) finds that lower-income students are more responsive to institutional grant aid than students who are likely to be higher income.[28] Linsenmeier, Rosen, and Rouse (2006) examine the impact of replacing loan aid with institutional grants on the matriculation of low-income students to a selective Northeast university, and find positive but statistically insignificant impacts, with larger and marginally significant increases for minority students.[29] However, Hillman (2013) finds that similar policies increased the enrollment of Pell Grant recipients in selective institutions.[30]

Research examining how institutional aid affects students' choice of major is more limited. Rothstein and Rouse (2011) find small and insignificant impacts of replacing loans with institutional grants on major choice among students attending an elite nonprofit university.[31] Stange (2013) examines whether tuition differentials between majors affects students' choices and finds some evidence that when the price of pursuing an engineering major increases, enrollment falls.[32]

Persistence and Attainment

Ultimately, we are interested in understanding how institutional aid affects educational attainment, where enrollment and choice of college and major are important intermediate steps. The best evidence comes from studies of the impacts of federal and state need-based grant aid on persistence and degree receipt. Although few papers specifically focus on institutional aid, these results may be generalizable to the case of institutional grant aid programs with similar timing and structure. Bettinger (2004) provides suggestive evidence that Pell Grant aid increases persistence.[33] Castleman and Long (2013) show that Florida's need-based grant program increases enrollment, persistence, and degree receipt.[34] Goldrick-Rab et al. (2012) find that grant aid targeting low-income students in Wisconsin increases persistence.[35]

Grant aid may be most effective when paired with other requirements or supports. Scott-Clayton (2011) finds that a state merit aid program in West Virginia that required recipients to meet minimum GPA and credit requirements to receive aid increased educational attainment and graduation rates.[36] Angrist, Lang, and Oreopoulos (2009) study a program where students attending a nonselective Canadian public university were randomly assigned to earn aid based on maintaining a minimum GPA and course load.[37] The program led to small increases in female students' GPAs when these students received additional services, such as peer advising.

CROWD-OUT OF FEDERAL AND STATE NEED-BASED GRANT AID

Federal and state governments provide substantial need-based financial aid with the intention of increasing college affordability and access to higher education. Some students may face credit constraints and may be unable to borrow against future income to finance college attendance, leading to inefficiently low levels of education. Need-based grant aid aims to relax these constraints. Additionally, increases in aggregate education levels may have positive spillover effects on productivity and may help to reduce crime, increase political participation, and affect other important social outcomes.[38] Finally, financial aid for higher education may represent redistribution generated by a desire for equity.

Although students are the statutory recipients of need-based grants, a dollar of federal or state aid does not necessarily lead to a one dollar reduction in the recipient's final price.[39] Schools may also respond to outside need-based aid by increasing recipients' effective prices. In other words, reductions in institutional aid may crowd out the benefit of federal or state grant aid.

In 1987, Secretary of Education William J. Bennett raised a related concern—that colleges would respond to increases in federal student aid by increasing prices via tuition and fees. Empirical evidence of the original "Bennett Hypothesis" is mixed. Several studies find a positive correlation between published tuition and the Pell Grant generosity, but these effects are identified using time-series variation in the maximum Pell Grant award, which is likely related to concurrent economic trends.[40] Additionally, the majority of Pell Grant recipients attend public schools and, in many states, public institutions lack the ability to raise tuition without approval from their governing body. However, Cellini and Goldin (2012) provide evidence that the original Bennett Hypothesis may be applicable to for-profit institutions by showing that federal aid eligibility leads to tuition increases in this sector.[41]

Students must fill out a Free Application for Federal Student Aid (FAFSA) form to qualify for federal and many state financial aid programs. The FAFSA requires a complicated set of inputs, including information on income, assets, and family structure. Students also specify the institutions they are considering. Upon completing the FAFSA, students learn of their expected family contribution (EFC), the federal government's measure of need. The schools listed on the FAFSA receive all of this information. Schools put together a financial aid package by calculating the student's eligibility for federal and state grant aid and choosing how much institutional aid the student will receive. The student is then provided with the entire financial aid package (which may also include loans or work-study). Even though state, federal, and institutional grant aid is delineated, at this point the final price (tuition and fees minus grant aid from all sources) is likely the most salient component. The majority of prospective students only list one school, likely making it more difficult to distinguish between the sources of aid the school controls and federal and state aid that is not tied to any specific institution.

Long (2004) and Turner (2012) test for crowd-out of state grant aid and tax-based aid, respectively. Long (2004) examines the implementation of the Georgia HOPE scholarship program, which provides substantial assistance to students in Georgia who achieve a 3.0 GPA.[42] Results suggest that private nonprofit institutions captured 30 percent of HOPE aid by increasing tuition and fees and reducing institutional aid. Turner (2012) focuses on tax-based aid provided by the Hope and Lifetime Learning credits.[43] Using individual-level data from the NPSAS and comparing students with similar levels of income before and after the tax credits were implemented, he finds evidence that four-year public and nonprofit institutions reduce institutional aid dollar for dollar with estimated education tax benefits.

I test whether Pell Grant aid crowds out institutional grant aid.[44] I take advantage of the nonlinearities in the Pell Grant program's formula and use regression kink and regression discontinuity designs to examine how differences in Pell Grant generosity affect the provision of institutional grant aid for students attending the same institution, in the same year, with essentially the same level of need (table 7.4). I find that for every dollar increase in Pell Grant aid, schools reduce institutional aid by 15 percent ($0.15) on average, an amount totaling approximately $5 billion in 2011.

However, this result masks substantial variation in crowd-out across sectors (defined by institutional control and selectivity). The majority of Pell Grant recipients attend public institutions, and in this sector, net crowd-out is approximately zero (table 7.4, second row). Additionally, public schools *increase* institutional aid provided to some Pell Grant recipients—those

TABLE 7.4   Estimated crowd-out of Pell Grant aid via price discrimination

	Percent captured	95% Confidence interval
All Institutions	0.148	[0.093, 0.203]
Public Institutions	0.038	[0.006, 0.070]
Nonselective Private Institutions	0.179	[0.056, 0.301]
Selective Nonprofit Institutions	0.677	[0.425, 0.930]

Source: 1996, 2000, 2004, and 2008 NPSAS.
Note: See Turner (2013) for estimation details.

near the program's eligibility threshold. On average, Pell Grant recipients attending nonselective public schools receive an additional $200 in institutional aid (a 92 percent increase) and those attending more selective public schools receive an extra $860 (a 120 percent increase). However, even in the public sector, additional Pell Grant aid crowds out institutional aid by 11 to 13 cents on the dollar. Overall, these two responses result in a transfer of institutional grant aid from the most needy Pell Grant recipients (those with the lowest EFC) to the least needy recipients (those near the Pell Grant eligibility threshold).

Conversely, I estimate that reductions in institutional grant aid crowd out close to 70 percent of Pell Grant aid for students attending more selective nonprofit institutions. Crowd-out is smaller among nonselective nonprofit and for-profit institutions—these schools appropriate around 18 percent of students' Pell Grant aid.

Ultimately, the effectiveness of the Pell Grant program in raising educational attainment for low-income students depends on both the degree of crowd-out and how institutions use these funds. Schools may use these funds to increase the quality of education and improve the probability that Pell Grant recipients graduate. On the other hand, these additional funds may be used to increase discounts provided to higher ability students. My results suggest that the majority of Pell Grant aid increases affordability for the targeted population, but future research is needed to untangle these additional questions.

POLICY IMPLICATIONS

The federal government has developed several tools to help students understand the difference between listed tuition and college costs net of federal, state, and institutional grant aid. The 2008 Higher Education Opportunity Act required schools participating in federal student aid programs to post a *net price calculator* by October 2011.[45] The calculator is intended to approximate an individual's EFC and provide individualized price estimates. Prospective students enter information relating to their income and other characteristics. Outputs include a breakdown of the total cost of attendance, estimated grant aid, and a "net price" equal to the cost of attendance minus grant aid from all sources. However, schools are not required to differentiate between portable grant aid that follows a student and discounts tied to the specific institution. Moreover, there is no standardized format or centralized location for calculators; many are difficult to locate, without links from institutions' financial aid Web sites.[46]

Beginning in 2013, each school participating in federal student aid programs receives an annual *college scorecard*.[47] Ultimately, a school's scorecard will contain five key pieces of information on college costs and quality, including average cost of attendance (net of grant aid from all sources), the percentage of students graduating within 150 percent of expected time to degree, three-year federal student loan cohort default rates, median student loan debt, and employment outcomes. Currently, no employment outcomes are reported. Students can search for specific institutions by name, location, program offerings, and size.[48]

Finally, the Department of Education and Consumer Financial Protection Bureau have developed a *financial aid shopping sheet* that schools voluntarily adopt.[49] This form provides a standardized method for reporting a student's financial aid package and is intended to facilitate cross-institution comparisons of net prices and financial aid. The form also contains measures of institutional quality, such as graduation rates and median student loan debt.

Key Considerations for Reforms Affecting Institutional Aid

Policies that affect the provision and distribution of institutional aid can target the behavior either of students (demand-side interventions) or of institutions (supply-side interventions). Demand-side interventions aim to reduce schools' ability to appropriate outside grant aid through price discrimination. Schools' ability to capture outside grant aid should decrease as competition grows. Conversely, supply-side interventions aim to directly affect the behavior of institutions either by mandating or incentivizing low (net) prices. Currently, institutions receiving federal student aid face a limited set of requirements, none of which relate to institutional aid.[50] However, any additional regulations placed on institutions should not provide incentives for schools to avoid admitting low-income students such as Pell Grant recipients or reduce their ability to target needy students with institutional aid.

The majority of prospective students only list one school on their FAFSA, effectively limiting their ability to gain information on distribution of net costs across institutions.[51] Federal and state governments can encourage students to "shop around" by either decreasing students' cost of accessing information or by incentivizing students to apply to multiple institutions. The tools described above all aim to reduce the cost of accessing information on net prices across institutions. Ultimately, the effectiveness of these tools will depend on whether the information they contain is easy for students to access and understand. Hoxby and Turner's (2013) Hamilton Project proposal provides a detailed framework for providing customized information to high school students.[52] The ongoing FAFSA Completion Project, where high schools are provided student-level information on FAFSA filing, is an example of an intervention that could be modified to incentivize students to apply to multiple institutions.[53]

Incremental reforms to the Department of Education's current tools could further decrease the cost of accessing information on prices. For instance, most net price calculators do not differentiate between institutional grant aid and fungible federal and state grants. Providing more information to students about their options and how far their Pell Grants will take them at various schools could increase pressure on schools to lower prices. At a minimum, the net price calculator should distinguish between federal, state, and institutional grant aid and which sources of aid are tied to a specific school.

Currently, each school maintains its own net price calculator. To compare prices across schools, students must first locate each school's calculator and then enter information required by the specific school. Alternatively, the Department of Education could develop and maintain a centralized net price calculator and require schools to submit a standardized set of inputs, such as listed tuition and institutional grant aid for students in a given range of adjusted gross income (AGI) and dependency status. Since Pell Grant and most state grant aid programs are not tied to a specific institution, the Department of Education use its own formula to provide estimates of Pell Grant eligibility. State governments could likewise submit simplified formulas that would allow for an estimate of the expected state grant awards. Students would then be able to go to one Web site and enter a set of search criteria (e.g., zip code, state, sector, maximum net price) and compare prices across a number of schools.

Even this approach requires students to understand the purpose of the net price calculator, have knowledge of their family's financial circumstances, and have some idea of which schools they would like to consider. A more ambitious approach would be to further reduce the cost of accessing this information by automatically providing families containing high-school-aged children with personalized information on college costs and quality. For example, parents with high-school-aged children could be allowed to indicate on their annual tax return that they would like to receive personalized information on college costs and options.[54] The IRS would provide information from the family's tax return to the Department of Education. The Department of Education would provide each participating family with a unique link and password to the online net cost calculator prefilled with the family's individualized inputs and outputs from local institutions.[55] Students and their families would also be allowed to generate new lists of schools based on other criteria such as predicted net price, sector, or size.

What are potential supply-side policies that aim to increase institutional aid targeting low-income students or reduce crowd-out of federal student aid? Schools could be required to offer multiyear institutional aid packages. Students may be more likely to enroll in college and invest their time in coursework if they receive a guaranteed net price for their expected period of attendance. Schools could agree to not increase tuition or decrease institutional aid for students after enrollment, conditional on meeting specific goals related to GPA or progress toward their degree. This requirement would reduce one potential avenue for crowd-out of outside aid, as students who experience an increase in need and a resulting increase in Pell Grant aid will continue to also receive their initial institutional aid package.

The federal government could incentivize school spending on needy students by offering a match for institutional aid spent on Pell Grant recipients. Similarly, schools that enroll (and graduate) a sufficiently large number of Pell Grant recipients could be given bonuses. In both of these cases, however, we should be concerned about unintended consequences. First, a matching requirement might lead schools to further increase overall tuition to generate sufficient revenue for the match. Providing bonuses linked to graduation outcomes may incentivize schools to reduce requirements for degree receipt.

Ideally, whether in the form of carrots or sticks, these policies should avoid providing incentives to schools to (1) avoid admitting Pell Grant recipients, or (2) treat Pell Grant recipients as cash cows (e.g., by focusing on enrollment over attainment and graduation). For instance, requiring institutions to provide a minimum amount of institutional aid per Pell Grant award may lead schools to reduce the number of Pell Grant recipients admitted.

The metric that schools are evaluated on should encompass efforts to both serve and support low-income students. Schools can achieve these objectives by providing additional institutional aid to these students, but they may also be able to more effectively serve needy students by providing noncash supports (e.g., access to tutoring) that increase graduation rates.

Ultimately, prices should not be the only factor in a student's decision of whether and where to go to college. Given the estimated returns on a college degree, price differentials are small in comparison to the present discounted value of future earnings. School quality matters for degree receipt. Cohodes and Goodman (2013) show that despite paying lower prices, students induced to attend lower-quality (defined by average graduation rates) public schools by the Massachusetts Adams Scholarship had lower educational attainment and were less likely to graduate than they would have been in the absence of scholarship.[56]

President Obama's recent proposal to tie student aid to college ratings includes a mix of mandates and incentives for institutions and increased information for students.[57] Schools would receive ratings based on prices and student outcomes, and federal student aid would be linked to colleges' performance along these metrics. Additional provisions include bonuses for schools that enroll and graduate Pell Grant recipients and incentives for states via a "Race to the Top" program. The college ratings, likely based on the current scorecard, would provide students with additional information on graduates' average earnings.

CONCLUSION

Institutional aid must play a larger role in the broader discussion of college affordability. Published tuition and fees do not provide an accurate picture of the prices students actually face or how affordable college is for students with different levels of need. Currently, much of the information schools are required to report does not distinguish between aid that the institution has control over and aid from outside sources, such as Pell Grants.

As tuition and fees have grown over the past three decades, schools' use of institutional aid to provide discounts to particular students has also increased. Price discrimination in higher education is not necessarily detrimental. For instance, tuition from higher-income students may allow a school to offer more institutional aid, effectively subsidizing lower-income students.

However, if students only respond to published tuition and lack an easy way to approximate their individual discount at a given university, price discrimination and the high-tuition/high-aid model may reduce low-income students' enrollment and attainment. Low-income students underestimate their eligibility for financial aid and likely face some of the highest costs of gathering information on the availability of institutional aid. Finally, the benefit of federal and state grant aid may be crowded out by reductions in institutional aid.

Proposals targeting students aim to decrease the cost of gathering information on college costs and quality, encouraging students to "shop around" for the best deal. Any policies that target the behavior of institutions, such as regulating prices or incentivizing the enrollment of Pell Grant recipients, should be carefully designed to avoid unintended consequences.

8

Managing Risk, Reaping Reward

The Case for a Comprehensive Income-Based Student Loan System

Stephen Crawford and Robert Sheets

INTRODUCTION

Weighing in at well over $100 billion per year, the federal government's student loan programs constitute by far the largest public investment in American higher education. As such, they offer a powerful tool for pursuing the goals of higher education policy. To date, however, that tool has been employed for just one purpose: expanding access. In today's environment, there are compelling reasons for adding two other goals: increasing college completion rates and ensuring that students gain sufficient economic value from their investments to pay off their loans without financial hardship.

To achieve these goals, this chapter[1] recommends a comprehensive, income-based loan system that builds on current income-contingent repayment proposals but focuses more attention on the "front end" of the loan cycle—the point at which students first receive guidance and take out loans. At the front end, loan manageability would be determined by estimating the borrower's future income based on the experience of similar students who attended the programs and institutions being considered. Manageability would be facilitated while in college by providing students with "on-track" feedback and incentives for doing what is necessary to graduate and achieve success in their chosen field.

The chapter also proposes changes to the "back end" of the loan management cycle. In place of loan forgiveness provisions now included in many income-contingent loan models, it recommends "systemic risk" adjustments for economic downturns and shifts in demand beyond the control of institutions and students. It also recommends incentives to institutions to help students manage financial risks by addressing two major determinants of loan problems—program noncompletion, and insufficient income to repay loans without financial hardship. This proposed income-based system would require a new national data infrastructure that could support an open applications marketplace for consumer information, student-institutional matching, and institutional performance management. The chapter concludes with the outline of a road map of steps for beginning to put in place the envisioned new loan system.

BACKGROUND

Although higher education clearly enriches individuals in many ways not captured by financial rewards, the national conversation has increasingly focused on its economic value. Concerned about competing in a changing global economy and providing economic opportunity to those left behind, governments and foundations have launched major initiatives to increase the proportion of Americans with a postsecondary credential.[2] Educational institutions themselves have emphasized the higher lifetime earnings of college graduates. More broadly, students, their families, and most Americans have come to view higher education as critical for career success, and to regard borrowing to finance it as a smart investment.[3]

Yet growing numbers of Americans express doubts that investments in higher education are producing the desired returns. According to a recent survey, 57 percent of respondents say that the higher education system "fails to provide students with good value for the money they and their families spend."[4] President Obama acknowledged these doubts in his 2013 State of the Union speech when he called for reforms to the financial aid system and new efforts to enhance the "value" of higher education.[5]

The concern with economic value is not surprising when one considers the stagnation of middle-class incomes, the expansion of college enrollments to include more students from lower-income families, the growth in the proportion of students who are working adults, and the increase in the number of students and former students who have substantial loans to repay. The debt problems are significant. Since 2004, both the number of student borrowers and the amounts they borrow have increased by 70 percent.

One result is that three-fifths of the class of 2012 graduated with an average of $26,500 in student loan debt, and 4 percent of them owed more than $100,000.[6] Worse, many other students dropped out along the way, leaving college with substantial debts but not the credentials that would help them earn enough to repay their loans. Student loan debt now amounts to over one trillion dollars, four-fifths of which is owed to the federal government. The latest figure for defaulting on these debts within three years of beginning repayment is 14.7 percent.[7] While this figure is influenced by a very high rate at for-profit schools, the rate is still 13 percent at public colleges and universities.

More tellingly, the delinquency rate (payments overdue by more than ninety days) for those "in repayment" is now 30 percent—and 35 percent for those who are thirty years of age or younger.[8] Repayment problems are also rising among older students who invested in higher education late in life in connection with career changes (or those that have Parent PLUS loans on behalf of their children). The number of individuals whose Social Security checks are being garnished because of unpaid student loans now exceeds 119,000, up from just 6 such cases in 2000.[9]

Some experts note that the average burden of loan repayment relative to income has probably not increased in recent years, and that monthly repayments for a $20,000 debt (assuming a ten-year repayment period) are only $212, meaning that college graduates need earn only a modest $25,500 a year to keep their loan payments under 10 percent of their income, a common benchmark for loan manageability. Yet others expect default rates to reach 40 percent in the future, though the recent changes to income-based repayment and loan forgiveness programs make that less likely.[10] In any event, the trends in delinquency and default rates, combined with the sums now involved, raise serious questions about the risks that borrowers and lenders are running. Student debt may also undermine the broader economy, as recent graduates put off large purchases in light of their difficulties repaying their student loans. They may postpone further investments in higher education as well.[11]

The growing uncertainties about whether college is worth the expense do not alter the fact that, *on average*, it is.[12] However, aggregate figures on average lifetime earnings mask wide variations by school, major, and age at the time of graduation.[13] For example, 42 percent of individuals with some college but no degree earn more than the median for workers with an associate's degree, and 28 percent of those with an associate's degree make more than the median for workers with a bachelor's.[14] Moreover, bachelor's degree holders who majored in the humanities and social sciences earn considerably less on average than those who majored in engineering and science, and they have much higher loan-to-income ratios.[15] In addition, college-educated workers, especially those with bachelor's degrees and below, have experienced stagnant and declining real earnings even before the most recent recession.[16] Thus, in the words of economists Christopher Avery and Sarah Turner, "from a financial perspective, enrolling in college is equivalent to signing up for a lottery with large expected gains . . . but also a lottery with significant probabilities of both larger positive, and smaller or even negative, returns."[17]

The federal government has responded to the concerns about the cost and value of postsecondary education in a variety of ways. It has tried to improve consumer education and protection. It has warned institutions offering career-related programs to provide students with at least minimum levels of "gainful employment" if they wish to continue enrolling students receiving federal financial aid. It has urged all institutions to hold down costs and keep price increases near the rate of inflation. And it has revised repayment terms for income-contingent loans in ways that should help students better manage their debts. These efforts are promising. However, none of them addresses whether student loans are truly manageable. Nor do they address how to manage repayment risks at the back end of the loan cycle in ways that can be effectively underwritten by a system that is not dependent on public subsidies or eventual bailouts.

EXPANDING THE GOALS

We believe that more fundamental reform is needed, starting with the goals themselves.

Access *and* Completion

Since the 1960s, federal student financial aid has focused largely on expanding access to postsecondary education, including access for students facing financial barriers to attending top-flight institutions. Grant programs addressed the needs of low-income students, while federal loan programs addressed broader issues of affordability, liquidity, and credit that middle-income students and their families faced. Underlying these programs was an assumption that higher education "pays off" for the vast majority of students who attend accredited programs and institutions. Student grants and loans were viewed as ways to finance high up-front expenses whose value would be realized only gradually over many years. If there was a perceived problem, it was not one of value but rather of financing the growing investments needed to expand access and facilitate social mobility in the face of rising college tuitions, stagnant family incomes, and increasing economic inequality.[18]

Strategies for promoting access assume that once admitted to a college or university, most students will graduate. However, about 45 percent of students at two- and four-year institutions do not graduate in three or six years, much less on time. Moreover, many noncompleters leave with large debts.[19] Because high rates of noncompletion undermine efforts to increase the proportion of adult Americans with postsecondary credentials, there has been much discussion of how to improve completion rates and what role federal policy could play. To date, however, student loan programs have changed little in response. Thus, we recommend expanding the traditional goal of access to one of access and completion.

Economic Value and Loan Repayment Adjustment

For students going deeply into debt to finance their education, the critical question, however, is not just whether they graduate, but whether they earn enough after graduation to pay off their loans. We do not assume that all students seek to maximize their future earnings—much less that they should do so—but we do believe that they and taxpayers share a goal of student borrowers at least breaking even on the debt-financed portion of their investment. That means graduating with the kinds of knowledge, skills, and credentials needed to earn enough to repay their loans without personal hardship or making unwise tradeoffs, such as not saving for retirement.

Loans are likely to be manageable if students attend programs and institutions that provide good economic value to students like them. The concept of value compares the gains in lifetime earnings capacity attributable to education to the costs of obtaining that education.

Higher education's costs and returns vary widely by state, institution, program, and student. Prudent borrowing requires knowing the likelihood that people "like me"—people with similar educational backgrounds and abilities, work experience, goals, opportunity costs, and region of work and residence—will graduate from a specific program at a specific institution and subsequently earn enough to exceed the full costs "to me." For the sake of the student, the government lender (taxpayer), and the economy, student loan policy should provide the needed information and encourage students to act accordingly.

This is important for the large number of students who "undermatch" because they don't have the information needed to weigh the value of one option versus another. And it is especially important in the case of high achieving low-income students. Many students could realize better value by borrowing less for a lower-cost institution and program that enables them to cut back on paid employment while in college and thus graduate and start earning a graduate's salary sooner. In other cases, they may be better off borrowing more to attend a school that charges higher tuition but offers much greater long-term value.

In addition, the loan system should help students manage their loans during the repayment process by offering the flexibility of income-based repayment, as many have proposed.[20] Income-based repayment addresses difficulties stemming from the fluctuations in income that many college-educated workers experience, especially early in their careers. However, they do not address the systemic risk of larger and longer-lasting reductions in future income due to severe recessions and structural changes in labor markets. Our repayment plan does, by adjusting loan balances accordingly. This is not only fair; it also combats loan aversion and enables students to make additional investments in higher education throughout their careers in the face of rising credential requirements, shifts in labor market demand, and the probability of high returns from investments in graduate and professional programs.

Thus, we recommend that it be a formal goal of federal student loan policy to enhance the ability of borrowers to obtain good value from their loan-financed investments in higher education and to enable students, institutions, and lenders to better manage the risks involved. Again, we are not advocating that the loan system encourage the highest lifetime earnings or highest rate of return. We are simply saying that it should discourage borrowing that is likely to result in unmanageable debt, and facilitate recognition of the differences in the economic value of various higher education options. Such a system would not only better protect students and taxpayers. It would incent educational institutions to align prices with the value delivered and to pay more attention to costs. To the extent that value reflects the supply of and demand for skills, it should also encourage more informed decisions about investments in human capital, with the likely result that there would be fewer occupational skills shortages and surpluses in the labor market.

TOWARD A MORE COMPREHENSIVE INCOME-BASED LOAN SYSTEM

How can these expanded goals of completion and economic value be accomplished without tradeoffs in terms of access? And how can the federal loan system help students, institutions, and public and private lenders manage the overall financial risks of investing in higher education in a rapidly changing economy? We think the answer lies in designing a more comprehensive income-based loan system that leverages recent advances in financial risk management and behavioral economics, especially regarding consumer choice architecture and performance-based underwriting. We also think key insights can be drawn from the seminal work of Yale economist and Nobel Laureate Robert Shiller on "income-linked loans" that can smooth fluctuations in future income and provide alternative mechanisms for settling loans without the threat of bankruptcy.[21]

By comprehensive income-based system, we mean a system that ties student loan decisions to expected or actual income *throughout the loan cycle—* from student guidance and loan origination to loan management while in college and final repayment after college. At the front end of the process, this system uses "expected income"—a projection of likely future earnings given the student's institution, major, and past performance—to ensure that students do not borrow more than they will be able to repay without financial hardship. Tying loans to expected income should also incent institutions to constrain tuition pricing, so that the prices charged for programs do not exceed the incomes likely to be earned by the vast majority of students completing those programs.

This front-end process would draw on leading innovations in financial risk management and behavioral economics, with special attention to choice architectures for novice investors, risk-based loan terms, and risk-based insurance requirements. During college, this system maintains the link to expected income by basing "satisfactory academic progress" on predictors of the student success needed to complete programs, transition to employment, and achieve expected incomes. This stage of the loan cycle could draw on innovations in performance-based insurance pricing now used in automotive and health-care insurance.

At the back end, the proposed loan system uses actual income to adjust loan payments, in much the way that current and proposed income-contingent repayment systems do. However, we take a different approach to loan forgiveness. Under our approach, forgiveness would apply only to that portion of a student's loan that reflects "systemic" risk factors—developments beyond the control of students or institutions, such as economic downturns and major shifts in the demand for their skills similar to what has been proposed by Shiller for income insurance.[22]

This comprehensive income-based approach addresses the most serious weaknesses of current and proposed income-contingent repayment programs. By focusing only on helping students manage loan debt after leaving college, the latter ignore the front end of financial risk management. They also neglect the serious moral hazard problems that their forgiveness provisions entail—hazards that are likely to result in higher-than-expected public subsidies and higher risks of taxpayer bailouts. Finally, existing repayment reform proposals do not fully address debt aversion, undermatching, and related barriers facing low-income students, or the special needs of post-traditional students.

This comprehensive income-based system would require six major reforms to current federal loan programs:

- Simplification and alignment of loan and grant programs
- Use of choice architecture in student information and guidance systems
- Flexible risk-based loan limits, pricing, and loan insurance
- Performance-based loan adjustments and satisfactory progress measures
- Income-contingent repayment and systemic risk adjustments
- Shared risk incentives for institutions

Let us examine each in turn.

Simplification and Alignment of Loan and Grant Programs

Most recent recommendations for redesigning federal student loan programs call for consolidating existing programs into a single direct loan program in which income-based repayment is the default option. They also call for the new program to be compatible with expanded federal grant programs, especially Pell Grants. In addition, most redesign proposals urge that government subsidies focus on making need-based grant programs such as Pell Grants true entitlements because grant programs have the most impact on access and affordability for low-income students.[23]

We agree, and would go one step further. We suggest that all government subsidies involved in current federal loan programs (e.g., interest rate subsidies) be moved into a unified need-based Pell Grant program and that all loan programs be consolidated into one unified income-based loan program. This loan program could then operate as a true market-based loan system without government subsidies and with the expectation that it would not need future bailouts due to poor underwriting or unsustainable loan losses due to extensive loan forgiveness. We also recommend that the new grant and loan programs be better aligned so that grant levels decline gradually as student incomes increase, rather than bump against fixed upper-income eligibility thresholds.

Student Information and Guidance

The time seems ripe for a new generation of student information and guidance systems that feature carefully tested choice architecture using new decision frames and anchors.[24] Behavioral economists note that there are no "neutral" frames of reference when providing information about investment decisions, including those about higher education. Effective decision "framing" should be based on a full-life-cycle approach to financial planning and risk management—one that reflects the diversity of post-traditional students, including parents and older students facing different financial constraints and planning horizons. It should help students weigh important financial tradeoffs, such as borrowing for education versus saving for retirement. Most importantly, we favor the use of risk-management frameworks and tools to highlight the distribution of risks, including the probability of significant losses, unmanageable debts, and loan defaults. Such anchors and benchmarks are needed to offset the tendency of first-time, long-term borrowers to underestimate the risks involved.

Finally, we recommend the use of "risk profiles" that better capture the personal risks students face in financing higher education, as well as more composite "risk indexes" that capture the combined risks for students with different risk profiles enrolling in various institutions and programs that produce different outcomes for similar students. These would be an improvement over the current use of such risk groups as Pell Grant recipients, which hide important within-group differences. We also suggest that all students, especially those considering high-risk loans, be given information on alternative institutions and programs that offer better value for students like them. Such information could help offset loan avoidance in cases where students choose institutions and programs with lower prices that provide lower value.

Flexible Risk-Based Loan Limits, Pricing, and Loan Insurance

A key feature of a more comprehensive income-based loan system is maintaining a strong connection and alignment between loan upper limits (how much students can borrow) and expected financial returns, especially the returns needed for students to at least "break even" on their investments. This alignment is important for preventing overborrowing. It also is important for discouraging students from underinvesting by choosing institutions with lower prices but lower value, or taking out higher-priced private loans because they have exceeded upper limits on federal loans.

These recommendations borrow in part from the Australian approach to student aid, which controls the upper limits of tuition pricing at publicly funded higher education institutions. The Australian system has been widely viewed as a model of how to design the repayment part or back end of income-based loan systems. Observers have paid less attention to the Australian system's front end, in which student loan amounts are based in part on the expected incomes associated with graduation from different categories or "bands" of programs. Australia defines three major bands, with an additional fourth band for national priorities. Band 1, with the lowest range of tuition pricing, includes units of study in the humanities, behavioral sciences, social studies, education, clinical psychology, foreign languages, visual and performing arts, education, and nursing. In contrast, Band 3, with the highest range of tuition pricing, includes largely professional and business units of study with the highest expected earnings, such as law, dentistry, medicine, veterinary science, and accounting.[25]

By aligning student loan amounts to their expected future incomes and ability to repay, this feature reduces the likelihood of unmanageable student debt. At the same time, there are some design problems with this system. One is the fixed and arbitrary thresholds represented by the boundaries of the four income categories. Another is that different institutions and programs may provide widely variable value for different types of students.

However, there is no reason that this approach cannot be improved upon by, for example, allowing loan amounts to vary according to the earnings projected for specific students in specific programs.

Skeptics worry that this approach will prevent or deter some students from pursuing degrees in relatively low-paying but socially important fields such as teaching and social work. These are valid concerns, but ones we believe our recommendation addresses in three ways. First, given the right incentives, most of these programs could be offered at lower prices than now because they cost less to provide than the average program. For example, social work and education programs should cost less because faculty members in these programs are usually paid less than business and engineering faculty, and faculty salaries are major cost drivers in higher education.[26]

Second, many students in these programs may seek and take unrelated jobs when they enter the labor market. This suggests that labor shortages are better addressed during the repayment period through incentives such as forgiveness or reduced interest rates based on years of service in a shortage-suffering field or region. This would be best done outside the proposed income-based loan system through more targeted and temporary federal and state initiatives.

Third, this approach should help address critical faculty shortages in other fields like nursing, information technology, and engineering. It would allow universities and colleges to charge more for higher-value programs that cannot find qualified faculty because of the differences in what they and private employers pay. Some states have found this to be a problem, for instance, in nursing programs.[27] Loan caps that vary according to expected earnings make sense in the context of the growing practice across institutions of charging higher tuition or fees for their high-demand and more costly but also more remunerative programs.[28]

Currently, federal loan terms and conditions, including loan limits and pricing (e.g., interest rates) and related conditions, are established through legislation and regulation. In the process, they are set at arbitrary and fixed levels without systematic underwriting and with only loose connections to financial market conditions and risk-management considerations. We would put much greater emphasis on systematic underwriting resulting in variable loan terms and conditions that take into account expected future earnings and related risks of nonrepayment, such as predicted persistence and completion. This would encourage the setting of more individualized and dynamic upper limits based on the latest risk conditions.

Therefore, we recommend variable loan terms and conditions, including variable loan limits and interest rates—all pegged to the expected ability of students to repay their loans, calculated using leading practices in financial risk management and underwriting. Further, we recommend that the determination of repayment ability be based on the *combined* risks for specific students enrolling in specific programs at specific institutions, rather than on the risk profiles of students alone. This combined risk level could be calculated with the help of new composite risk indexes based on real data measuring prior graduates' labor market fortunes. The collection of such data would be enabled by a national open data platform of the kind Shiller envisions for global risk management and that we discuss below.

In short, we believe that variable loan terms, including loan caps and interest rates, will "nudge" many students to make more prudent decisions about borrowing and investing in higher education. If true, they should obtain better loan terms than they would otherwise or could now receive. That in turn would enable poor but talented students to borrow and invest more than current caps allow without driving them into the private loan market or leading them to settle for a less selective institution than they could otherwise attend. Similarly, the availability of lower-interest loans for attending higher-value schools and programs would discourage under-matching and thus facilitate social mobility. However, as an additional consumer safeguard, we also favor exploring some type of upper limit on interest payments relative to the size of loan principal. Doing so could ensure that students never face interest payments that exceed their loan principals during the repayment period; this is similar to current income-based repayment system proposals.[29]

Any such risk-based loan limits and pricing should be complemented by loan insurance. Insurance would allow students with high-risk profiles to assume larger risks with higher potential returns while working to improve their risk profiles over time through demonstrated academic performance. This would work the way mortgage insurance does for qualified borrowers who do not have the up-front capital or credit rating to purchase their first choice in housing but have realistic plans to improve their financial situation and are willing to pay a small premium to take those risks. Some students with qualified scores on composite risk indexes may choose to take out additional voluntary insurance offered for certain occupations and programs that are susceptible to upward and downward swings in demand, similar to what Shiller has proposed for income-based loan systems.[30] Again, such risk-based loan limits, pricing, and insurance would require an open-data platform that both public and private loan systems could use for loan underwriting, thereby promoting innovation in the larger student loan market.

Performance-Based Loan Adjustments and Satisfactory Progress

Recently, the financial services industry has harnessed the power of behavioral economics and "big data" analytics to design financing systems that enable and encourage risk reduction. One example is the move to "performance-based" underwriting and pricing in the auto insurance market, where rate adjustments are now based on the behavior of drivers as measured through tracking devices. Another example is using financial incentives in employee health-care plans to encourage the adoption of healthy lifestyles and thereby reduce health-care costs. By contrast, federal student loan policy sets fixed interest rates, fees, and loan maximums, with the only performance-based variations being the minimal requirements for maintaining satisfactory academic progress.

These insights can be applied in the student loan system. Currently, federal student grant and loan policies provide only minimal incentives for students to work hard and do well in college. They do this through institutionally defined measures of satisfactory academic progress (SAP), which usually require no more than passing grades and continuous enrollment. Some recent reform proposals argue that student loans should provide stronger and more salient incentives for students to better prepare for postsecondary education. Others caution that students should have multiple opportunities to show they are college ready and have what it takes to complete college and pay back student loans—in a sense, improve their student risk profile. These competing perspectives are best addressed by providing a more dynamic, performance-based pricing system for student loans that allows students to constantly improve their loan terms and conditions (including removing the need for insurance) based on how well they do once enrolled.

We recommend allowing students to improve their loan rates and conditions when they perform at higher levels according to clearly defined criteria that are predictive of completion and future income for graduates of that institution and program. This would encourage students to work harder, which in turn would improve their completion rates and future income.[31] In designing such a system, policy makers could draw on the lessons learned from applying the insights of behavioral economics in health care—lessons showing that people behave differently when faced with highly salient and immediate losses, such as higher deductibles and co-pays, for behaviors that increase risks. In view of these lessons, we suggest that students be afforded a chance to demonstrate that they can perform well despite their risk profiles. This would require institutions to reevaluate their existing criteria for satisfactory academic progress—criteria that in most cases were established to maximize access, not encourage completion and economic value.[32]

Income-Contingent Repayment and Systemic Risk Adjustment

As discussed, income-contingent repayment plans address critical problems related to the timing and rigidity of loan repayments given the fluctuations in income that many college-educated workers experience. However, income-based repayment plans that allow loan forgiveness after a certain number of years—with the loan system absorbing the losses regardless of cause—create incentives for students to extend their loan repayment periods and qualify for some loan forgiveness. If many students respond accordingly, the student loan system may need higher levels of public subsidy and loan bailouts, especially if faced with higher-than-expected defaults due to an economic downturn or structural shifts in demand for college-educated workers.

However, a comprehensive income-based student loan system based on underwriting principles could be designed to enable forgiving the portion of student loans that are proving difficult to repay because of systemic risk factors that are beyond the control of students and the institutions they attend. Drawing from Shiller's work, the loan system could use indexes to determine what portion of future loans could be forgiven based on the impact of a severe economic downturn that had significant and measurable impacts on similar groups of students attending similar programs and institutions. However, portions of student loans would not be forgiven for students attending programs and institutions that experienced earnings losses greater than comparable students at comparable programs and institutions. In those cases, the loan program would require students to take responsibility for repaying their loans through income-contingent repayment systems and to take responsibility for defaults and any additional types of insurance coverage as discussed earlier.

Shared Risk for Higher Education Institutions

In higher education finance, colleges and universities do not share in repayment risks except in extreme cases when they are denied participation in the federal student loan system because of high student default rates. However, this risk of default will be greatly diminished in our proposed system because all loan amounts and repayment plans will be income-based and subject to systemic risk adjustment. What then will incent institutions to behave responsibly?

One option would be to hold institutions accountable for minimal performance on the two major drivers of loan repayment: time to credential as measured by on-time completion rates, and the economic value of the credentials they offer relative to tuition and fees as measured by actual-income-to-tuition-paid ratios. This approach would avoid the problem that institutions cannot control the size of the loan that students decide to take as long as the loan is under the threshold for total costs of enrollment.[33] However, it would require adjustments of institutional performance benchmarks based on the students they serve and the programs they offer—and maybe also the national and regional labor markets where they place students. This could be done through the use of risk indexes to adjust the expectations of institutions and programs, especially for those serving the highest-risk students. This option could also include rewards for institutions that exceed performance expectations on completion and economic value, including performance expectations for high-risk (e.g., low-income) students. This would provide further incentives for achieving the goals of completion and advancement.

BUILDING AN OPEN NATIONAL DATA PLATFORM

The recommendations above assume that students, institutions, and loan originators have the necessary risk information and are able to use this information as intended. Another assumption is that higher education service providers, including traditional institutions, have the flexibility to innovate in a more open and transparent market. This is not the place to discuss accreditation reform, but it and related policy changes may be needed to enable the kind of innovation implied by the suggested loan system reforms. What follows are recommendations for developing the needed data infrastructure.

Many observers agree that government should provide more complete, accurate, and up-to-date consumer information on higher education institutions and programs that would help potential students make prudent investment decisions.[34] However, there is no consensus on how this information should be provided given the limitations of current federal and state data systems, including limited linkages to income data contained in the federal tax system.

We recommend that the federal government provide widespread access to longitudinal, student-level data while protecting privacy and security through an "open data" platform similar to what Shiller envisions for managing global risks in advanced economies—what he calls "global risk information databases."[35] This data platform also should provide easy access to detailed, comparable electronic information on institutions and programs, including differential tuition pricing by program and requirements for program completion (e.g., satisfactory academic progress) now contained in university and college publications and Web sites (e.g., college catalogues). This data platform also should include regional and national labor market information related to economic growth and decline and structural shifts in demand for college-educated workers.

This data platform would provide the basis for the analytics needed to enable more personalized loan underwriting and performance incentives. It would also facilitate the development of a new generation of software applications in student information and guidance based on the new choice architecture critical for income-based loan systems described earlier. Finally, it would facilitate the development of needed software applications in student-institution matching and institutional performance management.

ROAD MAP FOR IMPLEMENTING AN INCOME-BASED LOAN SYSTEM

This proposed income-based loan system calls for major reforms that will require more research and experimentation along with major changes in existing loan programs and the consumer information and data systems that support them. These reforms must be carefully implemented over multiple years. We recommend that this system be implemented according to the following high-level road map.

Step 1: Performance Management and Satisfactory Academic Progress Criteria

The federal government should incent institutions to develop and validate student feedback systems that communicate whether students are "on track" in completing programs and achieving sufficient economic value. These systems should use criteria that predict completion and economic value and should go well beyond the minimal SAP requirements adopted by higher education institutions. The government should also establish new guidance for defining and validating SAP criteria and promote research and best practices through federal grant programs and experimental site initiatives with the goal of improving completion rates for students in federal loan programs.

Step 2: Research and Experimentation in Choice Architecture, Risk-Based Loan Terms, and Systemic Risk Adjustment

The federal government should promote research and experimentation on choice architecture, risk-based loan terms, and systemic risk adjustments to explore how they can best be designed and used to nudge student investment behavior to achieve the goals of completion, economic advancement (addressing undermatching), economic value, and risk management. This step should focus on the construction and use of risk indexes and the data infrastructure needed to support them. It could also involve experimental site initiatives to pilot-test alternative approaches for designing and implementing these key features of income-based loan systems.

Step 3: Developing an Open National Data Platform

The federal government should establish a commission of leading experts in financial risk management, federal and state data systems, labor market information, and information technology to develop a plan to design and implement a national data infrastructure that can support an income-based system based in part on the data requirements defined in Step 2. This commission should start from Shiller's vision for global risk information databases, and build on current federal initiatives to link education and tax system data for measuring economic value and default rates. It also should recommend how to make more detailed institutional and program pricing information available through the national data platform. Finally, the commission should propose how this public-private data platform should be implemented, managed, and sustained over time.

Step 4: Implementing the Income-Based Loan System and National Data Platform

The final step would be to implement the loan system and national data platform through federal legislation. This would establish an independent loan system that would be underwritten to achieve the proposed goals without federal subsidy. This system would then phase in variable loan terms and systemic risk adjustments over time based on research and experimentation of the kind discussed in Step 2. This could begin by introducing variable loan limits and implementing policies that would allow future increases in existing federal loan limits only when justified by higher or increasing economic value at specific institutions and programs.

CONCLUSION

The rapidly growing federal student loan system represents the nation's single largest investment in higher education. This chapter has argued that this system should be used not only to increase access and completion, but also to ensure at least minimum levels of economic value from investments in higher education and to improve risk management. We have suggested that this can best be done by establishing a more comprehensive, income-based loan system that abides by normal underwriting principles, with all public subsidies shifted to an expanded Pell Grant program that is fully aligned and integrated with this new loan system. Finally, we have provided a high-level road map that suggests how to implement this system.

This system promotes alignment between higher education pricing and financial returns (and related ability to repay loans) through a front-end process that makes sure students take out manageable loans based on expected income, and are asked to repay loans based on actual income through a back-end process that contains protections against excessive interest accumulation and systemic risks. If properly supported by an open national data platform and related policy reforms, it has the potential to expand access, enhance the value of the education students obtain, and improve the management of the risks that loans involve.

Fairness and Opportunity Issues

Further research is needed to ensure that the proposed system does not reduce access to higher education for high-risk low-income students. Income-contingent repayment systems around the world have been designed to partially shift the costs of higher education from taxpayers to students and parents while maintaining access and affordability and increasing the percent of the population attaining higher education credentials. Our proposed system builds on these models; it attempts to maintain access *and* promote higher levels of economic advancement for low-income populations by improving the matching of students with institutions and programs, which should increase program completion and lifetime earnings. However, more research needs to be done on the impact of such a system—and not just on access, but on overall economic advancement.

In discussions with colleagues of the loan system recommended here, a common reaction has been concern that low-income and minority borrowers will obtain worse loan terms than others, precisely because they represent a higher risk. We appreciate this concern, but believe that it overlooks key dimensions of both the current reality and our recommendations. The current reality is that large numbers of disadvantaged students are selling themselves short by attending institutions that have very poor graduation and employment outcomes, even though they could get into better performing institutions. This is not just a matter of the exceptionally talented poor youth who are the focus of most undermatching studies, but of average students who don't understand the risks involved when they decide to attend a fourth-tier college rather than a third-tier one, because it is cheaper, closer to home, better known to them (more people they know attended), or otherwise more comfortable.

The point of a risk-based loan system is to nudge these students to choose an institution that is better for them. The nudge will work, we believe, because the guidance and accompanying financial incentives (e.g., variable caps and loan terms) reflect not just the risks associated with the student, but the risks associated with the institution and program the student attends. That is, the risk-based system we recommend regards risk as a function of both the student (based on past performance, not demographics) *and* the institution involved, and as a risk that can be managed dynamically by the student and institution while the student is enrolled. We already know that some institutions achieve much better results than others with students who have similar risk profiles. The goal then is to encourage all students to attend institutions and programs that will serve them well.

At the same time, we recognize that the validity of our approach depends on how many students respond to the nudges. If many students ignore the guidance and financial incentives to attend institutions that would serve them better, then a risk-based loan system may have unintended and undesirable consequences. In short, it's an empirical question as to whether the system we are proposing will achieve the desired effects. We think it will, and that the evidence from Income Share Agreements is encouraging, but we acknowledge the uncertainty, and recommend various simulations and pilots before any wholesale implementation is attempted.[36]

These equity issues should remain front and center in exploring our proposed income-based loan system. However, this proposed system should also be investigated in a comprehensive way that considers not only its impact on access and equity, but also its potential for improving higher education innovation and performance, increasing the value of a college education, and better managing the investment risks faced by students who borrow to finance their education and the taxpayers who lend to them.

Making College Affordable

The Case for an Institution-Focused
Approach to Federal Student Aid

Sara Goldrick-Rab, Lauren Schudde, and Jacob Stampen

INTRODUCTION*

Nearly three in four Americans believe that higher education is unafford-able, and more than nine in ten college presidents agree.[1] While analysts have offered several explanations for this perception,[2] few have considered whether it stems from the financial aid system's strong focus on the behaviors of "student-consumers" rather than on the policies or practices of education providers.[3]

Financial aid in the United States is a $175-billion-per-year enterprise resting on a key set of principles and assumptions that have guided its operations for more than forty years without significant reexamination. Financial aid's existence asserts that college attainment is an important public good benefitting the populace. However, it also means the provision of higher education is the shared responsibility of both government and private citizens; aid is provided rather than taxpayer-supported, free higher education. Given this shared relationship and the origins of American higher education in private colleges and universities, the system allows postsecondary institutions almost complete autonomy in determining their costs of attendance. Finally, federal aid is primarily student aid. With an equity goal in mind,

* The authors thank Andrew Kelly and David Mundel for useful comments and feedback on an earlier draft. Paul Weinstein provided valuable assistance with the cost calculations. All errors remain our own.

the system assumes that financial barriers to college attainment can be over-come by means-tested vouchers that discount the price for some individuals.

Despite these goals, family income has increasingly become a stronger determinant of college attainment.[4] Among people born in the early 1960s, there was a 31 percentage point income gap in the likelihood of bachelor's degree attainment, with just 5 percent of those from poor families complet-ing college compared to 36 percent of wealthy students. Over the next twenty years, the gap grew to 45 percentage points primarily because the attain-ment of the wealthiest Americans raced ahead (up to 54 percent completing college) while Americans from more modest means made far smaller gains (increasing their chances to just 9 percent).[5] Even after controlling for cog-nitive achievement, family composition, race, and residence, the children of high-income families are 16 percentage points more likely to attend col-lege than those from low-income families.[6]

Reformers seeking to redesign or re-imagine financial aid usually focus on the form of the voucher provided to students (e.g., grant, loan, or tax credit), its amounts, or the attached incentives (how many credits are required to receive aid, when it is distributed, and so forth).[7] Yet his-torically such efforts have met with remarkably little success, much like their counterparts in K–12 school reform, where frantic schemes to cre-ate change often result in little more than "tinkering toward utopia."[8] This may be because, as Terry Sanford wrote in 1971, "much of what has passed for a national approach to higher education has in fact been a willy-nilly, piecemeal, programmatic, annually determined, tardily funded, and not-always-released formula for the support of higher education."[9] We have yet to find a worthy solution.

Finding a better way to make college affordable requires directly dealing with two major challenges: admitting many students who require more sup-port than is currently provided to complete their degrees, and discounting the price of education rather than controlling costs. The current student-focused approach to financial aid does little for either issue. In sharp con-trast to K–12 education, where the federal government contributes at most 10 percent of revenue and makes strong accountability demands, postsec-ondary arena colleges and universities receive up to 90 percent of their sup-port from student financial aid but are asked to account for very little in return. This is striking to many close observers of educational policy, includ-ing Stephen Burd of the New America Foundation, who recently reported that "federal officials, for the most part, appear to be operating under the [false] assumption that colleges are continuing to complement the government's efforts to make higher education more accessible and affordable for the neediest students."[10]

Given the national interest in college attainment paired with the substantial economic inequality in our society, we argue that it is time to address affordability concerns by refocusing financial aid policy on schools, rather than students, as the central unit of change. The litany of cost problems in higher education makes it unlikely that altering student behavior with vouchers will ever succeed in making college affordable. Instead, greater progress may come through focusing attention on the colleges and universities where students are educated and considering the role that government can play in improving student learning and life outcomes.

Making educational institutions the centerpiece of federal financial aid policy could also instigate a long overdue national conversation about the purposes of postsecondary education and highlight the most pressing problem areas, which are located at the schools where the most disadvantaged students are concentrated. The original formulation of financial aid, focused on students, has had unforeseen effects on state financing, institutional cost structures and behaviors, and families. With those effects now evident, it is time to consider a different model in which institutions of higher education are the locus of both public funding and public accountability. We briefly review the history and development of the current model, and then describe how a new one could be seeded.

THREE CRITICAL TASKS FOR ENSURING AFFORDABILITY

More than 90 percent of American tenth graders expect to attend college, up from just over 75 percent thirty years ago.[11] Making college affordable while ensuring that mass participation is possible will require (1) greater state investment and oversight, (2) institutional responsibility for keeping costs down while maximizing the inclusion of all students regardless of family background, and (3) an approach to financing that is aligned with the resources, capabilities, and beliefs of both today's and tomorrow's families and students. The current financial aid system fails to meet these requirements. Most importantly, extant federal (and most state) policy only requires that students be allowed to use their financial aid at an institution to help cover their college costs; it does not require that states (or colleges and universities) take steps to ensure that those students can fully participate in college so that they gain access to the range of benefits higher education is purported to offer.

The Importance of State Investment and Oversight

The federal Title IV student aid program provides resources to undergraduates throughout all fifty states without asking that state governments do much in return. Relative to federal spending on Title IV, state spending on higher education (both in terms of resources for financial aid programs and appropriations for instruction) has declined.[12] Diminishing state appropriations are tightly linked to increasing tuition at public institutions, and the waning purchasing power of state aid also reduces affordability at private institutions.[13]

Some analysts contend that these trends are occurring because federal policy provides incentives for this behavior, to which states are simply responding.[14] This is a very difficult claim to evaluate, but regardless of what drives their actions, states are effectively helping to make college less affordable. In addition, given that state actions most directly affect public institutions, they are helping to differentially advantage institutions with more control over their resources. Those private and for-profit institutions then compete with public institutions, which, unlike their peers, are held more accountable to the broader public.

The manner in which states allocate the limited resources they provide to higher education is also disconnected from the federal goal of reducing the linkage between family income and college attainment.[15] For example, states provide disproportionately more resources to flagship institutions, which educate the smallest number of the states' disadvantaged residents.[16] Moreover, instead of reinforcing the federal emphasis on need-based aid, states continue to distribute a substantial amount of aid based on "merit."[17]

For decades, the federal government has been virtually silent on the matter of state actions on higher education. This behavior is consistent with broader patterns of policy devolution. Time and again, colleges and university leaders—especially in the public sector—have pointed to disinvesting state legislatures as the key source of rising costs.[18] But it has been difficult to determine how to hold states accountable in a federal system that distributes its aid directly to students.[19] In the meantime, costs of higher education continue to rise in nearly all states, despite evidence that the students who are least likely to participate in higher education have greater educational opportunity in states that keep their costs down.[20]

A Clear Need for Institutional Responsibility

While the fortunes of public institutions are inextricably linked to the behaviors of both private institutions and states, those public institutions also possess substantial decision-making power. This is mainly, and especially, true for public flagship universities, which in recent years have substantially escalated many facets of the costs of attendance.[21] Such moves have been facilitated by changes in state governance structures, that give colleges and universities a remarkable level of autonomy, including their own boards to focus on institution-specific interests.

Are higher education institutions setting their costs based in part on the availability of federal financial aid, thus undermining efforts to promote access? This is another difficult question to examine, and most contemporary reviews on the topic find mixed evidence.[22] Many of these studies focus on the Pell Grant as a potential cost driver, however, while paying perhaps too little attention to the role of student loans. But the American public is quite clear: 77 percent of people surveyed believe that higher education institutions should reduce their tuition and fees. In comparison, 59 percent say state governments should provide more assistance, and 55 percent desire the federal government to provide more assistance.[23] Such polling data implies that even though schools often claim to use financial aid to hold needy students "harmless" from high costs, the discounting they provide is insufficient. Even the poorest students at public institutions are left with as much as $12,000 in unmet financial need each year, and many families from modest means but higher expected family contributions (EFCs) face expectations with which they simply cannot comply.[24] This may fuel the evident backlash against the use of student tuition for need-based financial aid;[25] drawing distinctions between haves and have-nots becomes more difficult when the average student and her family have relatively fewer resources.

Even as it provides enormous subsidies to institutions indirectly through multiple grant programs and by backing student loans, the federal government is silent on how institutions of higher education distribute their institutional aid. Research indicates that much of that aid requires students to be academically meritorious and far less often financially needy.[26] In part, this appears to be driven by state preferences that provide few incentives for schools to invest money in matching need-based financial aid or supportive programs for aided students. Thus it is fairly common for government and philanthropic aid to supplant institutional aid rather than supplement it, limiting aid dollars available for students.[27]

But in addition, four-year institutions have chosen to engage in an arms race over students, developing an industry of "enrollment managers" seeking to maximize prestige and revenue rather than promote college attainment and affordability. Financial aid has often become a weapon of choice, deployed to battle other schools rather than to serve students.[28]

Updating the Expectations for Students and Families

Whether or not a financial aid policy is effective at making college affordable depends on whether students and families embrace its requirements, norms, and values. Given the planned and effective massive expansion of college access, it is unsurprising that compared with their peers of the 1960s, today's undergraduates have lower average levels of high school preparation, more varied family experiences with education, smaller social networks, less familial wealth, but high expectations for a college education.[29]

There is a rigorous body of research demonstrating that existing mechanisms for distributing federal student aid are too complicated for current students, requiring unreasonably high levels of information and financial expertise for effective use.[30] While some informational interventions have produced changes in student behavior, those impacts have occurred for targeted groups of students and are relatively small compared with the magnitude of the overall problem.[31]

The needs analysis currently employed to assess eligibility for financial aid is also outdated, focusing on the computation of an expected family contribution that emphasizes intra-family transfers from parent to child. In fact, most undergraduates are not children (regardless of their age), are not receiving familial financial support (even when we might think they "should"), and are thus unable to come up with the EFC that is "expected" from them.[32] Less than one-third (27 percent) of Americans reported that their parents paid most of the costs of their college attendance (and just 22 percent said that grant aid paid most of the costs).[33] The difficulties for families created by this part of the aid system spill over into interactions with institutional financial aid officers that are often unhelpful and counterproductive to the overall goal of making college affordable. Perceived as agents of the federal government, financial aid officers are often put into the difficult position of denying resources to individuals despite clear and evident need. Evidence suggests that "the effect of a given subsidy may vary across groups due to relative differences in financial positions, academic preparation, access to information, the form taken by the subsidy itself, and interactions of these factors."[34] Yet even reformers advocate for further individualization of aid, rather than less. This sort of individual determination once again divides students and educators instead of encouraging educational institutions to find ways to collectively meet the needs of all students. The market-based approach also repositions students as consumers rather than pupils to be educated.[35]

A BRIEF HISTORY OF THE DECISION TO AID STUDENTS RATHER THAN SCHOOLS

As recently as the 1960s, the role of government in providing educational opportunity was, with few exceptions, limited to states creating and maintaining broadly accessible colleges and universities, funding a high percentage of the cost of instruction at public institutions, and maintaining tax-exempt status for private colleges and universities. Tuition at public institutions was very low, and private college tuition averaged only about double the rate charged by public institutions. Even so, there was concern about the high cost of college attendance, especially due to foregone income (the loss of income a student might have earned if working instead of attending college). Then, as now, it was widely believed that a substantial portion of young people from low-income backgrounds were capable of succeeding in college and that this constituted a source of talent that the nation could ill afford to squander.

The Benefits of a Robust Economy

In the 1960s, doing something to make a college education more accessible (as well as responding to many other domestic concerns) seemed feasible to political leaders at state and federal levels because it was a time of great national prosperity. President Lyndon Johnson captured the sense of the time by spearheading a nationwide effort to improve life in America through his "War on Poverty." His subsequent "Great Society" programs, together with programs initiated at the state level, made college more accessible for students from both low- and middle-income families. Congress responded to the president by passing legislation aimed at improving education at all levels and by reducing economic barriers to college attendance through student financial aid awarded on the basis of financial need.

Passage of the Higher Education Act of 1965 dramatically increased the federal investment in public higher education and provided grants and loans for students attending public and private nonprofit colleges. Initially, federal student aid was mainly in the form of grants awarded on the basis of demonstrated financial need. New legislation also contained incentives for banks to consider the future earnings of college graduates as collateral for student loans. In this way, banks came to play a major role in financing college attendance.

Development of a Student-Focused Policy

At first it seemed clear that federal aid to higher education would focus on institutions *and* students. In 1971, the Senate Subcommittee on Education debated a bill introduced by Senator Claiborne Pell that aimed to establish as a policy of the federal government "the right of every youngster, regardless of his family's financial circumstances, to obtain a postsecondary education." The bill provided $1,200 annually for each student to attend college, and institutional grants of $1,000 annually to lower the amount of tuition paid. Institutional leaders were, of course, widely supportive of those institutional grants, but while Pell reported that the subcommittee "was prepared to accept the thesis of student aid as a right," it changed its mind on institutional aid. In retrospect, he described the discussion this way:

> [It] was interesting to watch. At the outset the subject was approached from a "yes" or "no" position. The Administration's view was originally negative. Gradually the question changed from "yes" or "no" to one of "how." As the subcommittee went along, the Administration rethought its position and proposed institutional aid based on a percentage of the present student assistance funds received by the institution.[36]

But Pell grew concerned about the feasibility of institutional assistance because of questions about the constitutionality of aiding private institutions (a question that has since been resolved). He believed that once the concept of aid-to-students was firmly established, the concept of institutional aid "[could] then grow."[37] Successive amendments to the Higher Education Act, beginning in 1972 and accelerating after 1976, followed this trajectory, furthering the focus on students and away from institutions.[38] The 1972 amendments seem motivated primarily by liberal Democrats and moderate Republicans who assumed that higher education benefited society and were convinced that students from lower-income families should receive assistance.

But at the very end of the 1960s, many campuses were still in revolt over the unpopular Vietnam War, and protests on public university campuses polarized supporters and opponents. Before then, people on both sides had looked upon public institutions as developers of the best and the brightest in society. Now they blamed those same institutions for both supporting and opposing the war.[39]

Moreover, the nation was experiencing early signs of a weakening economy due to the rising cost of the war on top of spending for Great Society and other domestic programs. Even so, the push to expand educational opportunity continued through open enrollment policies, more flexible scheduling for part-time students, and an emphasis on recruiting minority students.[40] But in addition, there was widespread fear that many private colleges were in danger of closing because they could not compete with low-tuition public colleges.[41] In 1970, one admission officer at a private institution prognosticated that "by 1985, all private education will be state assisted."[42]

These challenges, and in particular stagflation (simultaneous inflation, high unemployment, and economic stagnation)[43] drew the attention of Milton Friedman and other economists, who later formed the Chicago School.[44] Friedman argued that the crisis could be resolved by relying more on the private sector rather than government. Encouraged by what became widely perceived as success in ending stagflation, Friedman further argued that the private sector could also replace government financing of higher education. Specifically, public and private higher education could—and, he argued, should—be financed almost entirely through loans to students. After all, he stated, society did not benefit enough from higher education (and particularly public higher education) to justify subsidizing students with low tuition.[45]

W. Lee Hansen and Burton Weisbrod modified Friedman's approach by calling, in a journal article, for increased public dollars in the form of grants (currently Pell Grants) awarded on the basis of demonstrated financial need. The core idea was that higher education would be financed through students rather than institutions, and the approach was easy to explain: from each according to their ability to pay and to each according to their need for assistance. Hansen and Weisbrod argued that low tuition in public higher education was wasteful because well-to-do families could afford to pay more for their children's education and that it caused a sizeable redistribution of income from students from low-income families to students from high-income ones.[46] Again, other opponents of low tuition in the public sector and proponents of student loans were concerned that it permitted public institutions to compete "unfairly" with the private sector.[47]

Thus, the student-aid-focused approach appealed to the many fiscally conservative but socially liberal Republicans, then a major wing of the party, who thought that financing higher education in this way would primarily aid individuals and make institutions compete more for students, and that this in turn would hold down college costs and increase instructional quality. The approach also appealed to many liberal Democrats who favored redistribution of resources in favor of the poor. The members of Congress who thought this way were mostly from New England and Midwestern states. Together they formed the nucleus of a majority coalition in Congress that enacted the Higher Education Amendments of 1972 and a great deal of student aid legislation thereafter.[48]

The idea of means-tested student-focused grants also represented a refinement and moderation of recommendations of the more than 37 policy reports and 137 research reports of the Carnegie Commission on Higher Education, as well as studies by Alice Rivlin.[49] Clark Kerr was especially adamant that financial barriers could only be effectively removed by providing aid directly to students; institutional grants could not succeed. He was also concerned that other approaches would pit states and institutions against one another, exacerbating the political nature of the process.[50] These recommendations, however, lacked supporting empirical evidence, for as Rivlin noted there was almost a complete absence of behavioral information—no one knew how students (let alone states or institutions) would react to changes in higher education financing.[51]

But in 1971, there was already evidence of congressional distrust of public institutions,[52] and many people were coming to believe that higher education might be better financed through students. Thereafter, students attending private, for-profit institutions also became eligible to receive federal student aid.[53] Proponents argued that in this way the federal government could assist in reducing the public-private tuition gap that private institution leaders alleged was placing the future of many colleges at risk of failure.[54] Predictions by M. M. Chambers and others that a student-aid-centered system would encourage institutions to raise tuition, and that this would result in an ever-increasing escalation of college attendance costs and dependence on loans, were simply not deemed credible.[55]

After passage of the Higher Education Amendments of 1972, attention shifted to more specific questions about *how* aid should be distributed to students. Differential price sensitivity of students at public and private institutions came to take center stage as a source of debate. Some argued that since resources are limited, public institutions should gradually raise tuitions and place greater reliance on student aid.[56] The Higher Education Amendments of 1972 also sought to involve state governments in substantive, although meagerly funded, ways. For example, the State Student Incentive Grant Program was established to provide matching funds to encourage the states to create and expand student aid programs. But the federal program imposed no requirement that the federally matched scholarship be geared to tuition costs, nor was it even required until 1976 that state programs be open to students in private institutions.[57] Another provision of the 1972 Amendments limited the amount of aid the lowest-income students attending public institutions could receive to one-half of the total cost of tuition, room, board, books, and other expenses. The same formula allowed students attending higher-priced private institutions to receive more aid. Federal student aid became increasingly price sensitive.

By 1979, even the associations representing public colleges and universities agreed to support higher and more-price-sensitive maximum Basic Education Opportunity Grants, later renamed Pell Grants. Although several members of Congress and public college associations called for a balance between student and institutional aid, it became increasingly clear that the federal government's role in financing higher education would be to only fund students. However, that conclusion was reached through a process that many questioned. As Chester Finn wrote at the time (quoting James Perkins), "With respect to higher education, the federal government has made no decision. It has made bits and pieces of decisions about specific and limited issues."[58]

REFOCUSING AID ON INSTITUTIONS

Instead of subsidizing colleges irrespective of how they spend their resources, the financial aid system needs to be reoriented such that federal and state governments reward institutions that focus on the public good by placing a premium on keeping college affordable for all students.[59] A multi-pronged approach is required to achieve this, recognizing that the federal government has the capacity to act as a unifying leader in goal-setting for states, while states are more effective at stimulating changes in the behaviors of their institutions.[60] In addition, we hypothesize that institutions may be more effective at producing changes in state behaviors if they act as coalitions with common interests.

Operationalizing and Funding the Model

Under this new approach—a modified version of some state performance-based funding frameworks for higher education—institutions would receive Title IV funds according to the needs of their students. In exchange, they would be held accountable for taking steps to develop and maintain an affordable and effective college experience. The success of this model relies on altering the political economy of financial aid, moving it from a market-driven, choice-based approach focused on consumers to one in which the public goods associated with affordable education are emphasized and institutions succeed by being responsive to government, not merely individuals.

In shifting to this new model, the federal government has to clarify that Title IV aid is meant to provide resources in service of national interests, ensuring that a college education is affordable to the qualified population. States and institutions must first establish that they possess sufficient financial resources to provide an "adequate" college education on average. (The determination of adequacy necessitates development at the federal level and needs to consider a range of outcomes. There are currently no parallels in higher education to state-level adequacy funding in K–12.[61]) For public institutions, this funding base should come from state appropriations. For private institutions, it should be provided by an endowment or tuition, with tuition constituting no more than half of the funds. In addition, private and for-profit institutions should not receive any Title IV financial aid unless public institutions in that state are *also* recipients. (In other words, aid to private and for-profit institutions ought to supplement, not supplant, aid to public institutions.) This should increase the incentive for all forms of postsecondary institutions and their constituents to collectively pressure state legislatures to invest in postsecondary education.

Title IV aid should be provided directly to qualified institutions in order to first discount the price charged to all students, and secondly, to increase the resources devoted to the postsecondary education of disadvantaged students (those within 200 percent of the poverty line). Nearly all studies on funding in K–12 education agree that more funds are required to educate economically disadvantaged students to proficiency. In exchange for these financial resources, institutions ought to be held accountable for monitoring growth in the overall costs of attendance (including room and board), focusing the most resources to support students at greatest risk of non-completion, and demonstrating growth in the completion rates of students from all family backgrounds, adjusted for high school preparation and/or placement scores. Financial aid officers currently employed to administer student-focused financial aid could be redeployed in an effort to assist colleges and universities in achieving these goals.

We can afford this new approach to financial aid. The current array of federal support for higher education is spread across ten different tax incentives (not including 529 plans), grants programs, and loans. The student loan program, though providing the bulk of financial support, is a revenue producer for the federal government as it is currently constructed (and accounted for under federal budget rules). The various tax incentives and grant programs, on the other hand, currently require expenditures of approximately $83 billion.[62] Consolidating these various programs into a single, institution-focused investment would help to leverage federal investment more effectively. For example, with the same amount of funds presently available, it would be possible to make tuition at public community colleges free for any student who wants to go and still have money left over for other institution-based investments. Or the existing dollars could be used to provide every public institution of higher learning with additional federal aid worth $4,000 per student.

Feasibility

President Barack Obama recently began to discuss a plan to hold institutions accountable for making college affordable; however, it does not reflect the critical elements of this plan as described above. Its centerpiece is the creation of a college ratings system that would, in theory, help students and parents better assess the value of attending different colleges and universities. Unfortunately, this is a purely informational solution to a systemic problem that goes far beyond the decision of individual students. It requires a systemic solution that includes accountability metrics and money tied to those metrics in order to generate institutional responses.

Conditions today are very different from what they were in the early 1970s, when the current financial aid system took shape. The social benefits of a college-educated populace are evident, if not readily quantifiable.[63] Moreover, concerns about the transfer of resources from non-users to users have been greatly alleviated by the very high rates of college participation now observed. Instead of one-third of the public enjoying subsidized college-going at the expense of the two-thirds not engaged in higher education, we face a future where 80 percent of children can expect to be consumers of higher education, with the vast majority headed for public higher education. That great majority will share the expense, and if this new system sufficiently increases demand among the poorest citizens, a head tax to fund it would be progressive—not regressive. It would be even more so if tax reform helped to ensure it. Even the non-users would stand to benefit, as the greater taxes paid by users can be used to finance the security of the relatively smaller fraction of non-users. Another benefit of this approach is that it will likely create more allies for financial aid, especially among middle-class families who are feeling squeezed and yet have little aid to which to turn.

How might the institutions respond to a shift from student to school subsidies? We would anticipate the public sector to be supportive. For example, Mark Yudof of the University of California has called for an expanded federal role in higher education that includes funding for core and operating expenses.[64] Moreover, some leaders in the private sector have proposed versions of these ideas over time, most notably in Michael McPherson and Morton Shapiro's call for "cost of education" grants.[65] That said, this refocusing moves far beyond the scope of those original ideas, and is intended to come with significant accountability, rendering it far less popular among powerful players. Back in 1971, Derek Bok, then president of Harvard University, rejected proposals for federal institutional subsidies, arguing that they would add administrative costs and bureaucracy.[66] We might expect similar objections from the American Council on Education today.

It is also possible that some will resist this refocusing on the grounds that it is regressive, rather than progressive, or that it will provide resources to the students or institutions that need them the least. While additional analysis is undoubtedly required (and intended, as this is merely an instigating piece), we suspect this is not true, and it is certainly not the intention. It is the schools with the most disadvantaged students that need the greatest investments, and those are the schools that should receive them if the policy is correctly implemented. Certainly, costs will be reduced for some students who can pay more than they will be charged, but history (and lessons from the K–12 sector) indicate that most of these students will instead turn to more expensive, private options, regardless—and in doing so essentially pay twice for higher education (once through taxes, again through tuition).

There are many other possible scenarios that could result from a switch to an institution-focused aid model, and given their potential effects perhaps it is best to try these ideas in the context of a demonstration program. For example, rather than working in tandem with the public sector, for-profit and private institutions may close en masse, restricting access (at least temporarily). States could fail to provide their required match, either because other costs preclude it or because their leaders do not find value in postsecondary education. Students and families could misunderstand the changing landscape and fear that without student-focused aid, their opportunities for college would disappear. All change of course comes with risk, but continuing the status quo is clearly just as risky.

Conclusion

Andrew P. Kelly and Sara Goldrick-Rab

INTRODUCTION

The contemporary conversation about student financial aid is both an empirical debate and a political football. It is also destined to become a historical artifact. That is why we teamed up to assemble a volume that aims to move beyond mere rhetoric and shortsighted fixes to tackle the bigger question: how can policy makers create a system of student financial aid that is able to meet the demands of a new century? Collectively, these chapters deepen and invigorate discussions of financial aid reform and root them more fully in the realities of both Washington policy making and (far more importantly) the lives of students and families across the nation.

Several times a year, this book's editors meet at events convened by think tanks, foundations, government agencies, and academic associations. We sit next to each other, scribbling notes (and tweeting) in an ongoing debate about the various higher education policy topics of the day. Because we come from dissimilar disciplinary backgrounds, run in different political circles, and espouse disparate values, we often disagree. For example, Andrew places a high priority on innovation, competition, and incentives, while Sara emphasizes the importance of using policy levers that increase social equity through systemic change and do not compromise a commitment to access and opportunity. Sometimes our exchanges create more heat than light, but when it comes to student financial aid policy, more often than not we agree on the need for reform. In particular, we concur that today's federal, state, and institutional systems of allocating and distributing aid are not meeting students' needs, and that change is required. We also agree that the route to reformation or transformation needs to be grounded in empirical evidence about the needs and decision-making habits of all affected parties. The current priority—political expediency—may be doing untold harm to the college attainment prospects of individuals across the country.

But it is not all sweetness and light between the two of us; when it comes to particular policy solutions, we often disagree. Andrew believes that the system needs more market-based reform, not less, while Sara argues that our reliance on individual choice and flawed theories of market accountability facilitated the current crisis in college affordability. Instead, she and her coauthors propose aid policies that would fund and regulate the behavior of colleges more directly.

This volume grew out of these continuing debates and discussions, as well as our shared frustration with the shortsighted, evidence-free, and politically expedient policy making that often passes for financial aid reform. In choosing the authors, we explicitly sought out voices and perspectives within the higher education community that are frequently underrepresented in Washington policy debates. Too often, policy makers call on the most published and recognized authors again and again to express their views, while those with new ideas and people who question old ones are left unheard. While this volume actively engages with the ideas of these established and respected scholars, it also provides a platform for authors who have not yet influenced the policy conversation but will do so in the years to come.[1]

In this book we identified several areas in which there seems to be a growing consensus, mainly among policy makers, about the aspects of the financial aid system that are in need of reform. They all deserve serious debate and discussion. We tried to model this approach by working together to craft the introduction and conclusion of this volume, assemble the authors, and edit their work. Naturally, however, there are also key distinctions and disagreements in our thinking about the necessary next steps. Thus in the next two sections, we take the opportunity to provide input in our own voices, before rejoining in the final segments to talk collaboratively about ways to move forward.

IN MY VIEW: ANDREW P. KELLY

As a political scientist, I view financial aid reform—and the obstacles to it—as a political problem first and foremost. On many dimensions, existing financial aid programs have not worked as intended. Yet policy makers have done little to reform existing programs. What gives?

Put simply, there is little to be gained politically—and perhaps much to be lost—from pushing for reforms that would fundamentally change the incentives for students, institutions, and states. To borrow from the great James Q. Wilson, the benefits of existing aid programs are concentrated, while the costs are diffuse. Higher education is a big, heavily subsidized industry, and it happens to be extremely equitably distributed across every congressional district in the country. Student advocates and the higher education lobby keep a close eye on policy making, while the average taxpayer is unlikely to notice or care when student aid spending increases.

Hence, policy makers on the left respond to rising tuition costs in the same way they always have: by spending more on student aid. If only the Pell Grant were larger, interest rates were lower, or repayment plans more generous, they argue, the problem of college affordability would be solved. Spending more feels good, is a political winner, and satisfies important constituencies. And anyone who questions the logic of simply spending more is labeled anti-student. Policy makers on the right also shoulder the blame here. With some exceptions, conservatives have also been reticent to push for major change, choosing instead to push for cuts to existing programs or a return to private lending, both of which would leave existing incentives in place. When select Republicans have pushed for more fundamental reforms, they have sometimes sparked opposition within their own party.[2] At other times, Republicans have seemed just as willing to pander to student advocates as Democrats; in the 2012 campaign, for instance, Mitt Romney joined President Obama to support a costly extension of the 3.4 percent interest rate on subsidized student loans.

But trying to spend and lend our way to college affordability is Sisyphean: federal policy makers spend and spend until that rock is nearly at the top of the hill, only to have it come crashing down again when states cut higher education funding and colleges increase their tuition. Then, at the behest of student advocates and the higher education lobby, they start pushing all over again. Though scholars and advocates have debated whether federal aid causes tuition increases, the broader point is often ignored: increasing students' and families' ability to pay relaxes the incentive to keep tuition affordable. When faced with a choice between raising tuition and containing costs, the former is simpler and less controversial on campus, and federal loans ensure that students will continue to clamor for admission. The result is predictable: tuition growth begets more student aid that drives more tuition growth, and federal policy makers have no way to prevent it.

But all is not lost. The deepening college cost crisis has spawned new, bolder ideas, many of which are contained in this volume. Though these ideas will run into the same thorny politics, they provide what critiques of student aid reform have often been lacking: an alternative vision for design and delivery. At the risk of overgeneralizing, the most forward-thinking ideas fit into one of two categories. The first category, which includes the Goldrick-Rab et al. chapter, suggests that a shift away from the traditional, voucher-based approach to student aid is necessary to get control of college costs. According to these arguments, the disappointing results of the last forty years reveal that we cannot rely on consumer choices and market forces to discipline the behavior of colleges, so the state must step in. Specifically, the government should fund colleges and universities directly, not through student vouchers, presumably in exchange for more accountability and control over their behavior. Some go so far as to argue that all existing subsidies be plowed into a free "public option" for higher education, creating a system similar to the one we have in K–12 education, where public schools are funded directly and privates receive little or no public money. (The recent book by Bob Samuels, president of the American Federation of Teachers' University Council, and a policy paper by Sara Goldrick-Rab and Nancy Kendall, are two prominent recent examples of this argument.)[3]

Proposals in the second category go in the opposite direction, arguing that we need more market forces and individual-level incentives, not fewer. How could we expect individuals to make the kind of informed decisions market accountability requires when we've never bothered to provide them with the information about cost, quality, and likely outcomes they need to do so? Unlike other lending products, where eligibility and terms vary according to the risk, identical federal loans are handed out for any accredited program. No surprise, perhaps, that students often invest in programs from which they are unlikely to reap a return; the lender sent them no signal to avoid those programs. Likewise, why should we expect individuals to complete college on time when the definition of "full-time" enshrined in federal law—twelve credits—would not allow a student to finish his degree in "normal time"? Individual-level interventions like underwriting and risk-based pricing (Crawford and Sheets), income-based loans (Hillman), and performance-based scholarships (Richburg-Hayes) fit into this category.

In my view, the second route to reform is more promising for a couple of reasons. First, I do not believe that a public option will fix a primary driver of poor student outcomes: low-quality colleges and programs.[4] Is the logic that the federal government will be better able to force institutions to improve simply because they are funding them directly? Based on what evidence should we draw that conclusion? And what would be the cost, in terms of innovation and diversity, of moving to a more centralized model? The federal Title I program, which provides direct funding for disadvantaged students in K–12 public schools, suggests the limits of federal power in this regard.[5] Washington can tell public organizations to do something, but it cannot tell them to do it well.

Such a public option could also jeopardize access goals. Samuels argues that current federal investments could cover the cost of public higher education *today*. But what happens as the inexorable rise in the cost of delivering higher education (the so-called "cost disease") crashes headlong into finite public budgets? Increased rationing is the likely answer. Should we aspire to be more like the public university systems in Europe, where demand often outstrips supply and access is tightly rationed?

Second, it is not as though institutions do not respond to consumer demand; it is just that consumer demand is both woefully underinformed and distorted by easy access to federal loans. Indeed, campuses have invested millions of borrowed dollars in costly amenities in an effort to attract students. In the absence of objective information about the quality of the schooling provided and its cost—the value of the education—consumers decide where to attend on the basis of other things, many of which have nothing to do with education.[6] A student aid system that informed consumers about their options, tailored aid terms to reflect risk, and eliminated loan programs that drive tuition growth (like Parent PLUS) would invigorate market accountability.

In the push to improve student aid, all of these new ideas should be on the table. Indeed, it is a lack of experimentation and creativity that has put us here in the first place. To avoid more of the same, policy makers should look for opportunities to experiment with a blend of individual- and institution-level policy ideas. That is the only way to learn.

IN MY VIEW: SARA GOLDRICK-RAB

The most significant problem with contemporary discussions about financial aid policy, in my view, is that they are disconnected from the daily experiences of financial aid recipients. As I read policy papers on redesigning, reimagining, or reforming financial aid, I often wonder if any of the authors have ever received financial aid or spoken to anyone who did. While there are important exceptions, for the most part policy reforms and even financial aid research appear to be guided by an assumption that a lack of motivation undergirds the low college completion rates of financial aid recipients. Moreover, the fundamental problem of student debt, some reformers suggest, is not the debt itself, but the difficulty in repaying it,[7] while the reason for poor institutional performance is the failure to maintain high academic standards, rather than the failure to learn how to support the needs of a broader group of students.

The diagnosis of the problem coupled with a strong theory of change leads rather rapidly to policy prognosis. The results of efforts to fix the current problems suggest that our diagnoses are often wrong to begin with. For example, take the discussion of performance-based scholarship programs presented in chapter 5. This is an ambitious and expensive effort to try and leverage financial aid dollars to provide students with additional incentives to take more credits and achieve better grades. It is aimed at a motivation problem and tries to instill motivation to solve it. But while the author does detect some program impacts using a rigorous experimental evaluation, a closer examination reveals that the impacts are rather small. For example, rarely do performance-based scholarships have a statistically significant effect on increases in credit attainment, and they hardly ever improve retention rates. Thus, while it is indeed exciting to find any positive impacts that are unlikely to be due to chance alone, the fact is that the intervention is not moving the dial very much at all. The policy question is therefore, could we do better with an intervention aligned to a different problem diagnosis?

What if, for example, instead of attributing low credit attainment to a lack of motivation, researchers thought it was due to inadequate financial support? The performance-based scholarships are aimed at students from working poor families, who often have to commit half or even three-quarters of their annual income to the costs of college attendance in order to enroll each year. Is it possible that more significantly offsetting those costs so that students and their families can make ends meet while supporting schooling would be more effective? This is the approach taken by the national free and reduced price lunch program, which acknowledges that even families valuing education often still can't afford the basics. Such supportive programs are demonstrably good at increasing academic achievement, given that health is a precursor to learning.[8] It is incorrect to claim that we do not have the funds for these kinds of efforts; we are simply spending them now in the private sector, facilitating choice among schools that appear to do little to promote degree completion, rather than concentrating taxpayer dollars in the public sector where most students choose to enroll. What might be the impacts of programs like Single Stop USA or the Working Families Success Network, if they brought additional supportive benefits to struggling undergraduates at public institutions who are pursuing college degrees? This is a good area for research and development, but more importantly, it takes as a starting point a very different definition of the problems facing low-income students who currently do not finish college.

Another example of a misaligned definition of the problem comes from the chapters about repayment options for student loans. These chapters view the challenge of reducing default rates as primarily one of program design and information. In other words, if only repayment were better crafted to align with the earning cycles of individuals, and if only students possessed good information, their debt situations would be resolved. Possibly, yes. But equally possible is a scenario in which low-income students continue to default on relatively small loans because they did not complete college, they are funding significant financial needs in their own families, they are avoiding formal governmental institutions because of other constraints on their lives (including penal rules), or they are loath to deal with a debt that they felt forced into taking. Under these conditions, in which students borrow out of a feeling of significant constraint rather than a sense of choice, where student loan money is the only source of support available to desperately poor families, and where government officials take punitive actions at least as often as supportive ones, the debt itself is a problem—not just the repayment situation. There are also many students who do not take on any debt at all, despite facing large amounts of unmet financial need. Instead, trying to juggle school with heavy work hours, they face time constraints that cost them their degrees. My research suggests that they are declining to borrow not because of a fear they cannot repay but because they object to using debt as a mechanism for achieving goals. They do not align with expectations set up by policy makers, and as the number of these students grows (they are predominately Hispanic and Southeast Asians) it may be that policy needs to shift as well.

Understanding the complex realities of students' lives and grounding ourselves in those rather than in idealized assumptions will also help the federal government build a viable accountability system for colleges and universities. The evident instinct of higher education institutions when faced with accountability, especially around the outcomes of low-income students, is to "raise the bar" to exclude these students—using either financial need or (more often) academic "standards" to do it. Recognizing that students from low-income families are far more likely to be from the academic middle—read B/C students—than to be "high achievers" will help policy makers ensure that schools take the right steps to increase completion rates while maintaining access. For example, institutions need to be rewarded for increasing the number of students with financial need and average high school profiles while also increasing the number of these students who graduate. Process measures are needed to ensure that the number of credits required isn't simply reduced or credentials otherwise devalued, and stipulations should require the integrated provision of academic, social, and financial services delivered in bundled fashion. The problem, as properly diagnosed, is how to help schools meet the needs of the students they have, rather than pushing them to rethink whom they admit.

The research and development agenda that helps to build these sorts of policies is one that recognizes the value of detailed qualitative inquiry coupled with rigorous quantitative statistical testing. In my own work, I marry the two on a daily basis, embedding surveys, interviews, and even ethnographic methods inside randomized experimental designs in order to understand whether and how the intervention approaches actually meet the needs of the individuals involved. This type of mixed method work is risky for researchers, who must be open to learning that they are wrong at least as often as they are right—but it is the sort that must be funded and valued if we are serious about finding effective solutions, rather than simplistic silver bullets.

BIPARTISAN CONSENSUS: A DISTINCT POSSIBILITY?

Despite these significant differences in worldview, we believe the chapters in this book illustrate areas in which it may be possible to bring together both political parties in order to improve the effectiveness of student financial aid. For example, most of the authors value an incremental, research-driven approach to policy change that allows for adaptation over time. With student demographics continually shifting, old funding mechanisms gradually eroding, and institutions of higher education dealing with calls for innovation and transformation, it seems unwise to develop a financial aid strategy just for the next decade. Instead, the nation needs a financial aid system that ensures educational opportunity and economic competitiveness for the next century. Such a long-term approach can move us away from periodic flurries of activity and lay the groundwork for a sustained, stable effort to buttress and regrow the middle class.

In addition, each of the chapters argues that financial aid policies must catch up with the needs of today's students. Originally designed in an era of robust state support for public education and reasonable institution prices, our existing financial aid policies were geared toward dependent students living at home with financially supportive parents. But these same policies are now ill designed to cope with students, states, and institutions that no longer reflect these outdated assumptions. As Mundel and Goldrick-Rab, Stampen, and Schudde point out in their chapters, when the system was originally created, policy makers did not adequately consider how these key actors would behave in response to aid policy over time, which left the system without sufficient safeguards. As the federal government invested more, states disinvested. While the federal government focused on distributing financial aid, institutions focused on raising prices. As the federal government emphasized the "traditional" student, students became more nontraditional. State and institutional aid policy is no better. In short, there is a mismatch between aging financial aid policies and the needs of contemporary students.

Finally, the chapters each argue that this conversation must continue far beyond a single cycle of reauthorization of the Higher Education Act. The original student aid system was crafted after more than a decade of social upheaval and debate about the importance of postsecondary education, the fight for civil rights, and robust arguments about how best to distribute finite resources. This is another such moment, and the nation will be best served by revisiting aid policies regularly, dispassionately, and with careful attention to evidence.

LESSONS LEARNED

The nine chapters in this book took shape over the course of a tumultuous eighteen months in the debate over how to reform federal financial aid. During that time, federal student loan debt surpassed $1 trillion for the first time, Congress and President Obama bickered over minor changes to interest rates on a subset of student loans (twice), the Gates Foundation funded sixteen separate financial aid proposals, and the president announced a proposal to link federal funding to institutional performance. The resulting chapters benefited from and reflect these growing debates. Although they are all quite different, and in some cases disagree with one another, we drew five key lessons from the many ideas presented.

1. Changes to financial aid must be informed and guided by rigorous evidence. First, the road to student aid reform (or in Sara's preferred term, transformation) must reflect the lessons and research from the past and present, along with their limitations. As is so often true, an ahistorical perspective in policy making will repeat many of the same mistakes that led us here in the first place. Many of today's leaders are young and new to the conversation, and as higher education policies age, it becomes increasingly easy to forget how they began. Critical figures who shaped the foundation of today's policies during the 1960s and 1970s are now retired, yet they have useful lessons that tomorrow's policy makers and researchers would be wise to learn from. This is why we invited critical thinkers such as David Mundel, Daniel Madzelan, Jacob Stampen, and W. Lee Hansen to contribute to this book.

But the hard fact is that despite attending to decades of scholarship on student aid, we still know far too little about how student aid programs affect the behavior of students, institutions, and states. We know even less about how potential changes to aid programs would affect these things. This lack of Mundel's *actionable knowledge* handicaps our ability to reform the system and leads to the kind of opportunistic tweaking and iterating that has not solved the problems. Reform will require focused, problem-oriented research that can inform the policy-making process going forward.

Fortunately, a recent set of rigorous randomized experiments (many of which are profiled in the preceding chapters) has begun to improve our understanding of student aid effects. Carefully designed studies of incentive-based scholarships, need-based grants, and Promise Programs are adding to our stock of actionable knowledge with each month that passes.[9] At the same time, policy makers should be careful not to extrapolate too much from any single study, given the wide range of students, schools, and financial aid policies and practices that exist across the nation. For example, Lashawn Richburg-Hayes cautions against grafting performance-based scholarships (which have been tested in a handful of specific sites around the country) onto a large federal program like the Pell Grant because the programs are fundamentally different. While both grant programs provide money to students, performance-based scholarships are small amounts of aid distributed *after* all other need-based aid is allocated. In contrast, the Pell Grant program forms the core of financial aid packages and is the base on top of which performance-based scholarships are built. Therefore, the estimated impacts of performance-based scholarships reflect the baseline support provided by the Pell Grant program. Simply applying performance criteria to the Pell Grant itself could lead to very different effects than those achieved by the scholarships MDRC has examined.

Rodney Andrews's comprehensive overview of Promise Programs suggests a similar lesson. These interventions appear to hinge on a community's commitment to the effort as well as on the effect—both economic and psychological—that such commitment has on the motivation of local students to pursue college. The wide variation in how these programs are implemented makes it difficult to predict how bringing such efforts to scale—through, say, a federal program—would fare. As such, federal policy makers should be wary of assuming that the lessons learned from local interventions will necessarily translate to a federal Promise effort.

The most urgent areas for greater research and development fall into three categories around which there is currently a great deal of reform energy: performance-based funding of financial aid to states or institutions, alterations in the structure of student loans, and student-focused incentives. Rather than a growing body of work in which estimated impacts all run in the same direction, evidence from each of these subfields suggests that effects vary considerably across different types of students and institutions and that there is tremendous variation in the design and implementation of the policies themselves. In other words, what seems to work in one experimental site or one state context appears to generate little positive benefit in another. Moreover, there has been a tendency to rush to make large investments in big new ideas, rather than use systematic replication, rapid prototyping, and mixed-method studies to build a robust body of knowledge that can guide the development of innovative and effective interventions.

For this reason, the federal government should invest in a systematic research and development effort geared at student financial aid policy. Such an effort is critical to the success of both our postsecondary system and the economy as a whole. Financial aid policies lie at the intersection of changing student demographics, public spending priorities, and important questions about how to promote human capital development and economic mobility.

The lessons learned from systematic efforts to experiment with, test, and scale well-developed policies will bear fruit not only for those working in higher education policy making but also for those who are focused on growing the economy.

2. Colleges and universities need to be active partners working in tandem with the federal government. When debating and designing student aid policy, policy makers have typically focused on students as the most important actors in the system: can they afford a school they want to attend, and can aid help them succeed in college? Institutions themselves and the states they reside in are thought to behave according to the maxims of market competition—working to attract students by providing the best possible product at the lowest possible price.

The result is a myopic focus on the ways in which aid influences student behavior, and how tweaks to eligibility and benefit levels can make marginal improvements. In the process, these reform debates have often ignored an equally important question: how do institutions respond to these same policies? Nicholas Hillman touches on this tension as he discusses the recent attention given to high default rates and student loan indebtedness. Students are borrowing more and more money to finance their educations, and stakeholders everywhere are calling for lower student interest rates and better repayment plans. But debates about interest rates and repayment plans fail to tackle the real source or the problem: the relentless increase in tuition prices. Sure, placing all student loan borrowers on a universal income-based repayment plan would improve default rates. But will it create any more incentive for institutions to keep their tuition prices affordable?

The same goes for the Pell Grant program: by tying the money to the decisions of individual students, institutions are effectively absolved from any responsibility for how that money is spent. After all, students chose to spend their voucher there. But relying on market mechanisms to ensure accountability has allowed institutions to spend federal investments however they want, whether it promotes student success or not. As Lesley Turner shows in her chapter on institutional aid, schools pay close attention to how much money students receive from federal and state aid programs. These grant programs often allow institutions to substitute public dollars for institutional aid they would have otherwise spent on needy students. As federal and state grant aid increases, institutions often shift their own scholarships and tuition discounts to merit aid designed to attract affluent students. This substitution effect, which is especially evident at private institutions, blunts the impact of federal grant programs.

In other policy areas "supplement not supplant" or "maintenance of effort" provisions prohibit this type of substitution effect (and often cause their own share of regulatory headaches). Not so in higher education, where institutions have been free to capture as much federal aid as possible. Thus a second key lesson is that future changes to federal student aid must acknowledge the incentive structure that aid programs set up for institutions and extend accountability for results beyond the student. Under the current system, students shoulder most of the responsibility for their own success—they must show academic progress, finish degrees in a timely fashion, and pay back their loans even if they fail to finish a degree. The assumption is that individuals will hold institutions accountable via their choice of where to enroll. Meanwhile, outside of accountability for their cohort default rate, colleges and universities are paid in full regardless of how successful their students are. Colleges can continue to increase tuition and spend money on amenities, trusting that federal student aid will continue to fund their students.

The results of this system are all too predictable. Turner's chapter shows that some institutions have used federal need-based aid as a way to free up their own resources—resources that they then spend on merit aid for students without financial need. Robert Sheets and Stephen Crawford echo similar sentiments, arguing that the existing student loan programs do not provide enough incentive for institutions to keep tuition low and serve their students effectively. By forcing institutions to have skin in the game, Sheets and Crawford argue, they will have greater incentive to keep prices low and ensure that students succeed. Specifically, they propose putting institutions on the hook when students default on their loans; defaults are correlated with student success in the labor market, an outcome for which both institutions and students bear responsibility.

Meanwhile, Sara Goldrick-Rab, Lauren Schudde, and Jacob Stampen's chapter challenges the basic assumption that financial aid should be given out to students as a voucher, arguing that this policy design compromises our ability to hold institutions accountable. If aid instead flowed directly to institutions, the authors argue, policy makers would be better able to ensure that institutions behave in ways that promote public goals. Without a radical shift in policy design, institutions will continue to behave in ways that maximize grant and loan revenue without necessarily maximizing student success.

3. Reforms should build a sense of shared responsibility between federal, state, and local governments. Federal policy is necessarily a blunt instrument when it comes to reforming America's diverse array of colleges and universities. There are millions of students with different aspirations and academic profiles attending different types of institutions, yet the same basic grant and loan programs cover all of them. The federal government can cut checks to cover voucher and loan amounts, but it currently has few levers to compel institutions to behave in ways that promote public goals or to create the kinds of "college-going cultures" that take root in K–12 schools and districts. In an effort to ensure that aid is appropriately targeted and that students hold up their end of the bargain, federal policy makers have constructed a complex system that is both difficult to navigate and critical to all the stakeholders in the system.

In federal policy debates, it is easy to lose sight of the fact that other levels of government must also play a role in financing and governing higher education. In fact, federal student aid policy is unique among social policies in how little it expects of state or local governments. This dynamic is particularly striking in contrast to K–12, where federal policy asks a lot of state and local governments even though it provides just a small share of public school funding. Unfortunately, as David Mundel points out, we know little about how to use federal policy levers to encourage state and local actors to take on some of this responsibility. Federal efforts to promote state investment—through matching grant funds or the like—have tended to disappoint. And we still know almost nothing about how aid programs affect the behavior of schools and school districts, if at all. As a result, federal policy debates have tended to think of financial aid in isolation from other layers of government. But the responsibility for college access and affordability cannot fall entirely on the federal government.

Rodney Andrews highlights the important role that local organizations and governments can play in promoting college affordability. Promise Programs are remarkable in both their simplicity and their potential to help us better understand how a critical set of actors—K–12 schools and districts—might respond to innovative financial aid policies. These programs reach down into the K–12 pipeline to communicate clear expectations early in a student's education: "graduate from high school and you get money for college." And because the local community is involved, the message reaches beyond schools to include churches, local businesses, and nonprofit organizations. Students are told from an early age that college is not just accessible but expected, and the local public schools are tasked with helping students get there. We are still learning about how these programs affect students and schools, and the programs typically rely on private funding that may not be available in perpetuity. But the emerging insight here is an important one: state and local governments can do things that federal financial aid policy cannot, and policy makers must find ways to encourage these actors to join in the effort to make college affordable. Rather than trying to make every new idea into a federal program, policy makers should instead find ways to incentivize this kind of state and local activity, perhaps via competitive grant programs or demonstration projects that provide states and local governments with the flexibility to try new ideas.

4. Access to completion is required. The Pell Grant program, the bedrock of federal student aid, was created to help students *obtain*—not just start—a college degree.[10] Thus, a dual focus on both college access and college completion has been present from the start, and yet many students who begin college do not go on to complete a degree. To address this, some reformers have proposed to alter student aid in ways that emphasize student progress *and* completion—for example, by conditioning aid on prior academic ability or performance or providing more aid to students who take more credits, get better grades, or persist longer in their programs. These well-intentioned ideas, however, have the potential to compromise the program's other mission: access. Democratizing college opportunity is central to ensuring that the American Dream remains achievable. At the same time, a system of open doors and second chances necessarily entails some rate of failure among students who enter, which runs counter to much of the current "completion agenda."

The chapters in this volume do not resolve this tension, but they bring it to the fore. And there are no easy answers. Stephen Crawford and Robert Sheets grapple with this tension in their proposal for student loan reform. A more dynamic system of student loans that accurately reflects students' "risk profiles" would likely be more efficient and limit the likelihood of default. For students, better information about the likely consequences of taking on debt for particular programs might help them make more informed decisions about where to invest their time and money. But Crawford and Sheets admit that such a system must be careful to ensure that at-risk students still have access to aid and postsecondary education. Increased underwriting based on student and program characteristics would bias the loan system in favor of the "best" students and against those with less academic preparation, with consequences for access.

The tension between access and success also emerges in discussions about what we should expect of undergraduates receiving federal aid. Recipients have long had to meet academic benchmarks at the end of each term, but recently some have argued that aid should be distributed based on intermediate (within-term) benchmarks as well. This is a basic premise in Lashawn Richburg-Hayes's chapter, since performance-based scholarships would only go to students who meet certain criteria for a given term. Similarly, Crawford and Sheets suggest that individual students should be able to improve their own risk profile over the course of their time in college. By taking and passing more credits, students could obtain increasingly favorable loan terms.

However, more stringent academic standards could also push some students away from college altogether. As Regina Deil-Amen and Cecilia Rios-Aguilar point out, for many students, life often gets in the way of school. If aid recipients can no longer pay their tuition bill because they have not met academic benchmarks, they face a choice: work more outside of school to earn money, drop out altogether, or spend more time on schoolwork to improve their academic performance in time for next semester. While raising academic standards is politically attractive, it may work at cross-purposes with the push to increase educational attainment.

5. Policy reform must move beyond politics. Higher education is a big industry, and like most big industries it entails its own politics. Various stakeholders clash over what is best and for whom, but institutions and their trade associations tend to wield the most power. Institutions, students, the Department of Education, Congress, and the executive branch all have different ideas about the goals of federal student aid policy and the policy designs that are likely to get us there. The result is what author Daniel Madzelan calls an ad hoc policy process "driven by near-term political exigencies rather than systematic policy development." This is a recipe for more of the same.

IN SUMMARY

As the reader can see, there is still much to be debated and discussed when it comes to aid reform. Such debate and discussion is not only healthy, it is critical. For too long, cherished programs and traditional assumptions have avoided the kind of hard questions that are common in other areas of social policy. But these days are coming to an end. In their place, policy makers must take the long view and embark on a systematic, evidence-based effort to transform the system. Collectively, the chapters in this volume begin to lay the groundwork for this long-term process.

Notes

Foreword

1. The Library of Congress, *Thomas Jefferson to George Wythe, August 13, 1786*. The Thomas Jefferson Papers Series 1. General Correspondence 1651–1827, http://hdl.loc.gov/loc.mss/mtj.mtjbib002184.
2. *Act of July 2, 1862 (Morrill Act)*, Public Law 37-108, which established land grant colleges; Enrolled Acts and Resolutions of Congress, 1789–1996; Record Group 11; General Records of the United States Government; National Archives. It is interesting to note that full passage of the Morrill Act required an amendment that colleges would offer courses in military tactics and engineering.
3. Higher Education for American Democracy, *A Report of the President's Commission on Higher Education* (Washington, DC: Government Printing Office, 1947–1948).
4. Harry S. Truman Library and Museum, *Commencement Address at Howard University*. Public Papers of the Presidents, Harry S. Truman, 1945–1953, http://trumanlibrary.org/publicpapers/index.php?pid=2402.
5. U.S. Department of Commerce, Census Bureau, *2012 National Population Projections: Summary Tables*, http://www.census.gov/population/projections/data/national/2012/summarytables.html.
6. See chapters 4 and 5 for more information about performance metrics and simplification related to student financial aid reforms.
7. Thomas Jefferson, "The administration of justice and description of the laws," in *Notes on the State of Virginia* (1785), http://xroads.virginia.edu/~hyper/jefferson/ch14.html.

Introduction

1. The examples abound. April 26, 1976, *Newsweek*: the cover features two graduates, still in cap and gown, operating jackhammers on a construction site with the headline "Who Needs College?" June 23, 1991, *New York Times*: "Grimly, Graduates Are Finding Few Jobs." March 17, 1997, *Time*: "How Colleges Are Gouging U" (cover) and "Why Colleges Cost Too Much." For more on this pattern see Kevin Carey, "Bad Job Market: Why the Media Is Always Wrong About the Value of a College Degree," *The New Republic*, June 9, 2011. http://www.newrepublic.com/article/economy/89675/bad-job-market-media-wrong-college-degree
2. Barack Obama, "Remarks of President Barack Obama—As Prepared for Delivery. Address to Joint Session of Congress. Tuesday, February 24th, 2009," http://www.whitehouse.gov/the_press_office/Remarks-of-President-Barack-Obama-Address-to-Joint-Session-of-Congress.
3. CNN Political Ticker, "Obama continues college cost pitch in weekly address," CNN, August 24, 2013, http://politicalticker.blogs.cnn.com/2013/08/24/obama-continues-college-cost-pitch-in-weekly-address/.

4. Congressional Budget Office, "The Federal Pell Grant Program: Recent Growth and Policy Options," September 2013, http://www.cbo.gov/sites/default/files/cbofiles/attachments/44448_PellGrants_9-5-13.pdf.

5. College Board, "Trends in College Pricing," 2012, http://trends.collegeboard.org/sites/default/files/college-pricing-2012-full-report_0.pdf.

6. Barack Obama, "Full Transcript: President Obama's remarks on the economy at Knox College," *Washington Post*, July 24, 2013, http://www.washingtonpost.com/politics/full-text-of-president-obamas-remarks-on-the-economy-at-knox-college-as-prepared-for-delivery/2013/07/24/fd580f6a-f47f-11e2-a2f1-a7acf9bd5d3a_story_4.html.

7. Mark Kantrowitz, "Pell Grant Historical Figures," Finaid.org, http://www.finaid.org/educators/pellgrant.phtml.

8. U.S. Department of Education, "Trends in Undergraduate Borrowing II: Federal Student Loans in 1995–96, 1999–2000, and 2003–04," Postsecondary Education Descriptive Analysis Report, February 2008, http://nces.ed.gov/pubs2008/2008179rev.pdf; College Board, "Federal Loan Programs in Current and Constant Dollars Over Time," Trends in Higher Education, September 2013, http://trends.collegeboard.org/student-aid/figures-tables/loans-federal-loan-programs-current-and-constant-dollars-over-time.

9. College Board, "Federal Loan Programs."

10. U.S. Department of Education, "Student Loans Overview," Fiscal Year 2013 Budget Request, http://www2.ed.gov/about/overview/budget/budget13/justifications/r-loansoverview.pdf; Quick Takes, "Study: Majority of Students Now Have Federal Aid," *Inside Higher Ed* (Aug. 20, 2013), http://www.insidehighered.com/quicktakes/2013/08/20/study-majority-students-now-have-federal-aid.

11. College Board, "Total and per FTE Student State Appropriations and Public Enrollment over Time," Trends in College Pricing, http://trends.collegeboard.org/college-pricing/figures-tables/total-and-fte-student-state-appropriations-and-public-enrollment-over-time; College Board, "Tuition and Fee and Room and Board Charges over Time," Trends in College Pricing, http://trends.collegeboard.org/college-pricing/figures-tables/tuition-and-fee-and-room-and-board-charges-over-time.

12. College Board, "Tuition and Fee and Room and Board Charges over Time."

13. College Board, "Tuition and Fee and Room and Board Charges over Time, 1973–74 through 2013–14, Selected Years," Trends in College Pricing, http://trends.collegeboard.org/college-pricing/figures-tables/tuition-and-fee-and-room-and-board-charges-over-time-1973-74-through-2013-14-selected-years.

14. Brian Jacob, Brian McCall, and Kevin M. Stange, "College as Country Club: Do Colleges Cater to Students' Preferences for Consumption?" (National Bureau of Economic Research Working Paper 18745, 2013).

15. Martha J. Bailey and Susan M. Dynarski, "Gains and Gaps: Changing Inequality in U.S. College Entry and Completion" (Working Paper 17633, National Bureau of Economic Research, 2011).

16. Emily Dai, "Student Loan Delinquencies Surge," *Inside the Vault* (Federal Reserve Bank of St. Louis, spring 2013), http://www.stlouisfed.org/publications/itv/articles/?id=2348.

17. John Gittelsohn, "Mortgage Delinquency Rate in U.S. Fall to 2008 Levels," *Bloomberg* (May 16, 2012), http://www.bloomberg.com/news/2012-05-16/mortgage-delinquencies-in-u-s-fall-to-lowest-since-2008.html.

18. Rohit Chopra, "A closer look at the trillion," *Consumer Financial Protection Bureau* (blog) (Aug. 5, 2013), http://www.consumerfinance.gov/blog/a-closer-look-at-the-trillion/.

19. Jamie Merisotis, "Meeting the Need for College Graduates in Texas" (speech at the Austin Economic Club, Austin, TX, March 8, 2013), http://www.luminafoundation.org/about_us/president/speeches/2013-03-08.html.

20. Bill Gates, "Morrill Act Sesquicentennial (speech)," Bill and Melinda Gates Foundation, http://www.gatesfoundation.org/media-center/speeches/2012/06/bill-gates-morrill-act-sesquicentennial.

21. Andrew P. Kelly and Mark Schneider, eds., *Getting to graduation: The completion agenda in higher education* (Baltimore: Johns Hopkins University Press, 2012).

22. Susan Dynarski and Judith Scott-Clayton, "Financial Aid Policy: Lessons from Research," *Future of Children* 23, no. 1 (2013): 86, http://futureofchildren.org/futureofchildren/publications/docs/23_01_04.pdf.

Chapter 1

1. Senator Morrill's statements (in which he noted the constraints facing his father who had only four years of schooling) indicate he wanted the colleges receiving these grants to aid disadvantaged youth.

2. Other sources consulted in the development of this chapter are as follows: Ronald G. Ehrenberg, "Is the Golden Age of the Private Research University Over?" *Change* May–June 2013; W. Lee Hansen, "Impact of Student Financial Aid on Access," in *The Crisis in Higher Education*, ed. Joseph Froomkin (The Academy of Political Science: 1984); Ron Haskins and Cecilia Elena Rouse, "Time for Change: A New Federal Strategy to Prepare Disadvantaged Students for College," in *The Future of Children* (Policy Brief, Spring 2013); HCM Strategists, "Doing Better for More Students: Putting Student Outcomes at the Center of Federal Financial Aid" (Washington, DC: 2013); Paul Jarvey, Alex Usher, and Lori McElroy, "Making Research Count: Analyzing Canadian Academic Publishing Cultures" (Toronto, Canada: Higher Education Strategy Associates, June 2012); Meir G. Kohn, Charles F. Manski, and David S. Mundel, "An empirical investigation of the factors which influence college-going behavior," *Annals of Economic and Social Measurement* May 1976 (also published by RAND Corporation: September 1974); Kevin Lang and Russell Weinstein, "Evaluating Student Outcomes at For-Profit Colleges" (National Bureau of Economic Research Working Paper 18201, June 2012); Robert E. Martin and R. Carter Hill, "Measuring Baumol and Bowen Effects in Public Research Universities" (unpublished manuscript: 2012); David S. Mundel, "Federal Aid to Higher Education and the Poor" (PhD thesis, MIT: 1971); David S. Mundel, "The Use of Information in the Policy Process: Are Social-Policy Experiments Worthwhile?" in *Social Experimentation*, ed. Jerry A. Hausman and David A. Wise (Chicago: University of Chicago Press, 1985); David S. Mundel, "What Do We Know About the Impact of Grants to College Students?" in *The Effectiveness of Student Aid Policies: What the Research Tells Us*, ed. Sandy Baum, Michael McPherson, and Patricia Steele (New York: College Board, 2008); Libby A. Nelson, "A Look at All 15 Reimagining Aid Design and Delivery Reports from the Gates Foundation," *Inside Higher Ed*, March 14, 2013; Richard Perez-Pena, "Colleges Show Uneven Effort to Enroll Poor," *New York Times*, March 31, 2013; Rethinking Pell Grants Study Group, *Rethinking Pell Grants* (College Board Advocacy and Policy Center: April 2013); U.S. Department of Health, Education, and Welfare, "Toward a Long-Range Plan for Federal Financial Support for Higher Education: A Report to the President" (Washington, DC: 1969 [note: also referred to as "The Rivlin Report"]); Pamela Barnhouse Walters, Annette Lareau, and Sheri H. Ranis, eds., *Education Research on Trial: Policy Reform and the Call for Scientific Rigor* (New York: Routledge, 2009).

3. College Board, *Trends in Student Aid 2012* (New York: College Board Advocacy and Policy Center, 2012).

4. These disappointing results have been documented in several policy-oriented reports including a series of recent reports supported by the Bill and Melinda Gates Foundation in its Reimagining Aid Design and Delivery (RADD) project.

5. The continuing problems include: (1) low rates of college-going and success (i.e., persistence and completion) among lower-income youth, (2) limited recruitment of aided students by many colleges, (3) increasing student reliance on borrowing and work to finance college, and (4) complexities in student aid programs and practices that have limited program impact.

6. This terminology is purposely similar to terminology used within foreign, defense, and intelligence communities—actionable intelligence.

7. Although highly statistically significant observations are less likely to be influenced by sampling-induced errors, other observations may be less subject to other errors (e.g., measurement errors) and thus more valid and useful.

8. These problems have been described as arising from market failures (by economists), non-market failures (by a range of social scientists focusing on organizational behaviors), and political system failures (by political scientists and many other observers).

9. Including economic, political, sociological, and demographic contexts.

10. In that book and elsewhere, Freidman argued that because investment in higher education produces benefits that cannot be captured by individual investors (i.e., "externalities and public goods"), individuals will underinvest in college. Another market failure arises because individuals planning to attend college are unable to borrow against their expected future income because they lack the collateral required by lenders.

11. It was implicitly assumed that the availability of federal guaranteed student loans would not reduce support provided by these parents.

12. In many instances these assumptions were essentially ignored, and in others, researchers, analysts, and/or policy makers presented their beliefs with greater certainty than was appropriate given limited available evidence.

13. See, for example: Charles Wolf, "A Theory of Nonmarket Failure: Framework for Implementation Analysis," *Journal of Law and Economics* 22, no. 1 (1979): 107–139; Charles Wolf, *Markets or Government: Choosing Between Imperfect Alternatives* (Cambridge, MA: MIT Press, 1988); Allison Graham and Philip Zelikow, *Essence of Decision: Explaining the Cuban Missile Crisis* (Boston: Little, Brown, 1971).

14. This discussion is largely theoretical or conceptual because the effect of these nonmarket factors on student aid policy and program effectiveness has not been specifically addressed in available research.

15. These differences have been discussed by many authors, most notably William J. Baumol, Howard R. Bowen, and Ronald G. Ehrenberg.

16. See chapter 7, by Lesley Turner, in this volume.

17. For example, although funding for the Pell Grant program increased dramatically during the recent recession, the structure of the program was not changed in response to a dramatically changed economic context. At the same time, important and potentially effective program changes that would have required small changes in resource allocations received little attention during this period of rapid and unsustainable program growth.

18. For example, see Baum, McPherson, and Steele, eds., *The Effectiveness of Student Aid Policies*; Susan Dynarski and Judith Scott-Clayton, "Financial Aid Policy: Lessons from Research," *The Future of Children* 23, no. 1 (2013): 67–92.

19. This review is based on a series of research reviews prepared by the author (David S. Mundel),

among others: David S. Mundel and Ann S. Coles, "Summary Project Report—An exploration of what we know about the formation and impact of perceptions of college prices, student aid, and the affordability of college-going and a prospectus for future research" (Boston MA: TERI, 2004); and Mundel, "What Do We Know About the Impact of Grants to College Students?" in *The Effectiveness of Student Aid Policies*, ed. Baum, McPherson, and Steele. This is in addition to other available research reviews.

20. David S. Mundel, "Do Increases in Pell and Other Grant Awards Increase College-Going Among Lower-Income High School Graduates?: Evidence from a 'Natural Experiment'" (Washington, DC: Brookings, 2008); David S. Mundel, "Observing the Impact of Changes in Net-of-Grant Prices on College-Going Among Lower Income Youth: Evidence from Two 'Natural Experiments'" (unpublished manuscript, 2011).

21. The potential college-goers that have been studied include college-oriented high school seniors who have not been actively involved in a college search or application process and high-achievement youth from high schools where graduates have rarely, if ever, attended more selective colleges and universities.

22. The best of these studies include: Eric P. Bettinger, Bridget Terry Long, Philip Oreopoulos, and Lisa Sanbonmatsu, "The Role of Application Assistance and Information in College Decisions: Results from the H&R Block FAFSA Experiment," *Quarterly Journal of Economics* 127, no. 3 (2012): 1205–1242; Caroline Hoxby and Sarah Turner, "Expanding College Opportunities for High-Achieving, Low-Income Students" (discussion paper, Stanford Institute for Economic Policy Research 12-014: 2013); Scott Carrell and Bruce Sacerdote, "Late Interventions Matter Too: The Case of College Coaching in New Hampshire" (unpublished manuscript: 2013).

23. There is much less evidence regarding the impact of more general, media-based marketing activities aimed at stimulating college preparation, completion of admission and aid applications, and college-going. Little research has been focused on these types of marketing, and the available research suggests weak and uncertain impacts. There is much more positive evidence about the impact of similar marketing efforts aimed at potential military recruits.

24. See Mundel and Coles, "Summary Project Report."

25. Sara Goldrick-Rab et al., "Need-Based Financial Aid and College Persistence: Experimental Evidence from Wisconsin" (unpublished draft: 2013).

26. The suggestion that federal student aid stimulated increases in college prices was made forcibly by the former Secretary of Education William J. Bennett in 1987; see William J. Bennett, "Our Greedy Colleges," *New York Times*, February 18, 1987.

27. See for example, Arthur M. Hauptman, "Class Differences in Room for Debate, Rising College Costs: A Federal Role?" *New York Times Room for Debate Blog*, February 2, 2010.

28. David S. Mundel, "Understanding the meaning and role of statistical significance" (unpublished, 2013).

29. Because these findings are rarely published, they are generally ignored in most research reviews that focus on articles published in peer-reviewed journals with reportedly "statistically significant" results.

30. For a fuller discussion of issues regarding the improper use of statistical significance testing results, see Mundel, "Understanding the meaning and role of statistical significance."

31. Within higher education, the use of insights and evidence derived from research in other sectors is extremely limited, and most higher education researchers act as if higher education is unique and there is little to learn from other sectors. As a result, potentially useful knowledge from other sectors—e.g., the health sector (which shares many characteristics with higher education)—is ignored. Similarly, knowledge derived from military recruiting and

training research could provide important insights useful in understanding student recruitment.

32. For example, the NCES NPSAS data sets.
33. For example, the Bureau of the Census CPS and American Community Survey data sets.
34. Much of the available observational student aid research is based on a single set of case study observations or a single set of data. This data-imposed limitation restricts the problem focus of research.
35. The National Health Insurance experiments (RAND) and the Income Maintenance Experiment (Institute for Research on Poverty) are examples of early-stage experiments that produced data used by several other researchers.
36. These changes have largely resulted from recession-induced changes in the economic context within which student aid programs operate, as well as legislative and budgetary forces.

Chapter 2

1. William W. Warner, *Beautiful Swimmers: Watermen, Crabs and the Chesapeake Bay* (Boston: Atlantic Monthly Press and Little, Brown Books, 1976).
2. In the much smaller Federal Perkins Loan program, college students borrow directly from their schools.
3. More specifically, lenders received quarterly "special allowance" payments equal to the difference between the market rate (generally the yield on a recently auctioned T-bill plus a markup) and the borrower's interest rate. During in-school and grace periods, lenders received payments equal to the market rate.
4. Donald G. Ogilvie, executive vice president of the American Bankers Association, quoted in Clifford Krauss, "House Panel Backs Clinton Student Loan Plan," *New York Times*, May 13, 1993.
5. Jeffords quoted in Clifford Krauss, "Skeptics and Lobbyists Besiege Student Loan Plan," *New York Times*, June 2, 1993.
6. Consider a $100 subsidized loan with a 5 percent interest where the "market rate" is 7 percent. Prior to the FCRA, that $100 lent to a borrower by the government would show up as a cost to the government of $100 in the year the loan was made. The government would realize revenue over time from borrower payments of principal and interest, but the first-year cost of a direct loan is $100. The same $100 lent as a guaranteed loan would "cost" much less, at least as far as the budget was concerned: because the bank lends a student $100 at 5 percent interest, the first-year cost to the government (because the borrower is in school) is the 7-dollar interest payment it pays the lender on behalf of the borrower. Once the borrower enters repayment, the cost to the government in the first year is just two dollars, or the gap between the 7 percent market rate and the subsidized rate on the loan (what is known as the "special allowance" payment to the lender). Of course the government will incur greater costs if the borrower defaults, but otherwise the annual cost is small.
7. Doug Lederman, "The Politicking and Policy Making Behind a $40 Billion Windfall; How Clinton, Congress, and colleges battled to shape Hope scholarships," *Chronicle of Higher Education*, Nov. 28, 1997.
8. TRA defined an institution of postsecondary education, to which tuition payments made by taxpayers would qualify for the new tax credits, by reference to the Higher Education Act definition: an institution of higher education whose students would be otherwise eligible to receive federal student aid funding under Title IV.
9. Quote from House Committee on Ways and Means, *President's Fiscal Year 1998 Budget: Hearings before the Committee on Ways and Means*, 105th Cong., 1st sess., Feb, 11–12, 1997.

Available online via: http://commdocs.house.gov/committees/ways/hwmw105-17.000/hwmw105-17_0f.htm.

10. However, there were still conforming amendments needed in the HEA to ensure the coordination of student-level benefits between the new tax expenditure and the existing student aid spending programs in the most advantageous way for families. This was accomplished the following year in the 1998 HEA Amendments.

11. The other being the Clinton administration's proposal for college tuition tax credits—enacted as the Taxpayer Relief Act of 1997.

12. Federal Supplemental Educational Opportunity Grants, the Federal Work-Study Program, and Federal Perkins Loans.

13. When it came to higher education policy, the tactic provided new administrations with some policy-making power even in periods between reauthorizations. The 1980 HEA Amendments preceded the 1980 election, precluding the incoming administration from participating in that effort. The 1992 HEA Amendments passed about four months prior to that year's presidential election, yet the Clinton administration was able to use the 1993 budget reconciliation process to expand the direct loan program. Likewise, the George W. Bush and Obama administrations began just after passage of the 1998 and 2008 HEA Amendments, respectively, and both used "off-cycle" legislation to advance their policy preferences.

Chapter 3

1. Ted C. Fishman, "Why These Kids Get a Free Ride to College," *New York Times Magazine*, Sept. 12, 2012.

2. Eligibility requirements for the West Virginia Promise are maintained at https://secure.cfwv .com/Financial_Aid_Planning/Scholarships/Scholarships_and_Grants/ West_Virginia_PROMISE.aspx.

3. The list of Promise Programs can be found at http://www.upjohn.org/Research/SpecialTopics/KalamazooPromise/PromiseTypeScholarshipPrograms.

4. Information on PromiseNet can be found at http://www.upjohninst.org/Research/SpecialTopics/KalamazooPromise/Community.

5. Information on the Pittsburgh Promise is located at http://www.pittsburghpromise.org. The Detroit College Promise is discussed at http://www.detroitcollegepromise.com. The El Dorado Promise is described at http://www.eldoradopromise.com. The Leopard Challenge is described at http://66.204.138.9/index.php?page=leopard-challenge.

6. The Jackson Legacy Scholarship is described at http://jacksoncf.org/Default. aspx?pageId=1431733. The Promise for the Future Scholarship is described at http://centralaz. edu/Home/About_Central/Foundation/Promise_For_the_Future.htm.

7. This information was obtained from http://www.peoriapromise.org/students.html.

8. Information obtained from the 2010 Decennial Census at http://factfinder2.census.gov/faces/nav/jsf/pages/community_facts.xhtml.

9. Information on the Peoria Promise may be found at http://www.peoriapromise.org/. The Great River Promise is discussed at http://www.pccua.edu/. The Promise for the Future program is described at http://www.centralaz.edu/Home/About_Central/Foundation/Promise_For_the_Future.htm.

10. Information on the Arkadelphia Promise was obtained from http://arkadelphiapromise.com/.

11. Information on the Sparkman Promise was obtained from http://www. sparkmanscholarshipfoundation.com/.

12. Ofer Malamud and Abigail Wozniak, "The Impact of College on Migration: Evidence from the Vietnam Generation," *Journal of Human Resources* 47, no. 4 (Fall 2012).

13. Maria D. Fitzpatrick and Damon Jones, "Higher Education, Merit-based Scholarships and Post-Baccalaureate Migration" (National Bureau of Economic Research Working Paper 18530, 2012).

14. Jeffery Groen, "The Effect of College Location on Migration of College-educated Labor," *Journal of Econometrics* 121, no. 12 (2004).

15. Information obtained (April 3, 2013) from http://www.upenn.edu/pennnews/news/ penn-announces-2012-13-financial-aid-budget-tuition.

16. Information retrieved (March 1, 2013) from http://www.eldoradopromise.com.

17. Eligibility criteria for the Northport Promise are located at http://www.northportpromise. com/eligibility.pdf.

18. Information on the College Bound Promise was obtained from http://collegebound.gohammond.com/index.php.

19. Fishman, "Why These Kids Get A Free Ride."

20. Joe Smydo, "Pittsburgh Promise Delivers on $15 million Fundraising Goal," *Pittsburgh Post-Gazette*, July 2, 2009.

21. Eleanor Chute, "Pittsburgh Promise Scholarship Fund Reaches $160 million," *Pittsburgh Post-Gazette*, June 14, 2012.

22. Quotation taken (Feb. 25, 2013) from http://www.detroitcollegepromise.com/dcpfaq.html.

23. Information retrieved (Feb. 25, 2013) from http://www.detroitcollegepromise.com/dcpfaq. html.

24. Chelsea Schneider Kirk, "Hammond Working on Long-term Funding for College Bound," *Times of Northwestern Indiana*, May 26, 2012.

25. Douglas N. Harris, "Testing the Promise: A Randomized Controlled Trial of a Promise Scholarship for Urban Public Schools Students," Project Narrative, http://doku.iab.de/veranstaltungen/2012/field_2012_Orr.pdf.

26. Rodney J. Andrews, Steven DesJardins, and Vimal Ranchhod, "The Effects of the Kalamazoo Promise on College Choice," *Economics of Education Review* 29, no. 5 (Oct. 2010).

27. Susan Dynarski, "Does Aid Matter? Measuring the Effect of Student Aid on College Attendance and Completion," *American Economic Review* 93, no. 1 (March 2003).

28. Robert Kelchen and Sara Goldrick-Rab, "Accelerating College Knowledge: Examining the Feasibility of a Targeted Early Commitment Program" (Discussion Paper 1405-13, Institute for Research on Poverty, 2013).

29. James J. Heckman, "Schools, Skills, and Synapses," *Economic Inquiry* 46, no. 3 (July 2008).

30. James J. Heckman and Tim Kautz, "Hard Evidence on Soft Skills" *Labour Economics* 19, no. 4 (2012).

31. Susan Dynarski, "Hope for Whom? Financial Aid for the Middle Class and Its Impact on College Attendance," *National Tax Journal* 53, no. 3 (2000).

32. Susan Dynarski, "The New Merit Aid," in *College Choices: The Economics of Where to Go, When to Go, and How to Pay For It*, ed. Caroline Hoxby (Chicago: University of Chicago Press, 2004).

33. Stephen L. DesJardins, Brian P. McCall, M. Ott, and J. Kim, "A Quasi-Experimental Investigation of How the Gates Millenium Scholars Program is Related to College Students' Time Use and Activities," *Educational Evaluation and Policy Analysis* 32, no. 4 (2010).

34. Ralph Stinebrickner and Todd Stinebrickner, "Time Use and College Outcomes," *Journal of Econometrics* 121, no. 12 (2004); Ronald G. Ehrenberg and Daniel R. Sherman, "Employment While in College, Academic Achievement, and Postcollege Outcomes: A Summary of Results," *Journal of Human Resources* 22, no. 1 (1987).

35. Stinebrickner and Stinebrickner, "Time Use and College Outcomes."

36. Jennifer Iriti, William Bickel, and Jessica Kaufman, *Realizing "the promise:" Scholar Retention and Persistence in Post-Secondary Education* (Pittsburgh, PA: University of Pittsburgh's Learning Research and Development Center, 2012).

37. Office of Education Policy, "El Dorado Promise Impact Report—2013." [Note: this is an independent study conducted by the Office of Education Policy at the University of Arkansas (2013).]

38. Dynarski, "Does Aid Matter?

39. Judith Scott-Clayton, "On Money and Motivation: A Quasi-Experimental Analysis of Financial Incentives for College Achievement," *Journal of Human Resources* 46, no. 3 (2011).

40. Susan Dynarski, "Building the Stock of College Educated Labor," *Journal of Human Resources* 43, no. 3 (2008).

41. David L. Sjoquist and John V. Winters "Building the Stock of College-Educated Labor Revisited," *Journal of Human Resources* 47, no. 1 (2012).

42. Ronald G. Ehrenberg, "American Higher Education in Transition," *Journal of Economic Perspectives* 26, no. 1 (2012).

43. Information on the Promise Zones obtained from http://www.promisezones.org/.

44. Information on Georgia House Bill 1325 obtained from http://www.legis.ga.gov/legislation/en-US/display/20032004/HB/1325.

45. Information on changes in HOPE scholarship obtained from http://www.gsfc.org.

46. Enrico Moretti, "Estimating the Social Return to Higher Education: Evidence from Longitudinal and Repeated Cross-Sectional Data," *Journal of Econometrics* 121, no. 12 (2004).

47. Tom S. Dee, "Are There Civic Returns to Education?" *Journal of Public Economics* 88, vols. 9–10 (2004).

48. David Card, "The Causal Effect of Education on Earnings," in *Handbook of Labor Economics*, eds. O. Ashenfelter and D. Card (New York: Elsevier Science, 1999), vol. 3A; Mark Hoekstra, "The Effect of Attending the Flagship State University on Earnings: A Discontinuity-Based Approach," *Review of Economics and Statistics* 91, no. 4 (2009).

49. Thomas Lemieux, "Postsecondary Education and Increasing Wage Inequality," *American Economic Review* 96, no. 2 (2006).

50. Michelle Miller-Adams, *The Power of a Promise: Education and Economic Renewal in Kalamazoo* (Kalamazoo, MI: Upjohn Institute Press 2009).

51. Gary Miron, Jeffrey N. Jones, and Allison J. Kelaher-Young, "The Kalamazoo Promise and Perceived Change in School Climate," *Education Policy Analysis Archives* 19, no. 17 (2011).

52. Marianne Bertrand, Sendhil Mullainathan, and E. Shafir, "A Behavioral Economics View of Poverty," *American Economic Review* 94, no. 2 (2004).

53. Judith Scott-Clayton, "Information Constraints and Financial Aid Policy" (National Bureau of Economic Research Working Paper 17811, 2012); Susan Dynarski and Judith Scott-Clayton, "Financial Aid Policy: Lessons from Research" (National Bureau of Economic Research Working Paper 18710, 2013).

Chapter 4

1. Ron Haskins, Harry Holzer, and Robert Lerman, *Promoting Economic Mobility by Increasing Postsecondary Education* (Washington, DC: Economic Mobility Project, Pew Charitable Trusts, May 2009).

2. Eric P. Bettinger, Bridget T. Long, Philip Oreopoulos, and Lisa Sanbonmatsu, "The Role of Application Assistance and Information in College Decisions: Results from the H&R Block FAFSA Experiment," *Quarterly Journal of Economics* 127, no. 3 (Aug. 2012).

3. Adam S. Booij, Edwin Leuven, and Hessel Oosterbeek, "The Role of Information in the

Take-Up of Student Loans," *Economics of Education Review* 31, no. 1 (Feb. 2012); Alicia C. Dowd, "Dynamic Interactions and Intersubjectivity: Challenges to Causal Modeling in Studies of College Student Debt," *Review of Educational Research* 78, no. 2 (June 2008); Stephen L. DesJardins, Dennis A. Ahlburg, and Brian Patrick McCall, "An Integrated Model of Application, Admission, Enrollment, and Financial Aid," *Journal of Higher Education* 77, no. 3 (Jan./Feb. 2006); Don Hossler, Mary Ziskin, Jacob P. K. Gross, Sooyeon Kim, and Osman Cekic, "Student Aid and Its Role in Encouraging Persistence," *Higher Education New York* 24 (Apr. 2009); Louis Jacobson and Christine Mokher, *Pathways to Boosting the Earnings of Low-Income Students by Increasing Their Educational Attainment* (Washington, DC: Hudson Institute, 2009); Melissa Roderick, Jenny Nagaoka, Vanessa Coca, and Eliza Moeller, *From High School to the Future: Potholes on the Road to College* (Chicago: Consortium on Chicago School Research, 2008).

4. Reshma Patel and Lashawn Richburg-Hayes, *Performance-Based Scholarships: Emerging Findings from a National Demonstration* (New York: Manpower Demonstration Research Corporation, May 2012).

5. Ana M. Martínez-Alemán and Katherine Lynk Wartman, *Online Social Networking on Campus: Understanding What Matters in Student Culture* (New York: Routledge, 2009).

6. Community College Survey of Student Engagement, *Making Connections: Dimensions of Student Engagement (2009 CCSSE Findings)* (Austin, TX: The University of Texas at Austin, Community College Leadership Program, 2009), http://www.ccsse.org/publications/national_report_2009/CCSSE09_nationalreport-10-26.pdf.

7. Cecilia Rios-Aguilar, Manuel Sacramento González Canché, Regina Deil-Amen, and Charles H. F. Davis III, *The Role of Social Media in Community Colleges* (Tucson, AZ and Claremont, CA: University of Arizona and Claremont Graduate University, 2012), http://www.league.org/gettingconnected/files/The%20Role%20of%20Social%20Media%20in%20Community%20Colleges.pdf.

8. Charles H. F. Davis III, Regina Deil-Amen, Cecilia Rios-Aguilar, and Manuel S. González Canche, *Social Media in Higher Education: A Literature Review and Research Directions* (Tucson, AZ, and Claremont, CA: University of Arizona and Claremont Graduate University, 2012), http://www.league.org/gettingconnected/files/Social%20Media%20in%20Higher%20Education.pdf.

9. Kristan M. Venegas, "Internet Inequalities: Financial Aid, the Internet, and Low Income Students," *American Behavioral Scientist* 49, no. 12 (Aug. 2006).

10. Lavon Frazier, "An Admissions Process Transformed with Technology," *Educause Quarterly* 23, no. 3 (Sept. 2003).

11. Michael C. Poock and Virginia A. Bishop, "Characteristics of an Effective Community College Web Site," *Community College Journal of Research and Practice* 30, no. 9 (Nov. 2006).

12. Jonathan Margolin, Shazia R. Miller, and James E. Rosenbaum, "The Community College Website as Virtual Advisor: A Usability Study," *Community College Review* 41, no. 1 (Jan. 2013).

13. Ibid.

14. Healey C. Wittset and Rory O'Sullivan on behalf of Young Invincibles, *Lost without a Map: A Survey about Students' Experiences Navigating the Financial Aid Process* (NERA Economic Consulting, Oct. 11, 2012).

15. Ibid.

16. The survey data was not disaggregated by type of institution, so we do not know if findings differ between two- and four-year college students.

17. Bettinger, Long, Oreopoulos, and Sanbonmatsu, "Role of Application Assistance and Information."

18. Alberto F. Cabrera, Kurt R. Burkum, and Steven M. La Nasa, "Pathways to a Four-Year Degree: Determinants of Transfer and Degree Completion," in *College Student Retention: A Formula For Success*, ed. Alan Seidman (Westport, CT: ACE/Praeger Series on Higher Education, 2005); DesJardins, Ahlburg, and McCall, "Integrated Model"; Patricia A. Pérez and Patricia M. McDonough, "Understanding Latina and Latino College Choice: A Social Capital and Chain Migration Analysis," *Journal of Hispanic Higher Education* 7, no. 3 (July 2008).

19. Sara Goldrick-Rab, "Challenges and Opportunities for Improving Community College Student Success," *Review of Educational Research* 80, no. 3 (Sept. 2010); Roderick, Nagaoka, Coca, and Moeller, *From High School to the Future*.

20. Sara Goldrick-Rab, Douglas N. Harris, and Philip A. Trostel, "Why Financial Aid Matters (or Does Not) for College Success: Toward a New Interdisciplinary Perspective," *Higher Education New York* 24 (Oct. 2009).

21. The complete title of the study is Getting Connected: Harnessing the Power of Social Media Technology to Enhance Community College Students' Success; see http://www.league.org/gettingconnected/.

22. For more details about Schools App see http://www.uversity.com/solutions/schools-app/.

23. John M. Braxton, Amy S. Hirschy, and Shederick A. McClendon, *Understanding and Reducing College Student Departure: ASHE-ERIC Higher Education Report* (San Francisco: Jossey-Bass, 2004); Regina Deil-Amen, "Socio-Academic Integrative Moments: Rethinking Academic and Social Integration among Two-Year College Students in Career-Related Programs," *Journal of Higher Education* 82, no. 1 (Jan./Feb. 2011); Scott L. Thomas, "Ties That Bind: A Social Network Approach to Understanding Student Integration and Persistence," *Journal of Higher Education* 71, no. 5 (Sept./Oct. 2000); Vincent Tinto, *Leaving College: Rethinking the Causes and Cures of Student Attrition* (Chicago: University of Chicago Press, 1993); Vincent Tinto, "Classrooms as Communities: Exploring the Educational Character of Student Persistence," *Journal of Higher Education* 68, no. 6 (Nov./Dec. 1997).

24. We also conducted regression analyses examining relationships between app usage, re-enrollment rates, and GPA. For these results see Loris Fagioli, Cecilia Rios-Aguilar, and Regina Deil-Amen, "Changing the Context of Student Engagement: Using Facebook to Increase Community College Student Persistence and Success" *Teachers College Record* (forthcoming).

25. Ingo Feinerer, Kurt Hornik, and David Meyer, "Text Mining Infrastructure in R," *Journal of Statistical Software* 25, no. 5 (Mar. 2008).

26. For more information on exact procedures of the Text Mining analyses see Regina Deil-Amen, Manuel González Canche, and Cecilia Rios-Aguilar, "University Students Using Social Networking Spaces to Forge Virtual Community in Community Colleges," paper presented at Association for the Study of Higher Education conference (Las Vegas, NV: Nov. 2012).

27. Ana M. Martínez-Alemán, Heather T. Rowan-Kenyon, and Mandy Savitz-Romer, "Social Networking and First-Generation College Student Success: A New Means of Engagement," paper presented at American Educational Research Association Annual Meeting (April 2013).

28. White House, *College Scorecard*, College Affordability and Transparency Center, n.d. accessed at http://www.whitehouse.gov/issues/education/higher-education/college-score-card.

29. U.S. Department of Education, 2012.

30. Katrina Reichert, *Aid and Innovation: How Federal Financial Aid Policy Impacts Student Success and How States Can Respond* (Boston: Jobs for the Future, 2012).

31. Ibid.

Chapter 5

1. Title IV of the Higher Education Act of 1965 references the purpose of financial aid in this way.

2. Enrollment management refers to the consolidation of recruitment, admission, and retention under a single leader or office. Among other things, many enrollment managers systematically test financial incentives to maximize enrollment yield with targeted groups of students or to increase net tuition revenue. Harrison Keller and Nate Johnson, "Completion Management: Using Aid and Price to Improve Results," Working Paper: Report of the Institutional Working Group (Indianapolis: Lumina Foundation, 2013).

3. The size of federal, state, and institutional aid for both undergraduate and graduate students as cited in HCM Strategists, *The American Dream 2.0: How Financial Aid Can Help Improve College Access, Affordability, and Completion* (Washington, DC: HCM Strategists, 2013).

4. Edward St. John et al., *Meeting the Access Challenge: Indiana's Twenty-first Century Program* (Indianapolis: Lumina Foundation for Education, 2002); Thomas Kane, "Evaluating the impact of the D.C. Tuition Assistance Grant Program" (National Bureau of Economic Research Working Paper 10658, 2004); Susan Dynarski, "Hope for Whom? Financial Aid for the Middle Class and Its Impact on College Attendance" (National Bureau of Economic Research Working Paper 7756, 2000); Susan Dynarski, "Does Aid Matter? Measuring the Effect of Student Aid on College Attendance and Completion," *American Economic Review* 93, no. 1 (Mar. 2003); Christopher Cornwell, David B. Mustard, and Deepa J. Sridhar, "The Enrollment Effects of Merit-Based Financial Aid: Evidence from Georgia's Hope Program," *Journal of Labor Economics* 24, no. 4 (Oct. 2006).

5. Edward St. John, Shouping Hu, and Jeff Weber, "State Policy and the Affordability of Public Higher Education: The Influence of State Grants on Persistence in Indiana," *Research in Higher Education* 42 (2001); Susan Choy, *Access and Persistence: Findings from Ten Years of Longitudinal Research on Students* (Washington, DC: Center for Policy Analysis, American Council on Education, 2002); Stephen L. DesJardins, Dennis A. Ahlburg, and Brian P. McCall, "Simulating the Longitudinal Effects of Changes in Financial Aid on Student Departure from College," *Journal of Human Resources* 37, no. 3 (2002); Eric Bettinger, "How Financial Aid Affects Persistence," in *College Choices: The Economics of Where to Go, When to Go, and How to Pay for It*, ed. Caroline M. Hoxby (Chicago: University of Chicago Press, 2007); Larry Singell and Mark Stater, "Going, Going, Gone: The Effects of Aid Policies on Graduation at Three Large Public Institutions," *Policy Sciences* 39, no. 4 (2006).

6. For a summary, see Don Hossler et al., "Student Aid and Its Role in Encouraging Persistence," in J. C. Smart (ed.), *Higher Education: Handbook of Theory and Research* (Netherlands: Springer Science + Business Media B.V., 2009); also see Judith Scott-Clayton, "On Money and Motivation: A Quasi-Experimental Analysis of Financial Incentives for College Achievement," *Journal of Human Resources* 46, no. 3 (2011).

7. Random assignment creates two or more groups that are equivalent with respect to both measured and unmeasured characteristics. An evaluation using random assignment permits an intervention or "treatment" to be given to one group, while at least one other group experiences the status quo. In this way, the "control" group serves as the counterfactual, or what would have happened in the absence of treatment.

8. Therefore, the results of these studies are likely to reflect marginal returns to financial aid since the aid is on top of any other aid for which students are eligible.

9. That is, incentive theory is concerned with structuring a contract between a principal and agent in the face of asymmetric information. See Jean-Jacques Laffont and David Martimort,

The Theory of Incentives: The Principal-Agent Model (Princeton, NJ: Princeton University Press, 2001) for a comprehensive review.

10. For findings related to welfare exits, see Cynthia Miller et al., *Implementation and 18-month impacts of the Minnesota Family Investment Program* (New York: MDRC, 1997); Winston Lin et al., *When Financial Incentives Encourage Work: Complete 18-month Findings from the Self-Sufficiency Project* (Ottawa: Social Research and Demonstration Corporation, 1998); Charles Michalopoulos, Philip Robins, and David Card, *When Financial Work Incentives Pay for Themselves: Early Findings from the Self-Sufficiency Project's Applicant Study* (Ottawa: Social Research and Demonstration Corporation, 1999). For findings on crime, see Naci Mocan and R. Kaj Gittings, "The impact of incentives on human behavior: Can we make it disappear: The case of the death penalty" (National Bureau of Economic Research Working Paper 12631, 2006). For findings on smoking cessation, see Kevin Volpp et al., "A randomized, controlled trial of financial incentives for smoking cessation," *New England Journal of Medicine* 360, no.7 (2009).

11. For incentives used to encourage private school attendance, see Joshua Angrist et al., "Vouchers for Private Schooling in Colombia: Evidence from a Randomized Natural Experiment," *American Economic Review* 92, no. 5 (2002). For incentives used to increase test scores, see Eric Bettinger, "Paying to Learn: The Effect of Financial Incentives on Elementary School Test Scores," *Review of Economics and Statistics* 94, no. 3 (2012); Kirabo Jackson, "The Effects of an Incentive-Based High-School Intervention on College Outcomes" (National Bureau of Economic Research Working Paper 15722, 2010); Nuria Rodriguez-Planas, "Longer-term Impacts of Mentoring, Educational Services, and Incentives to Learn: Evidence from a Randomized Trial in the United States" (MOVE, IZA and FEDEA working paper, 2010). For incentives to increase attendance, see Michael Kremer, Edward Miguel, and Rebecca Thornton, "Incentives To Learn," *Review of Economics and Statistics* 91, no. 3 (2009); Amanda Pallais, "Taking a Chance on College: Is the Tennessee Education Lottery Scholarship Program a Winner?" *Journal of Human Resources* 34, no. 1 (2009). For incentives to increase test scores, attendance, and reading, see Roland Fryer, "Financial Incentives and Student Achievement: Evidence from Randomized Trials," *Quarterly Journal of Economics* 126 (2011). For incentives to graduate high school, see Joshua Angrist and Victor Lavy, "The Effects of High Stakes High School Achievement Awards: Evidence from a Randomized Trial," *American Economic Review* 99, no. 4 (Sept. 2009).

12. For evidence of cheating among teachers in response to an incentive to increase test scores, see Brian Jacob and Steven Levitt, "Rotten Apples: An Investigation of the Prevalence and Predictors of Teacher Cheating," *Quarterly Journal of Economics* 118, no. 3 (2003).

13. Edward L. Deci, Richard Koestner, and Richard M. Ryan, "Extrinsic Rewards and Intrinsic Motivation in Education: Reconsidered Once Again," *Review of Educational Research* 71, no. 1 (2001); Bruno S. Frey and Reto Jegen, "Motivation Crowding Theory," *Journal of Economic Surveys* 15, no. 5 (2001); Alfie Kohn, *Punished by Rewards: The Trouble with Gold Stars, Incentive Plans, A's, Praise, and Other Bribes* (Boston: Houghton Mifflin Harcourt, 1999).

14. Students must make satisfactory academic progress (SAP) to maintain any Title IV federal aid (including Pell Grants). SAP entails three components: passing 60 percent of courses attempted (to demonstrate academic progress), earning a GPA of at least 2.0 over these courses (to demonstrate academic performance), and, if these first two components are violated, increasing performance during the academic probation semester to be returned to good standing. While these criteria appear straightforward, in practice students may fail for several terms before their eligibility is restricted as two-year institutions are only required to check SAP annually for students in two-year programs (though they can check more frequently). In

addition, students may continue to be in violation of SAP, lose their Title IV eligibility, yet continue to stay enrolled if the cost of tuition and fees are very low (see Sue Scrivener, Colleen Sommo, and Herbert Collado, *Getting Back on Track: Effects of a Community College Program for Probationary Students* (New York: MDRC, 2009) for evidence of this in California). As a result, the incentive scheme may be weak in inducing students to alter their behavior. See U.S. Department of Education, *Federal Student Aid Handbook 2012–2013* (Washington, DC: U.S. Department of Education, 2012), ch. 1, for specific details.

15. In most instances, the GPA requirements are equivalent to those required to meet satisfactory academic progress (SAP); see note 14. The exception to this pattern is Opportunity Knocks, which offered an incentive for grades passing 3.7 (A-) for a subpopulation of high achieving high school students; see note 17.

16. The Wisconsin Scholars program (Sara Goldrick-Rab et al., *Need-Based Financial Aid and College Persistence: Experimental Evidence from Wisconsin* (Washington, DC: Institute for Education Sciences, 2012), which randomly offered an extremely generous need-based grant (worth $3,500 per year for up to 5 years) to freshmen Pell Grant recipients attending public universities in Wisconsin, is not included in the summary. While program group members need to meet satisfactory academic progress measures that include a 2.0 GPA (the requirements for continued eligibility for the federal Pell Grant), the program does not include additional activities to make the academic benchmarks (SAP) salient. As this is an important component of incentives and one of the likely mechanisms through which incentives work, the study is excluded from this summary. Similarly, four other studies of the effect of additional financial aid on postsecondary student enrollment and outcomes are not included in this review as these studies employ quasi-experimental methods: Dynarski, "Does Aid Matter?"; Thomas Kane, "A Quasi-Experimental Estimate of the Impact of Financial Aid on College-Going" (National Bureau of Economic Research Working Paper 9703, 2003); Jackson, "Effects of an Incentive-Based High-School Intervention"; Judith Scott-Clayton, "On Money and Motivation: A Quasi-Experimental Analysis of Financial Incentives for College Achievement," *Journal of Human Resources* 46, no. 3 (2011).

17. Specifically, students in the lowest quartile of high school GPA were eligible for $5,000 for grades of B (college GPA of 3.0) or $1,000 for grades of C+ (college GPA of 2.3). Students in the second quartile of high school GPA were eligible for $5,000 for grades of B+ (college GPA of 3.3) or $1,000 for grades of B- (college GPA of 2.7). Students in the third quartile were eligible for $5,000 for grades of A- (college GPA of 3.7) or $1,000 for grades of B (college GPA of 3.0). Students in the highest quartile were not eligible for the study. See Joshua Angrist, Daniel Lang, and Philip Oreopoulos, "Incentives and Services for College Achievement: Evidence from a Randomized Trial," *American Economic Journal: Applied Economics* 1, no. 1 (2009).

18. Since 10 courses constituted a full course load for a year, a student obtaining perfect scores qualified for $7,000 (10 × ($100 + (30 × 20))) or $700 per class. See Joshua Angrist, Philip Oreopoulos, and Tyler Williams, "When Opportunity Knocks, Who Answers? New Evidence on College Achievement Awards" (National Bureau of Economic Research Working Paper 16643, 2010).

19. Edwin Leuven, Hessel Oosterbeek, and Bas van der Klaauw, "The Effect of Financial Rewards on Students' Achievement: Evidence from a Randomized Experiment," *Journal of the European Economic Association* 8, no. 6 (2010).

20. MacDonald et al., *Final Impacts Report: Foundations for Success* (Ottawa: R.A. Malatest and Associates Ltd., 2009), http://malatest.com/CMSF%20FFS%20-%20FINAL%20Impacts%20 Report.pdf.

21. Each study was developed to be evaluated as an independent site and the sample sizes were

derived to have enough power for this separate analysis. As a result, findings are presented individually. See Lashawn Richburg-Hayes et al., *Rewarding Persistence: Effects of a Performance-Based Scholarship Program for Low-Income Parents* (New York: MDRC, 2009) and Lisa Barrow et al., "Paying for Performance: The Education Impacts of a Community College Scholarship Program for Low-Income Adults" (forthcoming) for Opening Doors Louisiana; Lashawn Richburg-Hayes et al., *Providing More Cash for College: Interim Findings from the Performance-Based Scholarship Demonstration in California* (New York: MDRC, forthcoming) for California; Cynthia Miller et al., *Staying on Track: Early Findings from a Performance-Based Scholarship Program at the University of New Mexico* (New York: MDRC, 2011) for New Mexico; Reshma Patel and Timothy Rudd, *Can Scholarships Alone Help Students Succeed? Lessons from Two New York City Community Colleges* (New York: MDRC, 2012) for New York; Paulette Cha and Reshma Patel, *Rewarding Progress, Reducing Debt: Early Results from Ohio's Performance-Based Scholarship Demonstration for Low-Income Parents* (New York: MDRC, 2010) and Reshma Patel et al., *Performance-Based Scholarships: What Have We Learned? Interim Findings from the PBS Demonstration* (New York: MDRC, 2013) for Ohio.

22. The calculation of effect sizes follows Fredic Wolf, *Meta-Analysis: Quantitative Methods for Research Synthesis* 59 (New York: SAGE Publications, 1986) and Robert Rosenthal, "Parametric Measures of Effect Size," in *The Handbook of Research Synthesis*, ed. Harris Cooper and Larry V. Hedges (New York: Russell Sage Foundation, 1994). It uses Cohen's d calculated as $= \frac{2t}{\sqrt{df}}$, where ω is a small sample correction term equal to $1 - \frac{3}{4N-9}$, where N is the sample size. Given the sample size of the studies in this chapter, the small sample correction is not necessary and approximates 1. The reported effect sizes are not adjusted for the inclusion of covariates or weighed in any manner. Other effect size estimates were calculated when possible and the results were qualitatively similar.

23. This effect size falls into the bottom third of the distribution empirically estimated by Mark W. Lipsey, *Design Sensitivity: Statistical Power for Experimental Research* (Newbury Park, CA: Sage Publications, 1990), as cited by Howard Bloom, Lashawn Richburg-Hayes, and Alison Rebeck Black, "Using Covariates to Improve Precision for Studies That Randomize Schools to Evaluate Educational Interventions," *Educational Evaluation and Policy Analysis* 29, no. 1 (2007). While there is not an equivalent empirical distribution based on postsecondary education interventions, Howard Bloom et al., *Performance Trajectories and Performance Gaps as Achievement Effect-Size Benchmarks for Educational Interventions* (New York: MDRC, 2008) find that the mean gain in effect size for grades 11–12 using nationally normed tests is 0.06 ± 0.11 (see table 1), which suggests that it is difficult to detect gains for older students. If this difficulty of moving the needle extends to postsecondary outcomes, then the interpretation of the 0.14 effect size may be reliably regarded as modest and effect sizes of 0.25 may be regarded as substantially meaningful.

24. Dynarski, "Does Aid Matter?"

25. The Social Security Administration payment to students upon the death of their parent was $6,700 in 1980 or $17,730 in 2010 dollars.

26. Larry L. Leslie and Paul T. Brinkman, "Student Price Response in Higher Education: The Student Demand Studies," *Journal of Higher Education* 58, no. 2 (1987).

27. Dynarski, "Does Aid Matter?"

28. There are administrative costs associated with any financial aid program and costs will be discussed below. However, for an equivalent amount of aid, incentive grants will generally be lower in direct costs.

29. See note 23 above for an interpretation of magnitude.

30. See Christopher Cornwall, Kyung Hee Lee, and David B. Mustard, "Student Responses to Merit Scholarship Retention Rules," *Journal of Human Resources* 40, no. 4 (2005) for undesirable behavioral changes in response to the Georgia HOPE lottery. Some of the studies summarized in this chapter have performed some sensitivity checks for unintended consequences such as changes in course-taking behavior to see whether program group students were less likely to take challenging courses (Lisa Barrow et al., "Paying for Performance: The Education Impacts of a Community College Scholarship Program for Low-Income Adults" (forthcoming)). In addition, motivation was examined, both pre-RA and post-RA, in order to see whether intrinsic motivation was compromised (Richburg-Hayes et al., *Providing More Cash for College*). In several sites, subgroups were examined to see whether certain groups were being harmed (Patel et al., *Performance-Based Scholarships*, and Richburg-Hayes et al., *Providing More Cash for College*). In none of these analyses was there evidence of unintended consequences.

31. Once effect size estimates from the Opening Doors Louisiana study are removed, the effect size patterns reported remain the same. Once both the Opening Doors Louisiana and PBS Demonstration studies are removed, the average effect size lowers and the confidence intervals shown in figure 5.1 span zero. While this is not an official test of whether the average effect size estimates from the PBS Demonstration studies are statistically different from the average effect size estimates from the other studies, the patterns are suggestive.

32. John A. List, "Why Economists Should Conduct Field Experiments and 14 Tips for Pulling One Off," *Journal of Economic Perspectives* 25, no. 3 (2011).

33. Sandy Baum et al., *Beyond Need and Merit: Strengthening State Grant Programs* (Washington, DC: Brown Center on Education Policy, Brookings Institution, 2012); Douglas N. Harris and Sara Goldrick-Rab, "Improving the Productivity of Education Experiments: Lessons from a Randomized Study of Need-Based Financial Aid," *Education Finance and Policy* 7, no. 2 (2012).

34. This did not occur at the PBS Demonstration sites, but it is unclear whether this is a factor for the other studies summarized in this chapter.

35. See Dean Karlan, Margaret McConnell, Sendhil Mullainathan, and Jonathan Zinman, "Getting to the Top of Mind: How Reminders Increase Saving" (National Bureau of Economic Research Working Paper 16205, 2010); Mural Kalayoglu, Michael Reppucci, Terrence Blaschke, Luis Marenco, and Michael Singer, "An Intermittent Reinforcement Platform to Increase Adherence to Medications," *American Journal of Pharmacy Benefits* 1, no. 2 (2009); Ximena Cadena and Antoinette Schoar, "Remembering to Pay? Reminders vs. Financial Incentives for Loan Payments"(National Bureau of Economic Research Working Paper 17020, 2011).

36. Reshma Patel and Ireri Valenzuela, *Moving Forward: Early Findings from the Performance-Based Scholarship Demonstration in Arizona* (New York: MDRC, 2013).

37. See Benjamin J. Castleman and Lindsay C. Page, *Summer Nudging: Can Personalized Text Messages and Peer Mentor Outreach Increase College Going Among Low-Income High School Graduates?* (Cambridge, MA: Harvard University Center for Education Policy Research, 2013); Eric Bettinger and Rachel Baker, "The Effects of Student Coaching in College: An Evaluation of a Randomized Experiment in Student Mentoring" (National Bureau of Economic Research Working Paper 16881, 2011).

38. Patel et al., *Using Financial Aid to Promote Student Progress*.

39. In fact, the effects could be larger and generate perverse outcomes if financial aid exhibits diminishing marginal returns.

40. Based on the maximum Pell Grant for the 2010–2011 aid year of $5,550. In 2010–2011 the median tuition and fees for all public institutions was $4,632; for all public four-year institutions it was $6,780, and for all public two-year institutions $2,537. This represents tuition and fees over a full year, but these would be roughly half for each semester.

41. College Board, *Trends in Student Aid 2012* (New York: College Board, 2012).

42. U.S. Department of Education, *Federal Student Aid Handbook 2012–2013* (Washington, DC: U.S. Department of Education, 2012).

43. Donald Heller and Patricia Marin, *Why Should We Help? The Negative Social Consequences of Merit Scholarships* (Boston: Harvard Civil Rights Project, 2002).

44. National Association of State Student Grant and Aid Programs, *42nd Annual Survey Report on State-Sponsored Student Financial Aid, 2010–2011 Academic Year* (Washington, DC: National Association of State Student Grant and Aid Programs, 2012). For example, need-based aid increased by about 85 percent over the 10 years from 2000 to 2010, while merit aid increased by 137 percent over the same period; see tables 4 and 5 of the report.

Chapter 6

1. Richard Fry, *A Record One-in-Five Households Now Owe Student Loan Debt* (Washington, DC: Pew Research Center, Social and Demographic Trends project, 2010).

2. U.S. Department of Education, *Default Rates for Cohort Years 2005–2009*, http://ifap.ed.gov/eannouncements/010512DefaultRates20052009.html.

3. Ibid.

4. Alan B. Krueger and William G. Bowen, "Policy watch: Income-contingent college loans," *Journal of Economic Perspectives* 7, no.3 (1993): 193–201.

5. Karl Shell, Franklin M. Fisher, Duncan K. Foley, and Ann F. Friedlander, "The Educational Opportunity Bank: An Economic Analysis of a Contingent Repayment Loan Program for Higher Education," *National Tax Journal* 21, no. 1 (1968): 2–45.

6. Evelyn Brody, "Paying back your country through income-contingent student loans," *San Diego Law Review* 31 (1994).

7. Karl Shell, "Notes on the Educational Opportunity Bank," *National Tax Journal* 23, no. 2 (1970): 214–220; Carnegie Commission on Higher Education, *Quality and Equality: New Levels of Federal Responsibility for Higher Education* (New York: McGraw-Hill, 1970).

8. Barbara Vobejda, "Students Would Pay Interest in New Loan Plan," *Pittsburgh Press*, Jan. 2, 1987.

9. Jason Delisle and Alex Holt, *Safety Net or Windfall? Examining Changes to Income-Based Repayment for federal Student Loans* (Washington, DC: New America Foundation, 2012).

10. D. Bruce Johnstone, *New Patterns for College Lending: Income Contingent Loans* (New York: Columbia University Press, 1971).

11. Libby Nelson, "An Underused Lifeline," *Inside Higher Ed*, http://www.insidehighered.com/news/2012/10/23/despite-student-debt-concern-income-based-repayment-lags. Also see *Student Loan Debt by Age Group*, Federal Reserve Bank of New York, http://www.newyorkfed.org/studentloandebt/. It is noteworthy that many of these borrowers were automatically enrolled into income-based or income-contingent repayment because of default.

12. U.S. Department of Education, *Default Rates for Cohort Years 2005–2009*.

13. Bruce Chapman, "Income-Contingent Loans for Higher Education: International Reforms," in *Handbook of the Economics of Education*, vol. 2, ed. E. Hanushek and F. Welch (Amsterdam: North-Holland, 2006), 1435–1503. Also see Bruce Chapman, *Higher Education Financing in Australia* (CESifo DICE Report, 2007).

14. Chapman, "Income-Contingent Loans."

15. Bruce Chapman and Chris Ryan, "The access implications of income-contingent charges for higher education: lessons from Australia," *Economics of Education Review* 24, no. 5 (2005): 491–512; Buly Cardak and Chris Ryan, "Why Are High Ability Individuals from Poor Backgrounds Underrepresented at University?" (LaTrobe School of Business Discussion Paper A06.04, Melbourne, 2006); Gary Marks and Julie McMillan, "Australia: Changes in Socioeconomic Inequalities in University Participation," in *Stratification in Higher Education: A Comparative Study,* (ed.) Yossi Shavit, Richard Arum, Adam Gamoran, and Gila Menachem (Stanford, CA: Stanford University Press, 2006).

16. U.S. Department of Education, *FY 2009 Official National 3-Year Cohort Default Rates* (Washington, DC: U.S. Department of Education, 2013).

17. David J. Deming, Claudia Goldin, and Lawrence F. Katz, "The For-Profit Postsecondary School Sector: Nimble Critters or Agile Predators?" *Journal of Economic Perspectives* 26 (2012).

18. Ibid. Also see Nicholas Hillman, "College on credit: a multilevel analysis of student loan default," forthcoming in *Review of Higher Education.*

19. U.S. Department of Education, "FY 2009 3-Year Cohort Default Rates."

20. Donghoon Lee, *Household Debt and Credit: Student Debt,* Federal Reserve Bank of New York, http://www.newyorkfed.org/newsevents/mediaadvisory/2013/Lee022813.pdf.

21. Anya Kamenetz, "An Inadequate Response," *New York Times,* July 21, 2013, http://www.nytimes.com/roomfordebate/2011/10/27/should-college-grads-get-a-break-on-their-loans/obamas-inadequate-response-on-student-debt.

22. *New York Times,* "Misleading Advice for For-Profit Student Borrowers," Oct. 8, 2012, http://www.nytimes.com/2012/10/09/opinion/misleading-advice-for-for-profit-student-borrowers.html.

23. Lee, *Household Debt and Credit.*

24. Alisa F. Cunningham and Gregory Kienzl, *Delinquency: the untold story of student loan borrowing* (Washington, DC: Institute for Higher Education Policy, 2011).

25. Ibid.

26. Congressional Budget Office, *Costs and Policy Options for Federal Student Loan Programs* (Washington, DC: CBO, 2010).

27. See IBRInfo.org for more detail.

28. U.S. Department of Education, *Education Department Launches "Pay As You Earn" Student Loan Repayment Plan,* http://www.ed.gov/news/press-releases/education-department-launches-pay-you-earn-student-loan-repayment-plan.

29. Income-sensitive repayment is an obscure program that few people participate in or know exists, and is often not included as a standard repayment option.

30. Andrew Martin, "Change to Student Debt Relief Will Help Well-Off the Most, Report Says," *New York Times,* Oct. 16, 2012, http://www.nytimes.com/2012/10/16/business/change-to-student-debt-relief-will-help-well-off-the-most-report-says.html.

31. Consumer Financial Protection Bureau, *Student Loan Affordability: Analysis of Public Input on Impact and Solutions* (Washington, DC: CFPB, 2013), http://files.consumerfinance.gov/f/201305_cfpb_rfi-report_student-loans.pdf.

32. Jen Mishory and Rory O'Sullivan, *Denied? The Impact of Student Debt on the Ability to Buy a House* (Washington, DC: Young Invincibles), http://younginvincibles.org/wp-content/uploads/2012/08/Denied-The-Impact-of-Student-Debt-on-the-Ability-to-Buy-a-House-8.14.12.pdf.

33. William Bowen, Matthew Chingos, and Michael McPherson, *Crossing the Finish Line:*

Completing College at America's Public Universities (Princeton, NJ: Princeton University Press, 2009).

34. Andrew Martin, "Debt Collectors Cash in on Student Loans," *New York Times*, Sept. 8, 2012, http://www.nytimes.com/2012/09/09/business/once-a-student-now-dogged-by-collection-agencies.html?pagewanted=all. Also U.S. Department of Education, *Default Rates for Cohort Years 2005–2009*.

35. Nicholas Hillman, "College on credit: a multilevel analysis of student loan default," forthcoming in *Review of Higher Education*.

36. Drawing from John Kingdon, *Agendas, Alternatives, and Public Policies* (Pearson, 2010).

37. Milton Friedman, "The Role of Government in Education," in *Economics and Public Interest*, (ed.) R. Solo (New Brunswick, NJ: Rutgers University Press, 1955).

38. Miguel Palacios, *Human Capital Contracts: "Equity-like" Instruments for Financing Higher Education*: (Washington, DC: CATO Institute, 2002). See also Miguel Palacios, *Investing in Human Capital* (Cambridge: Cambridge University Press, 2004).

39. Maureen Woodhall, *Funding Higher Education: the Contribution of Economic Thinking to the Debate* (Education Working Paper Series 8, World Bank, 2007), http://siteresources.world-bank.org/EDUCATION/Resources/278200-1099079877269/547664-1099079956815/Funding_HigherEd_wps8.pdf.

40. Chapman, "Income-Contingent Loans."

41. Ibid.

42. Ibid.

43. Erin Dillon, *Affordable at Last: A New Student Loan System* (Washington, DC: Education Sector, 2011). See also "Income Contingent Repayments by Repayment Cohort and Tax Year 2000/01 to 2009/10 Inclusive" (Provisional), by Student Loans Company, and the 2000–2010 study "Income Contingent Repayments by Repayment Cohort and Tax Year 2000/01 to 2009/10 Inclusive."

44. Edina Berlinger, "An efficient student loan system: Case study of Hungary," *Higher Education in Europe* 34, no. 2 (2009): 257–267.

45. Compiled from various sources: Berlinger, "An efficient student loan system"; Chapman, "Income-Contingent Loans"; and Jamil Salmi and Arthur M. Hauptman, "Innovations in tertiary education financing: A comparative evaluation of allocation mechanisms" (Education Working Paper Series 4, 2006).

46. According to the *Digest of Education Statistics* (table 219), total fall enrollment at all Title IV institutions was over 21 million in 2010. The OECD Country Statistical Profile reports Sweden's and New Zealand's total populations are 9.4 and 4.4 million, respectively.

47. See Chapman, "Income-Contingent Loans" for more details on country profiles.

48. Philip G. Schrag, "Federal Income-Contingent Repayment Option for Law Student Loans," *Hofstra Law Review* 29 (2000).

49. Danny Vinik and Minjae Park, "Got Student Debt?" *Washington Monthly*, Sept/Oct, http://www.washingtonmonthly.com/magazine/septemberoctober_2012/features/got_student_debt039356.php.

50. U.S. Department of Education, http://www.studentaid.ed.gov/repay-loans/understand/plans/income-based.

51. See Michael McPherson and Morton Schapiro, *The Student Aid Game* (Princeton, NJ: Princeton University Press, 1998) for more history.

52. National Consumer Law Center, "Borrowers on Hold" (2012), and U.S. Department of

Education, *Federal Student Aid Annual Report*, http://studentaid.ed.gov/sites/default/files/
FY_2012_FSA_Annual_Report_508version_Final.pdf.

53. William Bowen, Matthew M. Chingos, and Michael McPherson, *Crossing the Finish Line: Completing College at America's Public Universities* (Princeton, NJ: Princeton University Press, 2009).

54. Dillon, *Affordable at Last*.

55. HCM Strategists, "The American Dream 2.0" (2012).

56. Sandy Baum and Saul Schwartz, *How Much Debt Is Too Much? Defining Benchmarks for Manageable Student Debt* (New York: College Board, 2006).

57. Congressional Budget Office, *Costs and Policy Options for Federal Student Loan Programs* (Washington, DC: CBO, 2010), and HCM Strategists, "The American Dream 2.0" (2012).

58. As explained in Dillon, *Affordable at Last*.

59. D. Bruce Johnstone, *New Patterns for College Lending: Income Contingent Loans* (New York: Columbia University Press, 1971).

Chapter 7

1. Sandy Baum and Jennifer Ma, *Trends in College Pricing: 2013* (New York: College Board, 2013), http://trends.collegeboard.org/college-pricing.

2. Between 2008 and 2012, the maximum Pell Grant increased from $4,310 to $5,500, the number of Pell Grant recipients increased from 5.5 million to 9.4 million, and total expenditures increased from $14.7 billion to $33.6 billion. See the 2007–2008 and 2011–2012 Federal Pell Grant Program End of Year Reports, http://www2.ed.gov/finaid/prof/resources/data/pell-data.html.

3. Sandy Baum and Kathleen Payea, *Trends in Student Aid: 2013* (New York: College Board, 2013), http://trends.collegeboard.org/student-aid.

4. Judith Scott-Clayton, "Information Constraints and Financial Aid Policy," in *Student Financing of Higher Education: A Comparative Perspective*, ed. Donald E. Heller and Claire Callender (New York: Routledge, 2013).

5. Eric P. Bettinger, Bridget Terry Long, Philip Oreopoulos, and Lisa Sanbonmatsu, "The Role of Application Assistance and Information in College Decisions: Results from the H&R Block FAFSA Experiment," *Quarterly Journal of Economics* 127, no. 3 (2012): 1205–1242.

6. Caroline M. Hoxby and Christopher Avery, "The Missing One-Offs: The Hidden Supply of High Achieving, Low Income Students" (National Bureau of Economic Research Working Paper 18586, 2012).

7. Hill, Winston, and Boyd (2005) examine net prices by family income in 28 selective private institutions and find that while low-income students generally receive the largest institutional discounts, this group does not always face the lowest ratio of net prices to income. Catherine B. Hill, Gordon C. Winston, and Stephanie A. Boyd, "Affordability: Family Incomes and Net Prices at Highly Selective Private Colleges and Universities," *Journal of Human Resources* 40, no. 4 (2005): 769–790.

8. Donald Heller, Rodney Hughes, John Cheslock, and Rachel Frick Cardelle, "Institutional Selectivity, Family Finances, and the Distribution of Grant Aid: Findings from the NPSAS:08" (paper presented at the 27th Annual Student Financial Aid Research Network Conference, 2010).

9. See discussion of these studies in the section Impacts of Institutional Aid on College Enrollment and Educational Attainment.

10. Some schools also offer loans, but expenditures on these programs are quite small. Undergraduates receive the vast majority of federal and state grant aid. According to the

College Board, in 2011, undergraduate students received 97 percent of all federal grant funds and 99 percent of all state grant aid. Although graduate students received around 20 percent of all institutional grant aid in 2011, the distribution of institutional aid to graduate students is often decentralized to specific departments or colleges within a larger university. Sandy Baum and Kathleen Payea, *Trends in Student Aid: 2012* (New York: College Board, 2012), http:// trends.collegeboard.org/student-aid.

11. U.S. Department of Education, *Digest of Education Statistics* (Washington, DC: National Center for Education Statistics, 2013). Unless otherwise noted, all dollar amounts are adjusted for inflation and listed in constant 2013 dollars using the CPI-U.

12. In 1977, the average Pell Grant was approximately $3,100 (Basic Educational Opportunity Grant Program 1976–1977 End of Year Report, http://www2.ed.gov/finaid/prof/resources/ data/pell-historical/beog-eoy-1976-77.pdf). In 2012, the average award was approximately $3,800 (Title IV Program Volume Report AY 2011–2012, http://studentaid.ed.gov/about/data-center/student/title-iv).

13. Unfortunately, IPEDS suffers from two major limitations. First, despite being required for schools that distribute federal student aid, IPEDS data miss a large percentage of schools serving Pell Grant recipients prior to 2001: 34 percent of all schools attended by Pell Grant recipients, representing 14 percent of all Pell Grant recipients and 13 percent of Pell Grant funds (author's calculations using IPEDS and Pell Grant administrative data). For-profit schools serving Pell Grant recipients are the least likely to be represented: 69 percent of for-profit schools, 21 percent of nonprofit schools, and 26 percent of public schools with enrolled Pell Grant recipients are either completely missing from the data or missing information on institutional revenue, expenditures, or enrollment. For these reasons, I only present statistics from IPEDS using data collected in 2002 and later.

14. Baum and Payea, *Trends in Student Aid: 2012.*

15. All statistics using NPSAS data are generated from the Department of Education's PowerStats application, http://nces.ed.gov/datalab/powerstats/.

16. Students eligible for the maximum Pell Grant award had an expected family contribution (EFC) of zero. Students eligible for a Pell Grant below the maximum had an EFC between 1 and 4110. Pell-ineligible students had an EFC above 4110.

17. Ideally, this analysis would be conducted within each institution, rather than across institutions.

18. According to the 2008 NPSAS, most students submit an application for federal student aid. On average, 71 percent of Pell-eligible students applied for federal aid and 48 percent of ineligible students submitted an application. Institutions may require separate applications for institutional aid and in 2008, 81 percent of Pell-eligible students and 67 percent of Pell-ineligible students submitted some financial aid application.

19. In Winston's (2003) model, students pay a price (tuition) for the product they receive and also receive a wage (education subsidy) for their contribution to the production of education. Selective colleges generate excess demand by setting tuition below the marginal cost of supplying an education. This allows institutions to increase the quality of admitted students and potentially increase both reputation and students' contribution to the production of education; see Gordon Winston, "Towards a Theory of Tuition: Prices, Peer Wages, and Competition in Higher Education" (Williams Project on the Economics of Higher Education Discussion Paper 65, 2003.) This framework may be less applicable to nonselective schools, many of which offer open admissions. These schools' behavior may fit better with a model presented by Steinberg and Weisbrod (2005), where a nonprofit firm produces a merit good and chooses a schedule of prices for its customers to maximize consumer surplus; see Richard Steinberg and

Burton Weisbrod, "Nonprofits and Distributional Objectives: Price Discrimination and Corner Solutions," *Journal of Public Economics* 89 (2005): 2205–2230.

20. Ronald G. Ehrenberg and Daniel R. Sherman, "Optimal Financial Aid Policies for a Selective University" *Journal of Human Resources* 19, no. (1984): 202–230.

21. Caroline M. Hoxby, "The Changing Selectivity of American Colleges," *Journal of Economic Perspectives* 23, no. 4 (2009): 95–118.

22. According to Project on Student Debt, as of 2010, 28 schools (5 public and 23 nonprofit) implemented policies to fully cover unmet need with institutional grant aid. Several private schools have scaled back or plan to eliminate their "no-loan" pledges. See http://projectonstudentdebt.org/pc_institution.php.

23. David Deming and Susan Dynarski, "Into College, Out of Poverty? Policies to Increase Postsecondary Attainment of the Poor," in *Targeting Investments in Children: Fighting Poverty When Resources are Limited*, ed. Philip Levine and David Zimmerman (Chicago: University of Chicago Press, 2010).

24. Susan Dynarski, Judith Scott-Clayton, and Mark Weiderspan, "Simplifying Tax Incentives and Aid for College: Progress and Prospects," in *Tax Policy and the Economy*, vol. 27, ed. Jeffrey R. Brown (Chicago: University of Chicago Press, 2013).

25. Susan M. Dynarski and Judith E. Scott-Clayton, "College Grants on a Postcard: A Proposal for Simple and Predictable Federal Student Aid" (Brookings Institution Discussion Paper 2007-01, 2007).

26. See, for instance, Bettinger et al., "Role of Application Assistance."

27. Bridget Terry Long, "How Have College Decisions Changed over Time? An Application of the Conditional Logistic Choice Model," *Journal of Econometrics* 121 (2004): 271–296.

28. Wilbert van der Klauuw, "Estimating the Effect of Financial Aid Offers on College Enrollment: A Regression-Discontinuity Approach," *International Economic Review* 43, no. 4 (2002): 1249–1287.

29. David M. Linsenmeier, Harvey S. Rosen, and Cecilia Elena Rouse, "Financial Aid Packages and College Enrollment Decisions: An Econometric Case Study," *Review of Economics and Statistics* 88, no. 1 (2006): 126–145.

30. Nicholas W. Hillman, "Economic Diversity in Elite Higher Education: Do No-Loan Programs Impact Pell Enrollments?" *Journal of Higher Education* 84, no. 6 (2013): 806–833.

31. Jesse Rothstein and Cecilia Rouse, "Constrained After College: Student Loans and Early-Career Occupational Choices," *Journal of Public Economics* 95, no. 1–2 (2011): 149–163.

32. Kevin Stange, "Differential Pricing in Undergraduate Education: Effects on Degree Production by Field" (National Bureau of Economic Research Working Paper 19183, 2013).

33. Eric Bettinger, "How Financial Aid Affects Persistence," in *College Choices: The Economics of Where to Go, When to Go, and How to Pay for it*, ed. Caroline M. Hoxby (Chicago: University of Chicago Press, 2004).

34. Benjamin L. Castleman and Bridget Terry Long, "Looking Beyond Enrollment: The Causal Effect of Need-based Grants on College-Access, Persistence, and Graduation" (National Bureau of Economic Research Working Paper 19306, 2013).

35. Sara Goldrick-Rab, Douglas N. Harris, Robert Kelchen, and James Benson, "Need-Based Financial Aid and College Persistence: Experimental Evidence from Wisconsin" (Social Science Research Network Working Paper 1887826, 2012).

36. Scott-Clayton, "Information Constraints."

37. Joshua D. Angrist, Daniel Lang, and Philip Oreopoulos, "Incentives and Services for College Achievement: Evidence from a Randomized Trial," *American Economic Journal: Applied Economics* 1, no. 1 (2009): 136–163.

38. See, for instance, Enrico Moretti, "Workers' Education, Spillovers, and Productivity: Evidence from Plant-Level Production Functions," *American Economic Review* 94, no. 3 (2004): 656–690; Lance Lochner and Enrico Moretti, "The Effect of Education on Crime: Evidence from Prison Inmates, Arrests, and Self-Reports," *American Economic Review* 94, no. 1 (2004): 155–89; and Thomas S. Dee, "Are There Civic Returns to Education?" *Journal of Public Economics* 88 (2004): 1697–1720.

39. The economic incidence of subsidies provided via the Pell Grant and other programs may fall partially on institutions; see Don Fullerton and Gilbert E. Metcalf, "Tax Incidence," in *Handbook of Public Economics*, vol. 4, ed. Alan J. Auerbach and Martin Feldstein (Amsterdam: North-Holland, 2002).

40. See, for instance, Larry D. Singell and Joe A. Stone, "For Whom the Pell Tolls: The Response of University Tuition to Federal Grants-in-Aid," *Economics of Education Review* 26, no. 3 (2007): 285–295.

41. Stephanie Riegg Cellini and Claudia Goldin, "Does Federal Student Aid Raise Tuition? New Evidence on For-Profit Colleges," *American Economic Journal: Economic Policy* (forthcoming).

42. Bridget Terry Long, "How Do Financial Aid Policies Affect Colleges? The Institutional Impact of the Georgia HOPE Scholarship," *Journal of Human Resources* 39, no. 4 (2004): 1045–1066.

43. Nicholas Turner, "Who Benefits from Student Aid: The Economic Incidence of Tax-Based Federal Student Aid," *Economics of Education Review* 31, no. 4 (2012): 463–481.

44. Lesley J. Turner, "The Road to Pell Is Paved with Good Intentions: The Economic Incidence of Need-Based Student Aid" (working paper, 2013), http://econweb.umd.edu/~turner/Turner_FedAidIncidence.pdf.

45. See https://nces.ed.gov/ipeds/resource/net_price_calculator.asp for more details.

46. TICAS, "Adding It All Up 2012: Are College Net Price Calculators Easy to Find, Use, and Compare?" 2012, http://www.ticas.org/files/pub/Adding_It_All_Up_2012.pdf. Schools could design their own calculator or use a template required by the Department of Education.

47. See http://www.whitehouse.gov/issues/education/higher-education/college-score-card.

48. As a precursor to the college scorecard, in 2011, the Department of Education began publishing lists of institutions in a given sector that reported the largest and the smallest increases in net prices; see http://collegecost.ed.gov/catc/.

49. See http://collegecost.ed.gov/shopping_sheet.pdf. Currently, 600 schools use this form for financial aid packaging.

50. See the 2013–2014 Federal Student Aid Handbook, available at http://ifap.ed.gov/fsahandbook /1314FSAHandbookCompleteActiveIndex.html.

51. For instance, 76 percent of 2007–2008 first-year students provided their FAFSA information to only one school, 9 percent only listed two schools, 5 percent listed three, and 10 percent listed four or more (author's calculations from the 2008 NPSAS).

52. Caroline M. Hoxby and Sarah Turner, "Informing Students About Their College Options: A Proposal for Broadening the Expanding College Opportunities Project" (Brookings Institution discussion paper 2013-03, 2013).

53. See http://www.ed.gov/news/ press-releases/92-new-school-districts-selected-project-help-more-students-complete-fafsa-and-a.

54. The Department of Education and IRS recently worked together to develop a link between tax return data and the FAFSA (http://www.irs.gov/uac/Automated-IRS-System-Helps-College-Bound-Students-with-Financial-Aid-Application-Process). Ideally, this intervention would be combined with the simplification of the federal aid application process proposed by Dynarski

and Scott-Clayton (2007) and Dynarski and Weiderspan (2012), where families would only need to check a box on their tax returns to apply for federal student aid.

55. Families should also be given the option to request hard copies of the results from their specific net price calculator so as not to exclude individuals with limited internet access.

56. Sarah Cohodes and Joshua Goodman, "Merit Aid, College Quality, and College Completion: Massachusetts' Adams Scholarship as an In-Kind Subsidy," *American Economic Journal: Applied Economics* (2014).

57. See http://www.whitehouse.gov/the-press-office/2013/08/22/ fact-sheet-president-s-plan-make-college-more-affordable-better-bargain-.

Chapter 8

1. This chapter has benefitted greatly from the suggestions of AEI's Andrew Kelly and KC Deane and the comments of discussants and reviewers participating in an AEI forum. It also draws from more recent work for a forthcoming white paper on "Designing a Comprehensive Income-Based Student Loan System in the United States," funded by the Lumina Foundation.

2. The Lumina Foundation's "big goal" is "to increase the proportion of Americans with high-quality degrees, certificates and other credentials to 60 percent by the year 2025." See http://www.luminafoundation.org/advantage/document/goal_2025/2013-Strategic_Plan-Executive_Summary.pdf. President Obama has set a similar goal, "that by 2020, America would once again have the highest proportion of college graduates in the world." See http://www.white-house.gov/issues/education/higher-education.

3. America's Call for Higher Education Redesign: The 2012 Lumina Foundation Study of the American Public's Opinion on Higher Education, the results of a survey conducted by the Gallup polling firm. See also www.northeastern.edu/innovationsurvey/pdfs/ InnovationinHigherEducationPresentation.pdf.

4. Paul Taylor, *Is College Worth It?* (Pew Research Center report based on a May 2011 survey).

5. Barack Obama, State of the Union Address, Feb. 12, 2013, available at http://www.whitehouse. gov/the-press-office/2013/02/12/remarks-president-state-union-address.

6. See College Board, *Trends in Student Aid, 2013.* This figure is somewhat lower than that produced by The Project on Student Debt, at The Institute for College Access and Success.

7. http://www.ed.gov/news/press-releases/default-rates-continue-rise-federal-student-loans.

8. Donghoon Lee, "Household Debt and Credit: Student Debt," written statement presented at press briefing, Feb. 28 2013, for the release of the Federal Reserve Bank of New York's Quarterly Report on Household Debt and Credit.

9. Stacey Patton, "I Fully Expect to Die with This Debt," *Chronicle of Higher Education*, April 15, 2013; in providing these figures, Patton cites data from the U.S. Treasury Department's Financial Management Service.

10. Jackson Toby, "The One Trillion Dollar Misunderstanding," *Minding the Campus* (blog), http://www.mindingthecampus.com/originals/2011/05/the_one_trillion_dollar_misund. html; see also his book, *The Lowering of American Higher Education: Why Financial Aid Should be Based on Student Performance* (Santa Barbara, CA: Praeger, 2010).

11. For example, Texas Guaranteed Student Loan Corporation, *Balancing Passion and Practicality: The Role of Debt and Major on Students' Financial Outcomes* (Round Rock, TX: TGSLC, 2012), and Iowa Student Loan report, *Debt-to-Income Ratio Internal Study* (Iowa Student Loan, 2011), http://www.studentloan.org/Docs/Research/Debt-to-Income-Ratio-Internal-Study-Report.pdf.

12. Sandy Baum, *Higher Education Earnings Premium: Value, Variation, and Trends* (Washington, DC: Urban Institute, February 2014).

13. Anthony Carnevale, Ban Cheah, and Jeff Strohl, *Hard Times: College Majors, Unemployment and Earnings* (Washington, DC: Georgetown University Center on Education and the Workforce, Jan. 2012).

14. Anthony Carnevale, Stephen Rose, and Ban Cheah, *The College Payoff* (Washington, DC: Georgetown University Center on Education and the Workforce, 2011).

15. Anthony Carnevale, Jeff Strohl, and Michelle Melton, *What It's Worth: The Economic Value of College Majors* (Washington, DC: Georgetown University Center on Education and the Workforce, Jan. 2012); example of differential income-to-loan ratios, Texas Guaranteed Student Loan Corporation, *Balancing Passion and Practicality: The Role of Debt and Major on Students' Financial Outcomes* (Round Rock, TX: TGSLC, 2012).

16. Declining real earnings of college graduates before and during the recent recession, reported by the Economic Policy Institute in Lawrence Mishel, Josh Bivens, Elise Gould, and Heidi Shierholz, *The State of Working America*, 12th ed. (Washington, DC: Economic Policy Institute, 2012).

17. Christopher Avery and Sarah Turner, "Student Loans: Do College Students Borrow Too Much—Or Not Enough?" *Journal of Economic Perspectives* 26, no. 1(2012), p. 180.

18. Caroline Hoxby and Sarah Turner, "Expanding College Opportunities for High-Achieving, Low Income Students" (Stanford Institute for Economic Policy Research Discussion Paper 12-014); Caroline Hoxby and Christopher Avery, "The Missing 'One-Offs': The Hidden Supply of High-Achieving, Low Income Students," *Brookings Papers on Economic Activity*, 2013.

19. Christina Chang Wei and Laura Horn (MPR Associates, Inc.), "Federal Student Loan Debt Burden of Noncompleters," *Stats in Brief* (National Center for Education Statistics, April 2013).

20. Comparisons of income-contingent proposals can be found in Susan Dynarski and David Kreisman, *Loans for Educational Opportunity: Making Borrowing Work for Today's Students* (Hamilton Project, 2013); Sarah Ayres, *10 Models for Student-Loan Repayment* (Washington, DC: Center for American Progress, 2013); and Stephen Burd, Kevin Carey, Jason Delisle, Rachel Fishman, Alex Holt, Amy Laitinen, and Clare McCann, *Rebalancing Resources and Incentives in Federal Student Aid* (Washington, DC: New America Foundation, January 2013).

21. Robert J. Shiller, *The New Financial Order: Risk in the 21st Century* (Princeton, NJ: Princeton University Press, 2003); see especially ch. 10, "Income-Linked Loans: Reducing the Risks of Hardship and Bankruptcy."

22. Ibid.

23. This is one subject of the recently released white papers commissioned by the Bill and Melinda Gates Foundation's Reimagining Aid Design and Delivery (RADD). Links to all the papers can be found at http://americandream2-0.com/aid-reports/.

24. The definition of choice architectures and its major components draws from Richard Thaler and Cass Sunstein, *Nudge: Improving Decisions About Health, Wealth, and Happiness* (New York: Penguin Books, 2009).

25. See the Australian website, http://studyassist.gov.au/sites/studyassist/helppayingmyfees/csps/pages/student-contribution-amounts.

26. Robert B. Archibald and David H. Feldman, *Why Does College Cost So Much?* (New York: Oxford University Press, 2011).

27. There is widespread agreement that shortages of nursing faculty are a major reason for nursing shortages. See the 2005 report by the Maryland Statewide Commission on the Crisis in Nursing, *Nursing Faculty Shortage: Causes, Effects, and Suggestions for Resolution*, http://www.mbon.org/commission/nsg_faculty_shortage.pdf. Also see the undated but recent Nursing

Faculty Shortage Fact Sheet, released by American Association of Colleges of Nursing (contact Robert J. Rosseter, at rrosseter@aacn.nche.edu).

28. Ronald Ehrenberg, "American Higher Education in Transition," *Journal of Economic Perspectives* 26, no.1 (Winter, 2012): 193–216.

29. U.S. Representative Tom Petri (R-WI) recently introduced a bill with exactly this provision; see The Earnings Contingent Education Loans (ExCEL) Act.

30. See reference to "aggregate risks" beyond the control of individuals on p. 112 of Robert J. Shiller, *The New Financial Order: Risk in the 21st Century* (Princeton University Press, 2012). Aggregate risks are similar to what we refer to as "systemic risks" in student loan policy.

31. Audrey Light and Wayne Strayer, "Determinants of College Completion: School Quality or Student Ability?" *Journal of Human Resources* 35, no. 2 (Spring, 2000): 299–332.

32. See our working paper with Winona Hao, available April 2014 and provisionally titled "Revising SAP Policies for Income-based Student Loan Systems" at www.gwu.edu/~gwipp, by clicking on the author's projects.

33. Some proposals argue that institutions should be able to control the level of loans within limits. For example, National Association of Student Financial Aid Administrators (NASFAA), "Reimagining Financial Aid to Improve Student Access and Outcomes" (Washington, DC: NASFAA, 2013).

34. See for example the recent white papers commissioned by the Gates Foundation, the bipartisan "Know Before You Go" bill before Congress, and the publications of Mark Schneider, the president of College Measures.

35. Shiller, *New Financial Order*.

36. Miguel Palacios, Tonio DeSorrento, and Andrew P. Kelly, *Investing in Value, Sharing Risk: Financing Higher Education Through Income Share Agreements* (Washington, DC: American Enterprise Institute, February, 2014).

Chapter 9

1. Lumina Foundation, *America's Call for Higher Education Redesign* (Indianapolis: Lumina Foundation for Education, 2013); Gallup, *College and University Presidents' Panel: Inaugural Survey Findings* (Washington, DC: 2013).

2. Sandy Baum and Saul Schwartz, *Toward a Realistic Conception of Postsecondary Affordability* (Washington, DC: George Washington University, 2012).

3. The federal aid system distributes financial aid directly to students rather than institutions. States also distribute aid directly to students, but in addition they aid students indirectly by subsidizing public institutions of higher education. However, those appropriations are rarely accompanied by significant accountability for keeping costs down or ensuring the distribution of financial aid reinforces the federal focus on needy students. Arguably, the focus of federal and state direct aid systems on students rather than schools reinforces (or even contradicts) the emphasis of state appropriations on schools.

4. David Ellwood and Thomas Kane, "Who is getting a college education? Family background and the growing gaps in enrollment," in Sheldon Danziger and Jane Waldfogel (eds.), *Securing the Future* (New York: Russell Sage Foundation, 2000, 283–324); Robert Haveman and Timothy Smeeding, "The Role of Higher Education in Social Mobility," *Future of Children* 16, no. 2 (Fall 2006): 125–150.

5. Here, poor means bottom 25 percent of the distribution of family income, and wealthy means top 25 percent of the distribution of family income. Martha Bailey and Susan Dynarski, "Gains and Gaps: A Historical Perspective on Inequality in College Entry and Completion," in

Greg Duncan and Richard Murnane (eds). *Whither Opportunity?* (New York: Russell Sage, 2011).

6. Philippe Belley and Lance Lochner, "The Changing Role of Family Income and Ability in Determining Educational Achievement," *Journal of Human Capital* 1, no.1 (2007): 37–89.

7. See the set of 15 papers issued by the Gates Foundation's Reimagining Aid Design and Delivery initiative, and the overview by Libby Nelson, "Reimagining Financial Aid," *Inside Higher Ed*, Washington DC, March 14, 2013. Papers that do address institutional incentives include those by the National Association of Student Financial Aid Administrators, the National College Access Network and the Institute for Higher Education Policy, which advocate for tying the relatively small fraction of funds in campus-based aid to college completion rates. The New America Foundation also calls for a small number of institutions (those charging poor students relatively high prices) to provide matching funds on the Pell Grant, and several other groups pushed for incentives to encourage institutions to focus grant aid on financial need. But overall, most proposals are variations on the current theme of student aid, with none seeking an overhaul of that fundamental approach.

8. David Tyack and Larry Cuban, *Tinkering toward Utopia: A Century of Public School Reform* (Cambridge, MA: Harvard University Press, 2005).

9. Terry Sanford, "Who Should Pay the Bill?" *Change* 3, no. 3 (May 1971): 6–7, 71.

10. Stephen Burd, *Undermining Pell: How Colleges Compete for Wealthy Students and Leave the Low-Income Behind* (Washington, DC: New America Foundation, 2013).

11. National Center for Education Statistics, *Youth Indicators 2005: Trends in the Well-Being of Youth, Indicator 18* (Washington, DC: NCES, 2005). But also note that a Gallup poll taken in 1968 found that 97% of all parents wanted their children to go to college—see Sanford, "Who Should Pay the Bill?"

12. Delta Cost Project, *Revenue: Where Does the Money Come From? A Data Update: 2000–2010* (Washington, DC: American Institutes for Research, n.d.).

13. Robert Toutkoushian and Nicholas Hillman, "The Impact of State Appropriations and Grants on Access to Higher Education and Outmigration," *Review of Higher Education* 36, no. 1 (Fall 2012); F. King Alexander, "Comparative Study of State Tax Effort and the Role of Federal Government Policy in Shaping Revenue Reliance Patterns," *New Directions for Institutional Research*, no. 119 (2003): 13–25.

14. For a review, see David Longanecker, Cheryl D. Blanco, and Bridget Terry Long, *The Impact of Federal Aid Policies on the Funding, Design, Operation, and Marketing of State and Institutional Financial Aid Policies and Practices: A Review of the Literature* (Boston: TERI, 2004).

15. Don Hossler, et al., "State Funding for Higher Education: The Sisyphean Task," *Journal of Higher Education* 68, no. 2 (1997): 160–190.

16. Michael K. McLendon, Christine G. Mokher, and William Doyle, "Privileging public research universities: The political economy of state appropriations to higher education," *Journal of Education Finance* 34, no. 4 (2009): 372–401; Michael K. McLendon, James C. Hearn, and Christine G. Mokher, "Partisans, professionals, and power: The role of political factors in state higher education funding," *Journal of Higher Education* 80, no. 6 (2009): 686–713.

17. Sandy Baum et al., *Beyond Need and Merit: Strengthening State Grant Programs* (Washington, DC: Brookings Institution, 2012).

18. F. King Alexander et al., *"Maintenance of Effort": An Evolving Federal-State Policy Approach to Ensuring College Affordability* (Washington, DC: American Association of State Colleges and Universities, 2010).

19. Michael Mumper, *Removing college price barriers: What government has done and why it hasn't worked* (Albany, NY: State University of New York Press, 1996).

20. Burd, *Undermining Pell.*

21. College Board, *Trends in College Pricing: 2012* (Washington, DC: 2012).

22. Longanecker, Blanco, and Long, *Impact of Federal Aid Policies*; Donald Heller, *Does Federal Financial Aid Drive Up College Prices?* (Washington, DC: American College on Education, 2013); Andrew Gillian, *Introducing the Bennett Hypothesis 2.0* (Washington, DC: Center for College Affordability and Productivity, 2012); Arthur Hauptman and Cathy S. Krop, *Federal Student Aid and Tuition Growth: Examining the Relationship* (New York: Council for Aid to Education, 1998); Bridget Terry Long, *What is Known About the Impact of Financial Aid? Implications for Policy* (Cambridge, MA: National Center for Postsecondary Research, 2008).

23. Lumina Foundation, *America's Call for Higher Education Redesign.*

24. Sara Goldrick-Rab, *Testimony to the United States HELP Committee* (Washington, DC: 2013), http://www.help.senate.gov/hearings/hearing/?id=58f4674b-5056-a032-5244-d855725503e9; Burd, *Undermining Pell.*

25. Eric Kelderman, "Iowa Bill Bars Use of Resident Tuition Funds for Financial Aid," *Chronicle of Higher Education*, June 3, 2013, http://chronicle.com/blogs/bottomline/ iowa-bill-bars-resident-tuition-for-financial-aid/.

26. William Doyle, "Changes in Institutional Aid, 1992–2003: The Evolving Role of Merit Aid," *Research in Higher Education* 51, no. 8 (2010):789–810; Burd, *Undermining Pell.*

27. William Doyle, Jennifer Delaney, and Blake Naughton, "Does Institutional Aid Compensate for or Comply with State Policy?" *Research in Higher Education*, 50, no. 5 (2009): 502–523; National Scholarship Providers Association, "White paper on scholarship displacement," not yet released.

28. Burd, *Undermining Pell.*

29. Andrew Delbanco, *College: What It Was, Is, and Should Be* (Princeton, NJ: Princeton University Press, 2012).

30. Sandy Baum et al., *Rethinking Pell Grants* (New York: College Board, 2013); Susan Dynarski and Judith Scott-Clayton, "Financial Aid Policy: Lessons from Research," *Future of Children* 23, no. 1 (Spring 2013); Judith Scott-Clayton, *Information Constraints and Financial Aid Policy*, (Working Paper 17811, National Bureau of Economic Research, Cambridge, MA, Feb. 2012).

31. Eric P. Bettinger, Bridget T. Long, Philip Oreopoulos, and Lisa Sanbonmatsu, *The Role of Simplification and Information in College Decisions: Results from the H&R Block FAFSA Experiment*, (Working Paper 15361, National Bureau of Economic Research, Cambridge, MA, Sept. 2009); Caroline Hoxby and Sarah Turner, *Expanding College Opportunities for High-Achieving, Low-Income Students* (Stanford, CA: Stanford Institute for Economic Policy Research, 2013).

32. Julie Minikel-Lacocque and Sara Goldrick-Rab, *Cash Transfer and College Attainment: How Kinscripts Affect Decisions of College Students from Low-Income Families* (New Orleans: American Education Research Association Conference, 2011); Meta Brown, John Karl Scholz, and Ananth Seshadri, "A New Test of Borrowing Constraints for Education," *Review of Economic Studies* 79, no. 2 (2012): 511–538.

33. The Pew Research Center for the People and the Press Poll Database, Pew Social Trends Poll, March 2011.

34. Susan Dynarski, "The Behavioral and Distributional Implications of Aid for College," *American Economic Review* 92, no. 2 (May 2002).

35. Sara Goldrick-Rab, "Following Their Every Move: How Social Class Shapes Postsecondary Pathways," *Sociology of Education* 79, no. 1 (Jan. 2006): 61–79.
36. Claiborne Pell, "Washington: A New Precedent in Federal Aid," *Change* 3, no. 7 (1971): 7, 58.
37. Ibid.
38. Carnegie Commission on Higher Education, *Higher education: Who pays? Who benefits? Who should pay?* (New York: McGraw-Hill, 1973).
39. Bruce W. Speck, ed., "Changing public attitudes toward higher education," *ASHE-ERIC Higher Education Report* 16, no. 6 (Sept. 1987): 13–30 (see especially p. 13, "The confidence of the general public in colleges and universities, as in other social institutions, however, diminished between 1965 and 1985, a period of time in which pressures for accountability made the public and elected officials looked critically at higher education").
40. David Breneman, *The Uneasy Public Policy Triangle in Higher Education* (New York: MacMillan, 1991); Jacob Stampen, *The Financing of Public Higher Education* (Washington, DC: American Association for Higher Education, 1980), 41.
41. R.A Freeman, *Last chance to save the private college: A special report on the financing of higher education* (Washington, DC: American Conservatives Union, 1969).
42. No Author, "Open Admissions: Unfair Competition?" *Change* 2, no. 5 (Oct. 1970): 20.
43. Between 1900 and 1970, average annual inflation was approximately 2.5%. From 1970, the average rate accelerated, reaching over 13% by 1979. Inflation and unemployment steadily increased, with interest rates rising to 12% per year.
44. Milton Friedman, "The Role of Government in Education," in *Economics and the Public Interest*, ed. R. A. Solo (New Brunswick, NJ: Rutgers University, 1954).
45. John P. Mallan, "The Student Loan Bank," *Change* 3, no. 2 (Mar.–Apr. 1971): 72–73; John P. Mallan, "The Cost of Education Controversy," *Change* 7, no. 5 (June 1975).
46. W. Lee Hansen and Burton A. Weisbrod, "The Distribution of Costs and Direct Benefits of Public Higher education: The Case of California," *Journal of Human Resources* 4 (Spring 1969): 176–191.
47. Mallan, "Student Loan Bank": 72–73; Mallan, "Cost of Education Controversy."
48. Jacob O. Stampen and Roxanne W. Reeves, "Coalitions in the Senates of the 96th and 97th Congresses," *Congress and the Presidency* 13, no. 2 (Autumn 1986): 187–208.
49. John Aubrey Douglass, *The Carnegie Commission and Council on Higher Education: A Retrospective* (Berkeley, CA: Center for Studies in Higher Education, 2005); Alice M. Rivlin, *Toward a long-range plan for federal financial support of higher education: A report to the President* (Washington, DC: Department of Health, Education, and Welfare, Jan. 1969); Lawrence E. Gladieux and Thomas R. Wolanin, *Congress and the Colleges* (Lexington, MA: Lexington Books, 1976).
50. Gladieux and Wolanin, *Congress and the Colleges.*
51. Mallen, "Student Loan Bank": 72–73; Alice Rivlin, *Systematic Thinking for Social Action* (Washington, DC: Brookings Institution, 1971).
52. Gladieux and Wolanin, *Congress and the Colleges.*
53. Timothy Engen et al., *National Commission of the Financing of Postsecondary Education* (Washington, DC, 1973), 83.
54. Carnegie Commission on Higher Education, *Higher education: who pays?*
55. M. M. Chambers, *Higher education: Who pays? Who gains?* (Danville, IN: Interstate Printers and Publishers, 1968); Mallen, "Student Loan Bank": 72–73; Joseph A. Pechman, "Notes on the Intergenerational Transfer of Public Higher-Education Benefits," *Journal of Political Economy* 80, no. 3 (1972): 256–259.

56. David Breneman and Chester Finn, *Public Policy and Private Higher Education*, (Washington, DC: Brookings Institution, 1978).

57. Gladieux and Wolanin, *Congress and the Colleges*.

58. Chester Finn, *Scholars, Dollars, and Bureaucrats* (Washington, DC: Brookings Institution, 1979).

59. Equity should not be mistaken for equality. This is not a radical call for ensuring *equivalence* in outcomes for all students but rather the adoption of a commitment that places a policy *priority* on raising prospects for college attainment of the currently disadvantaged, while also providing room to improving attainment of other students. It means that ensuring access to those resources, inputs, and services necessary to provide the "opportunity to learn"—that is, the opportunity to make progress toward established outcome goals in higher education. This will necessarily require *inequality* in inputs, as clearly demonstrated in K–12 education.

60. Bradley Curs and Luciana Dar, "Does state financial aid affect institutional aid? An analysis of the role of state policy on postsecondary institutional pricing strategies" (Social Science Research Network working paper, 2010).

61. A Century Foundation task force on which the lead author of this paper served recently called for the U.S. Education Department to commission a rigorous study of how much more colleges educating disadvantaged students should be provided compared with their peers, noting that a 25% premium is common at the state K–12 level; pp. 40–41 of the task force's report outlines strategies for pursuing adequacy lawsuits for higher education. See Century Foundation Task Force on Preventing Community College from Becoming Separate but Unequal, *Bridging the Higher Education Divide* (New York: Century Foundation, 2013).

62. The $83.2 billion includes the following FY 2013 expenditures: (1) federal education tax benefits ($31.8 billion), namely the exclusion of scholarship and fellowship income (normal tax method), the exclusion of scholarship and fellowship income (normal tax method), American Opportunity Tax Credit/Lifetime Learning, deductibility of student-loan interest, deduction for higher education expenses, exclusion of employer-provided educational assistance, parental exemption for students aged 19 through 23, exclusion of Earnings of Qualified Tuition Programs (529 Plans), exclusion of Interest on Coverdell's, and exclusion of Discharged Student Fees; (2) Pell Grants ($35.2 billion according to the Congressional Budget Office baseline); (3) Work Study ($1 billion); (4) Supplemental Education Opportunity Grants ($0.7 billion); (5) TEACH grants ($0.03 billion); (6) aid for institutional development, ($0.6 billion); (7) aid for Hispanic institutions ($0.2 billion); (8) IEFLS ($0.074 billion); (9) TRIO ($0.8 billion); (10) GEAR-UP ($0.3 billion); (11) Institute of Education Sciences ($0.5 billion); (12) veterans and military education benefits ($12 billion).

63. There is a critical difference. We measure what we value, and we value what we measure.

64. Mark Yudof, *Exploring a New Role for the Federal Government in Higher Education* (California: Office of the President, University of California System, 2009), http://ucfuture. universityofcalifornia.edu/documents/fed_role_education.pdf

65. Michael S. McPherson and Morton Owen Shapiro, *Getting the Most Out of Federal Student Aid Spending—Encouraging Colleges and Universities to Promote the Common Good* (New York: National Dialogue on Student Financial Aid, College Board, Jan. 2003).

66. Eric Wentworth, "Washington: The Higher Education Act: And Beyond," *Change* 4, no. 7 (Sept. 1972): 10, 63–64.

Conclusion

1. Of course, because of the book's length, we were not able to include every fresh voice in the field—and there are many others. For example, when it comes to rethinking how we support students to succeed despite severe economic disadvantage, the work of UCLA Professor Mike Rose deserves greater scrutiny. His rich on-the-ground descriptions of life in community colleges can help policy makers think about whether a given policy proposal will achieve its intended impacts, especially when it comes to altering student behavior. Similarly, scholars of workforce and job training programs like economist Jeffrey Smith of the University of Michigan can bring a great deal of insight to efforts linking financial aid to institutional accountability. And sociologist Tressie Cottom McMillan, currently a graduate student at Emory University, is fast becoming a critical voice in debates over the role of for-profit universities in Title IV, having spent years on the ground studying their interactions with African-American students. Clearly, while we have endeavored to widen the circle, it could and should be widened further still.

2. When the Spellings Commission called for increased accountability for colleges and universities receiving student aid, top Republican lawmakers threatened to stop the Department of Education from promulgating new rules. See Doug Lederman, "Key GOP Senator Warns Spellings," *Inside Higher Education* (May 29, 2007), http://www.insidehighered.com/news/2007/05/29/alexander.

3. Robert Samuels, *Why Public Higher Education Should Be Free: How to Decrease Cost and Increase Quality at American Universities* (New Brunswick, NJ: Rutgers University Press, 2013). See also Sara Goldrick-Rab and Nancy Kendall, *Redefining College Affordability: Securing America's Future with a Universal Two-Year College Option* (Indianapolis: Lumina Foundation, 2014).

4. On the effect of college choice on the outcomes of similarly qualified students, see William Bowen, Matthew Chingos, and Michael McPherson, *Crossing the Finish Line: Completing College at America's Universities* (Princeton, NJ: Princeton University Press, 2009); Sara Cohodes and Joshua Goodman, "Merit Aid, College Quality, and Completion: Massachusetts' Adams Scholarship as an In-Kind Subsidy," *American Economic Journal: Applied Economics*, forthcoming, 2014.

5. See, for example, Geoffrey D. Borman and Jerome V. D'Agostino, "Title I and Student Achievement: A Meta-analysis of Federal Evaluation Results," *Educational Evaluation and Policy Analysis* 18, no. 4 (Winter, 1996), 309–326; Wilbert Van der Klaauw, "Breaking the Link Between Poverty and Low Student Achievement: An Evaluation of Title I," *Journal of Econometrics* 142, no. 2 (Feb. 2008), 731–756.

6. Brian Jacob, Brian McCall, and Kevin M. Stange, *College as Country Club: Do Colleges Cater to Students' Preferences for Consumption?* (National Bureau of Economic Research Working Paper 18745, Jan. 2013).

7. Susan M. Dynarski and Daniel Kreisman, *Loans for Educational Opportunity: Making Borrowing Work for Today's Students* (Washington, DC: Brookings Institution, The Hamilton Project, 2013).

8. See P. Hinrichs, "The Effects of the National School Lunch Program on Education and Health," *Journal of Policy Analysis and Management* 29, no. 3 (Summer 2010), 479–505.

9. For examples, Sara Goldrick-Rab recently led a statewide randomized evaluation of a private need-based aid program in Wisconsin, and in fall 2014 she is launching a randomized evaluation of another private need-based grant focused on students in STEM fields. With J. Michael

Collins, she is also conducting an experiment with loan counseling and online students (see www.wihopelab.com for more information). Also under way is an experimental test of a private promise program based in Milwaukee, conducted by Douglas N. Harris. MDRC is also experimentally evaluating performance-based scholarships, as noted in chapter 5 in this volume, by Lashawn Richburg-Hayes

10. Claiborne Pell, "Washington: A New Precedent in Federal Aid," *Change* 3, no. 7 (1971): 7, 58.

Acknowledgments

M ore than ever before, college students in America rely on federal financial aid dollars to finance their postsecondary education. As the economy began its slow recovery after the Great Recession, family incomes remained stagnant while tuition at two- and four-year public and private institutions continued to rise. Students and their parents, told all their lives that a college education was the ticket to prosperity, must make a calculation that, on face value, appears risky: is the current cost of a college education worth the future benefits? For too many students, the end result is indebtedness without a degree. This is where our volume began. After years of conversations—at meetings, during conferences, on the phone, and over e-mail and Twitter—we sought to articulate what it is about the design of federal financial aid that does so little to ease the pain of high tuition, especially for the lowest-income students. How have the goals of the federal financial aid system changed over time, and has the system itself kept pace with these new goals?

In early 2013 we commissioned nine new pieces of research that, collectively, seek to ask not only how we can make existing financial aid programs more effective, but how we can retool the entire system for the next generation of students. As we began commissioning papers, student loan debt hit an alarming $1 trillion, while policy makers continued to bicker over the interest rate on subsidized Stafford loans, a relatively small portion of student loans that nevertheless amounted to a distraction from truly rethinking our financial aid systems. Federal financial aid was on everyone's mind, but the proposed solutions resulted in little more than tinkering with the tools that have undergirded the system since its inception in the 1960s.

Then, in June 2013, the authors we commissioned presented their work to an audience of over two hundred at a public research conference at the American Enterprise Institute. The authors were encouraged to ask the question: how can we reform student financial aid to fit the goals and needs of twenty-first century students? After the conference, the authors then incorporated new insights and feedback into their research, the final versions of which are included here. Presented as a whole, this volume offers readers a history of the development of the financial aid system, a critique of its weaknesses, and ambitious proposals for how to reform an outdated system that is no longer meeting the needs of students or taxpayers.

We would like to thank the authors for their excellent contributions as well as their patience during the editing process. We would also like to thank the following discussants for providing outstanding feedback throughout that day: Sandy Baum of George Washington University, Diane Auer Jones with Career Education Corporation, Justin Draeger of the National Association of Student Financial Aid Administrators, Ed Pacchetti with the U.S. Department of Education, Bob Shireman with California Competes, Debbie Cochrane with The Institute of College Access and Success, and Miguel Palacios with Vanderbilt University.

We are also indebted to the steadfast support provided by AEI and its president, Arthur Brooks. The Bill and Melinda Gates Foundation generously provided the financial support for this project; we are particularly thankful for our program officer Nick Lee for helping shepherd this project to completion. The terrific staff at AEI and the University of Madison-Wisconsin also deserve our appreciation. In particular, we'd like to thank KC Deane for her work managing and overseeing this project and coordinating the conference; Lauren Aronson for her efforts in promoting the conference, this volume, and all related publications; and Daniel Lautzenheiser, Taryn Hochleitner, Max Eden, and Sarah DuPre of AEI along with Alison Bowman at the University of Wisconsin-Madison for their vital assistance. Finally, we express our gratitude to the Harvard Education Press team, particularly director Doug Clayton and editor-in-chief Caroline Chauncey, who offered skillful and timely guidance throughout the course of this project.

About the Editors

Andrew P. Kelly is a resident scholar in education policy studies and the founding director of the Center on Higher Education Reform at the American Enterprise Institute in Washington, DC. His research currently focuses on higher education innovation, student aid reform, information and choice in education markets, and the politics of education. Kelly has published research on a variety of topics across K–12 and higher education, including postsecondary productivity and innovation, consumer information and transparency in education, K–12 principal preparation, charter school achievement, and collective bargaining in public schools. His scholarship has appeared in the *American Journal of Education, Teachers College Record, Educational Policy, Policy Studies Journal,* and various edited volumes. He has also published in popular outlets like *The Atlantic, National Affairs, U.S. News and World Report,* and *National Review,* and is a regular contributor to *Forbes.* He is coeditor of numerous edited volumes on education policy, including *Stretching the Higher Education Dollar, Getting to Graduation: The Completion Agenda in Higher Education,* and *Reinventing Higher Education: The Promise of Innovation.* He is an editorial consultant for *Phi Delta Kappan* magazine, and sits on the board of BASIS DC, a public charter school in Washington, DC. He holds a bachelor's degree in history from Dartmouth College and a master's and PhD in political science from the University of California, Berkeley, where he served as a National Science Foundation fellow and a graduate student instructor.

Sara Goldrick-Rab is a professor of educational policy studies and sociology at the University of Wisconsin–Madison. She is also the founding director of the Wisconsin HOPE Lab, senior scholar at the Wisconsin Center for the Advancement of Postsecondary Education, and an affiliate of the Center for Financial Security, Institute for Research on Poverty, the La Follette School of

Public Affairs, and the Consortium for Chicago School Research. Goldrick-Rab received the William T. Grant Faculty Scholars Award in 2010 for her project "Rethinking College Choice in America," and in 2014 she was given the Early Career Award by the American Educational Research Association. Goldrick-Rab has conducted several experimental studies on financial aid programs and written widely about the challenges facing undergraduates from low-income families. She provides technical assistance to more than a dozen foundations, think tanks, and nonprofits, and in 2013 she testified on college affordability before the United States Senate Committee on Health, Education, Labor, and Pensions. Dr. Goldrick-Rab earned her PhD in sociology from the University of Pennsylvania.

About the Contributors

Rodney J. Andrews is an assistant professor of economics in the School of Economic, Political, and Policy Sciences at the University of Texas at Dallas and director of the Texas Schools Project. He received his PhD in economics from The University of Michigan. His research interests are in the areas of the economics of education, labor economics, and public finance. He has published research on race-neutral alternatives to affirmative action and the impact of the Kalamazoo Promise on college choice. His current research projects examine a number of topics including the effects of college quality on the distribution of earnings, the relationship between the path to a degree and earnings, the returns to college major, the effects of tuition deregulation in Texas's college and universities on academic and labor market outcomes, the effects of targeted recruitment implemented by elite universities, and the impact of targeted prekindergarten programs on subsequent academic performance.

Stephen Crawford is a research professor at George Washington University's Institute of Public Policy. Previously he served as deputy director of the Brookings Institution's Metropolitan Policy Program; a division director at the National Governors Association; and executive director of the Governor's Workforce Investment Board in Maryland. Earlier he taught at Bates College and the University of Maryland; was executive director of research centers in Cambridge, Massachusetts, and College Park, Maryland; and served as an assistant dean at the University of Pennsylvania and a U.S. Army infantry officer in Vietnam. He also served as a special adviser to the Maryland Higher Education Commission, a member of the Frederick County Board of Education, and on the Obama-Biden transition team. His publications include *Technical Workers in an Advanced Society* (Cambridge University Press, 1987). His current research explores innovation in higher education, and includes publications with Robert Sheets in *Educause* (2012) and *Continuing Higher Education Review* (2013). Crawford holds a master's degree in business administration from the Wharton Business School and a PhD from Columbia University, and is a member of the board of the American National Standards Institute.

Regina Deil-Amen is an associate professor at the University of Arizona's Center for the Study of Higher Education. Her recent research explores strategies, challenges, and success among lower-income university students, including Latino students' social networks and career decision making. Through a Bill and Melinda Gates Foundation grant, she is currently exploring how community college students use social media to create community and enhance their success. Regina was formerly a research director for "College to Careers," a Northwestern University Institute for Policy Research study examining how community college occupational programs and comparable private career and technical colleges prepare students for sub-baccalaureate careers. Her coauthored book *After Admission: From College Access to College Success* (Russell Sage, 2007) details those study findings. Deil-Amen also completed a longitudinal qualitative study, sponsored by the NAEd/Spencer Foundation, of the transitions of students from high-poverty Chicago high schools to one-, two-, and four-year colleges. She has published in the *Journal of Higher Education, Review of Higher Education, Sociology of Education, Teachers College Record, Journal of Latinos and Education, Journal of Hispanic Higher Education, Community College Review,* and *Journal of Community College Research and Practice.*

Nicholas W. Hillman is an assistant professor of educational leadership and policy analysis at the University of Wisconsin–Madison. Hillman's research interests include higher education finance and financial aid policy analysis. His recent work has examined the impacts of state and institutional aid programs, Colorado's voucher reform, and state performance funding models. His research also examines trends in student loan default, college savings accounts, and student enrollment demand. Hillman is the associate editor of the *Journal of Student Financial Aid* and teaches courses on higher education finance, educational policy, and research methods. His work can be found in *Research in Higher Education,* the *Review of Higher Education, Education Finance and Policy,* the *Journal of Higher Education,* and *Teachers*

College Record, among other outlets. Previously Hillman worked as a policy analyst and researcher with State Higher Education Executive Officers and the American Association of State Colleges and Universities.

Daniel Madzelan began his federal career with the U.S. Department of Education in 1978 as a program analyst in the campus-based student aid program area. He retired in 2012 as the senior director of the strategic planning, analysis, and initiatives staff in the Office of Postsecondary Education (OPE), where he worked on a variety of program and policy issues including the development of the department's annual budget request for student financial aid and other programs administered by OPE. Between February 2009 and July 2010, Madzelan was the acting assistant secretary for postsecondary education. In this capacity, he was responsible for a staff of 210 in the management and oversight of an annual program budget of nearly $3 billion allocated via grant funding largely to colleges and universities to support students in undergraduate, graduate, and doctoral programs, both at home and abroad. He also had policy responsibility for the student financial assistance programs that provided $145 billion in grant, work-study, and loan assistance to fourteen million postsecondary education students and their families. In 2014 he accepted the position of associate vice president for government relations at the American Council on Education, where he helps advance the organization's advocacy on behalf of the higher education community, particularly the array of federal policies and issues critical to the missions of American colleges and universities and the students they serve. Between 2012 and 2014 Madzelan worked on areas of interest to higher education and consulting with a number of organizations contemplating reforms to the federal student aid programs to help achieve improved student outcomes. The views expressed in his chapter are his own.

David S. Mundel is an independent research consultant whose recent work has focused on higher education policy and the misuse and overuse of statistical significance testing. Before becoming an independent consultant, he was a professor and a senior executive in federal and local government organizations. Mundel's education research has focused on the design and evaluation of access-oriented higher education policies. His early papers include "Federal Aid to Higher Education and the Poor" (MIT, 1971) and "An Empirical Investigation of Factors which Influence College-Going Behaviors" (Rand,

1974). His recent publications include "What Do We Know about the Impact of Grants to College Students?" (College Board, 2008) and "Do Increases in Pell and Other Grant Awards Increase College-Going among Lower Income High School Graduates?—Evidence from a Natural Experiment" (Brookings Institution, 2008).

Lashawn Richburg-Hayes, director of the Young Adults and Postsecondary Education policy area of MDRC, works in higher education and focuses on finding ways to increase academic achievement and persistence among low-income students attending community colleges and less selective four-year universities. Richburg-Hayes is a quantitative methods expert and principal researcher of the national Performance-Based Scholarship Demonstration, which evaluates the effectiveness of performance-based scholarship programs to increase retention and persistence in higher education. She is also the project director and co-principal investigator of the Behavioral Inventions to Advance Self-Sufficiency project, sponsored by the Administration for Families and Children of the U.S. Department of Health and Human Services, which is geared to learning how tools from behavioral science can be used to improve the well-being of low-income children, adults, and families.

Cecilia Rios-Aguilar is an associate professor of education at the School of Educational Studies at Claremont Graduate University. Rios-Aguilar's research is multidisciplinary and uses a variety of conceptual frameworks (funds of knowledge and the forms of capital) and statistical approaches (regression analysis, multilevel models, GIS, and social network analysis) to study the educational and occupational trajectories of underrepresented minorities, including Latinas and Latinos, English learners, low-income, and immigrant and second-generation students. Rios-Aguilar's applied research also includes the design and evaluation of different programs and policies targeted to underrepresented students. She has been published in several journals, including *Teachers College Record*, *Higher Education: Handbook of Theory and Research*, *Language Policy*, *Community College Review*, and the *Journal of Latinos and Education*.

Lauren Schudde is a postdoctoral research associate at the Center for Analysis of Postsecondary Education and Employment at Teachers College of Columbia University. She received her PhD in sociology from the University of Wisconsin–Madison. Her research examines the causes and consequences of socioeconomic inequality in higher education.

Robert Sheets is a research professor at George Washington University's George Washington Institute of Public Policy and a long-time researcher and consultant in education, workforce, and economic development policy at the federal and state levels. He recently retired as the director of research at Business Innovation Services, University of Illinois at Urbana–Champaign. Sheets has conducted research and demonstration projects and consulted for the U.S. Departments of Education, Labor, and Commerce; the National Governors Association; foundations; and states. In addition to publications with those sponsors, he has published a book and numerous academic articles, including in *Administrative Science Quarterly* and *Public Policy Review*. He is currently working on a research project with Stephen Crawford at George Washington University's Institute of Public Policy on large-scale innovation in higher education. He is also conducting a research project on next-generation workforce development policy. His two most recent publications are "Harnessing the Power of Information Technology: Open Business Models in Higher Education" (*Educause Review*, March-April 2012, with Stephen Crawford); "Rethinking Higher Education Business Models" (Center for American Progress Policy, March 2012, with Stephen Crawford and Louis Soares); and "Creating Institutional Space for Business Model Innovation" (*Continuing Higher Education Review*, Fall 2013, with Stephen Crawford).

Jacob Stampen is emeritus professor of educational leadership and policy analysis at the University of Wisconsin–Madison and visiting researcher at the Wisconsin Center for the Advancement of Postsecondary Education. Stampen's forty-year career includes teaching history in high school; serving as director of special projects for the University of Wisconsin system; heading policy analysis projects serving the three major public higher education associations at the National Center for Higher Education in Washington, DC; and teaching and conducting research on educational planning, program evaluation, and higher education finance at the University of Wisconsin–Madison.

Lesley J. Turner, assistant professor of economics and faculty associate of the Maryland Population Research Center, received her PhD from Columbia University in 2012. Her research applies theory and methods from labor and public economics to topics in the economics of education and broadly considers the role government should play in providing and financing education. Dr. Turner received her BA from the University of Michigan in 2004 and her MPP from the Gerald R. Ford School of Public Policy at the University of Michigan in 2005. She was awarded the Upjohn Institute Dissertation award for the best PhD dissertation in labor economics in 2012.

Index

AASCU (American Association of State Colleges and Universities), 45–46
Achieving the Dream, 99
actionable knowledge, 14–15, 216
 See also research agenda design
Adams Scholarship, 69, 169
Allison, Graham, 17
American Association of State Colleges and Universities (AASCU), 45–46
American Council on Education, 204
American Opportunity Tax Credit (AOTC), 43, 47
American Recovery and Reinvestment Act, 51
American Taxpayer Relief Act (2012), 43
Applyful, 82
Arkadelphia Promise
 eligibility criteria, 60, 61
 last-dollar programs, 65
 subsidy focus, 58
Arkansas Challenge Scholarship, 61, 68
Australia, 137, 138, 180–181

back end of the loan cycle, 171–172, 178
badges in social media apps, 81
Basic Educational Opportunity Grant program. *See* Pell Grant program
Bay Area Commitment Fund, 58
Bennett, William J., 163
Bennett Hypothesis, 163
Bettinger, Eric, 8
Bill and Melinda Gates Foundation, 9
Bok, Derek, 204
Brinkman, Paul, 110
Bush administration, 2, 40, 46

California. *See* Performance-Based Scholarship (PBS) Demonstration
campus capital, 92
Canadian programs, 104, 108
Capitalism and Freedom (Friedman), 15
Carnegie Commission on the Future of Higher Education, 128, 200
Cavazos, Lauro, 48
Chambers, M. M., 200
Chicago School, 199
Clinton administration, 39–42, 46
Cohort Default Rates (CDRs) measures, 144
College Abacus, 80, 81
college access and degree completion
 attainment gaps between income groups, 6–7
 concern with the economic value of higher education, 172–173, 174
 educational-incentive from an income-related repayment model, 144
 history of interest in improving, 197–198
 institutional aid's implications for, 150–151
 lifetime earnings impact of college attendance, 173–174
 Promise Programs' impact on, 66–69
 recommendation for reform of goals for, 174–175
College Affordability and Transparency Center, 99
College Board, 3, 9, 82
College Bound Scholarship Program
 eligibility criteria, 61
 location, 57
 sources of funding, 63

College Cost Reduction and Access Act
(2007), 51, 139
CollegeGO, 82
Collegeology, 84
colleges and universities
argument for free public higher
education, 210, 211
complaints over education credits
reporting requirements, 44–45
degree attainment gaps, 6–7
disincentive to keep tuition affordable,
209
favoring of the status quo, 8, 19
federal-level concern with the economic
value of higher education, 172–
173, 174
federal proposal to change how
institutions receive aid, 4
as the focus of aid (*see* institution-
focused federal student aid)
history of federal support for higher
education, 13–14
income-related repayment plans impact
on, 146
increasing costs of tuition, 3, 6
institutional autonomy to determine
cost of attendance, 191
lack of accountability for controlling
costs, 2, 3–4, 192–193, 195–196,
213–214
need for incentives to keep tuition
affordable, 218–219
need to be actively involved in federal
efforts, 218–219
as the origin of aid (*see* institutional aid)
price discrimination in higher
education, 160–161
price sensitivity of college attendance,
161
response to policies, 218
responsiveness to aid programs, 16, 18
sharing loan risk with the institutions,
184–185
societal support for higher education,
72–73, 172, 197–198
support for tax credits from advocacy
groups, 45–46

usability problems with financial aid
web sites, 78
College Scorecard, 99, 166
Community colleges
federal policy's failure to account for
non-traditional students, 99–100
in the Schools App study, 87
survey of student engagement, 77
Community College Survey of Student
Engagement (2009), 77
Completion by Design, 99
ConnectEDU, 82
Consumer Financial Protection Bureau,
166
consumption smoothing, 129
Council of Economic Advisors, 43

debt, student loan. *See* student loan debt
defaults on student loans
consequences of for the student, 133
federal laws regarding, 134–135
in the proprietary sector, 145–146
protection against, 129
rates of, 127, 130–131, 133, 144, 173
deferment of loans, 132
Degree Project, 65
Department of Education, 35, 48, 99, 141,
147, 150, 154, 166
Detroit College Promise, 57, 63
Developmental Education Initiative, 99
direct lending program, federal, 40–42,
211
Domestic Policy Council (DPC), 35
Dynarski, Susan, 110

Earned Income Tax Credit, 45
Educational Opportunity Bank, 128, 136
Educational Opportunity Grant program,
13
EDUCAUSE, 77
Eisenhower, Dwight, 39
El Dorado Promise
eligibility criteria, 60
location, 57
retention rate, 68
sources of funding, 62
subsidy focus, 58

emergency protection plans for student
  loan repayment, 132
Expected Family Contribution, 48

Facebook, 87
  See also Schools App
FAFSA (Free Application for Federal
  Student Aid), 9, 61, 163
FAFSA Community, 80, 81
Federal Credit Reform Act (FCRA), 40–41
federal financial aid legislation
  Federal Credit Reform Act, 40–41
  HEA (*see* Higher Education Act)
  history of, 5
  Pell Grants (*see* Pell Grant program)
  tax credits creation, 43–46
  total spending on, 14
federal government and financial aid
  changing from a student- to an
    institution-focused approach (*see*
    institution-focused federal student
    aid)
  establishment of first federal student
    loan program, 13–14
  goals of loan programs, 171, 176–177
  imperative of an intra-governmental
    collaboration on aid, 141–142
  legislation regarding financial aid (*see*
    federal financial aid legislation)
  politics of aid (*see* politics of student aid)
  program reform recommendations
    (*see* financial aid policy reform;
    income-based student loan system
    reform)
  response to cost and value concerns of
    postsecondary education, 174
  shift towards federal versus state funded
    aid, 5
Federal Work-Study program, 13
financial aid policy reform
  active involvement of colleges and
    universities need, 218–219
  argument for free public higher
    education, 210, 211
  argument for market-based and
    individual-level incentives,
    210–211

assumptions made about faults in the
  current system, 212
building reforms on a sense of shared
  responsibility, 220–221
categories of needed research and
  development, 217
debates and discussions about, 207–208
disincentive to keep tuition affordable,
  209
folly of the current approach to college
  affordability, 209
innovations in programs (*see* incentive-
  based grants; Promise Programs)
interest groups' protection of the status
  quo, 2, 8
lack of consideration of alternatives,
  8–9
lack of political will to make changes,
  209
need for an accountability system for
  colleges and universities, 213–
  214
need to consider student views on
  incurring debt, 213
need to create incentives to keep tuition
  affordable, 218–219
need to go above politics, 222
need to reevaluate the problems facing
  low-income students, 212–213
path towards meaningful reform, 9–10
performance-based scholarships
  impact, 212
reform elements that enjoy a consensus,
  214–215
rigorous evidence requirement,
  216–218
shortfalls of federal direct funding, 211
student progress and completion
  emphasis need, 221–222
typical focus of, 7–8
financial aid program performance
  areas of focus of federal research efforts,
    25–26
  areas of focus of the research
    community, 25
  current knowledge of effectiveness of
    programs and approaches, 20–23

financial aid program performance *(Cont.)*
    design of an actionable knowledge
        research agenda (*see* research
        agenda design)
    impact of changes in economic and
        political contexts, 19–20
    market failures resulting from a reliance
        on incorrect assumptions, 15–17
    nonmarket failures that restrict
        program performance, 17–19
    scope of research favored by funders,
        24–25
    sources of gaps in available knowledge,
        23–24
financial aid shopping sheet, 166
Finn, Chester, 201
forbearance for a loan, 132
for-profit schools
    institutional aid dispersed by, 157
    proprietary sector default rate, 145–146
Foundations for Success, 108, 119
Free Application for Federal Student Aid
    (FAFSA), 9, 61, 163
Friedman, Milton, 15, 135, 199
front end of the loan cycle, 171, 177–178

GAO (Government Accountability
    Office), 45
Gates, Bill, 7
Gates Millennium Scholars Program, 67
Georgia, 67, 68, 70–72, 164
Getting Connected study. *See* Schools App
GI Bill, 5, 13, 39
Government Accountability Office
    (GAO), 45
GradGuru, 81, 84
graduate tax, 128, 136
Granholm, Jennifer, 69–70
Great River Promise, 58
Great Society programs, 197, 199
Guaranteed Student Loan program, 13

Hamilton Project, 167
Hansen, W. Lee, 199
HEA. *See* Higher Education Act
Health Care and Education Reconciliation
    Act (2010), 51

Helping Outstanding Pupils Educationally
    (HOPE) grant, 67, 70–72, 164
higher education. *See* colleges and
    universities
Higher Education Act (HEA)
    amendments process results, 47–49,
        200, 201
    impact of changes in the
        reauthorization process, 51
    impact on higher education, 39, 198
    income-related loans pilot, 128
    scope of, 33–34
Higher Education Amendments (1972),
    200, 201
Higher Education Opportunity Act
    (2008), 165
HOPE (Helping Outstanding Pupils
    Educationally) grant, 67, 70–72,
    164
Hope Scholarship, 43–44, 45
human capital contracts, 135–136
Hungary, 137

IBL (income-based loans), 136–138
IBR (Income-Based Repayment program),
    7–8, 133, 134, 139
ICR (Income-Contingent Repayment),
    133, 139
incentive-based grants
    communication's role in the program,
        123
    considerations for Pell Grant
        structuring, 123–124
    defined, 103
    impact on student performance (*see*
        student performance due to
        incentive-based grants)
    implications for private and employer
        grants, 125
    implications of benchmark selection,
        121–122
    importance of identifying the target
        group, 121
    incorporating stakeholders into the
        programs, 122
    integrating intervention efforts with
        existing programs, 122–123

potential for unintended consequences, 124–125, 126
promise of incentives, 102–103
research on incentive potential of financial aid, 101–102
selected characteristics of trial population, 108–109
state-based aid considerations, 125
structure of aid packages and, 122
study methodology, 104
study results, 120
summary of the study trials, 104–108
theory of behavioral change underlying, 103–104
income-based loans (IBL), 136–138
Income-Based Repayment program (IBR), 7–8, 133, 134, 139
income-based student loan system
access and completion goals and, 174–175
average amount of student loan debt, 173
back end of the loan cycle and, 171–172, 178
concern with the economic value of higher education, 172–173, 174
delinquency and default rates, 130–131, 173
described, 177
fairness and opportunity issues, 188–190
front end of the loan cycle and, 171, 177–178
goals of the federal student loan programs, 171, 176–177
lifetime earnings impact of college attendance, 173–174
loan repayment adjustment, 175–177
reform recommendations (*see* income-based student loan system reform)
road map for implementation, 186–188
societal support for higher education, 72–73, 172, 197–198
summary, 188
income-based student loan system reform
alignment of loan amounts with repayment potential, 180–181

creation of an open national data platform, 185–186
expansion of student information and guidance, 179–180
flexibility in loan terms and conditions, 180
implementation road map, 186–188
income-contingent repayment and risk adjustment, 184
loan insurance and, 182–183
performance-based loan adjustments, 183–184
pricing and systematic underwriting and, 181–182
sharing risk with the institutions, 184–185
simplification and alignment of programs, 178–179
viability of a system tying loans to predicted earnings, 181
Income-Contingent Repayment (ICR), 133, 139
income-related repayment plans
advocacy of by Clinton, 39, 41
argument that the loans introduce a moral hazard, 140–141
beneficial sensitivity to economic realities, 145
cohort default rates, 144
consequences of default for the student, 133
conventional repayment plans, 131–132
cost savings from a new repayment model, 142
default protection and consumption smoothing, 129
default rate on student loans, 130–131, 133
delinquency situations and, 127, 132–133
educational-incentive benefit from the new model, 144
emergency protection plans, 132
existing efforts in the U.S., 139–140
existing plans, international, 133–135, 137–138

income-related repayment plans *(Cont.)*
  federal laws regarding student loan
    default, 134–135
  graduate tax model, 128, 136
  history of, 128–129
  human capital contracts, 135–136
  imperative of an intra-governmental
    collaboration, 141–142
  implications of the funding model, 130,
    146
  income-based loans, 136–138
  interest cap options, 143–144
  loan collection costs and, 129–130
  loan forgiveness options, 143
  need for basic data on participating
    students, 140
  need for relevant research, 146–147
  plausible positive behavioral changes
    due to a new model, 142–143
  potential for fraud and abuse, 141
  potential impact on higher education,
    146
  potential to introduce simplicity and
    predictability into the aid system,
    145
  proprietary sector default rate
    considerations, 145–146
  suggested repayment model, 142
Income-Sensitive Repayment (ISR), 133
institutional aid
  analysis of dispersion of aid across
    students, 154–157
  analysis of its buffering effects on cost
    increases, 152–154
  college scorecard requirement, 166
  correlation between available aid and
    college cost increases, 163
  crowd-out of federal and state need-
    based grant aid, 162–165
  demand-side versus supply-side
    interventions, 166–167
  distribution based on levels of need,
    157–159
  effect on lower-income students' college
    and major choice, 161–162
  effect on persistence and degree
    attainment by students, 162
  financial aid award process, 163–164

financial aid shopping sheet
    requirement, 166
  grant aid receipt by sector, 155–156
  growth in the cost of college, 149, 152
  implications for affordability and access,
    150–151
  implications for equity and effectiveness
    for grant aid, 151
  need to decrease the cost of accessing
    pricing information, 167
  need to encourage students to attend
    higher-quality schools, 169
  net price calculator requirement, 165,
    167
  policy considerations for reforms,
    165–169
  price discrimination in higher
    education, 160–161
  price sensitivity of college attendance,
    161
  role in the college affordability
    discussion, 169–170
  supply-side policies that can help low-
    income students, 168
  unintended consequences to avoid, 168
  variation in crowd-out across sectors,
    164–165
institution-focused federal student aid
  affordability of the new model, 203
  appeal of a student-aid-focused
    approach for politicians, 200
  challenges for public institutions during
    the 1960s, 199
  concerns about transfer of resources,
    204
  economists' argument for student-based
    aid, 199–200
  family income's relationship to college
    attainment, 192
  history of interest in improving access
    to higher education, 197–198
  importance of state investment and
    oversight of affordability, 194–
    195
  inadequacy of reliance on a college
    ratings system, 203
  increasing price sensitivity of federal
    student aid, 201

institutional autonomy to determine cost of attendance, 191
institutional response to a shift from student to school subsidies, 204
lack of accountability for schools to control costs, 192–193, 195–196
past debate over the feasibility of institutional assistance, 198
Pell Grant origin, 198, 201
percent of American children expecting to attend college, 193
question of a correlation between costs and the availability of aid, 22, 195, 200
rationale for focusing on educational institutions, 193
risks of the model, 205
shortcomings of the current distribution of aid, 196–197
size of the financial aid industry, 191
state of reform efforts, 192
steps in operationalizing and funding a new model, 202–203
stipulations for success of the model, 202
Integrated Postsecondary Education Data Systems (IPEDS), 152
interest caps on loans, 143–144
Internal Revenue Service, 141
ISR (Income-Sensitive Repayment), 133

Jackson Legacy Program
eligibility criteria, 61
location, 57
subsidy focus, 58
Jobs for the Future, 99
Johnson, Lyndon, 197

Kalamazoo Promise
basis of the program's success, 72–73
eligibility criteria, 59–60
first-dollar program, 65
impact on access to postsecondary education, 66
location, 57
origin of, 55
as a source of inspiration, 56
sources of funding, 62

Kane, Thomas, 110
Kerr, Clark, 200

Legacy Scholars Program, 60
Leopard Challenge, 57, 60
Leslie, Larry, 110
Lifetime Learning tax credits, 43, 44, 164
loan forgiveness, 143, 178
Logrado, 81, 84
Louisiana programs, 108
lower-income students
consideration of inadequate Internet access, 86
degree attainment gaps between income groups, 6
degree that family income is a determinant of college attainment, 192
distribution of institutional aid based on levels of need, 157–159
impact of income requirements on the working poor, 99
institutional aid's effect on college and major choice, 161–162
need to reevaluate the problems facing, 212–213
Pell Grants and (*see* Pell Grant program)
supply-side policies that can help, 168
using social media to help inform (*see* Schools App)

Martínez-Alemán, Ana, 92
McPherson, Michael, 204
Merisotis, Jamie, 7
merit aid programs, 49–50, 59, 67, 104, 126
Michigan, 69–70
Morrill Act of 1862, 13
MyCoach, 81, 84
My College Dollars, 80

National Defense Education Act, 5, 39
National Defense Student Loans, 39
National Economic Council (NEC), 35
National Postsecondary Student Aid Study (NPSAS), 154
net price calculator, 165, 167

New Zealand, 137
Northport Promise, 60, 61, 72
NPSAS (National Postsecondary Student
     Aid Study), 154
Nunn, Sam, 47
Nvivo, 88

Obama administration, 2, 3, 4, 47
Office of Management and Budget
     (OMB), 35
Office of Postsecondary Education (OPE),
     33
Opening Doors Demonstration (OD
     Louisiana), 108, 116, 117, 119
Opportunity Knocks, 104, 108

Pay As You Earn (PAYE), 133, 139
PBS (Performance-Based Scholarship)
     Demonstration, 108, 110, 116, 117,
     119
PBS Ohio, 119
Pell, Claiborne, 198
Pell Grant Index, 48
Pell Grant program
     addressing shortfalls in funding, 36–
          37
     considerations for structuring around
          incentive-based grants, 123–124
     crowd-out of institutional grant aid,
          164–165
     effect on lower-income students' college
          and major choice, 162
     effect on persistence and degree
          attainment by students, 162
     erosion of its purchasing power, 3
     expansion under Obama
          administration, 3
     funding from the ARRA, 51
     history of, 5, 14
     impact of income requirements on the
          working poor, 99
     increase in effective value since
          inception, 152
     lessons learned about, 217
     origin of, 198, 201
     political focus on maximum awards,
          37–38
     positioning against tax credits, 44

potential for unintended consequences,
     124–125
potential institutional aid reforms
     involving, 168
size of and dollars spent by, 5
Peoria Promise
     eligibility criteria, 61
     location, 57
     sources of funding, 63
     subsidy focus, 58
performance-based loan adjustments,
     183–184
Performance-Based Scholarship (PBS)
     Demonstration, 108, 110, 116, 117,
     119
performance-based scholarships, 108
Perkins Loans, 39
Pittsburgh Promise
     eligibility criteria, 60, 61
     location, 57
     retention rate, 68
     sources of funding, 62, 69
place-based scholarships. *See* Promise
     Programs
politics of student aid
     adoption of direct loans, 41–42
     appeal of a student-aid-focused
          approach for politicians, 200
     budget process use as a policy-making
          tool, 50–51, 52–53
     challenges from relying on the tax code,
          46–47
     Congressional efforts to slow the direct
          loan program, 42
     Congressional positioning to set policy,
          35–36
     dynamic involved in trying to change
          federal policy, 34
     effect of advancing new policies and
          programs via reconciliation, 51–52
     executive branch positioning to set
          policies, 35, 39–42
     favoring of the status quo, 2, 8
     federal direct lending program
          replacement of guaranteed
          lending, 40–42
     HEA amendments process results,
          47–49

impact of changes in economic and
political contexts, 19–20
impact of changes in HEA
reauthorization process, 51
intra-agency divisions over merit aid,
49–50
lack of a single point authority on
federal financial aid, 33–34
lack of political will to make changes,
209
need to go above politics, 222
Pell Grant program (*see* Pell Grant
program)
tax credits for higher education, 43–46
themes evident in policy debates, 38–39
PossibilityU, 82
Presidential Merit Scholarships, 49–50
Project STAR, 104, 117, 119
Promise for the Future Scholarship
Program, 57, 58
PromiseNet, 56
Promise Programs
corporations' willingness to fund
programs, 62–63
described, 56
differences across programs, 58
eligibility criteria, 59–62
first program of its kind, 55
funding determination, 59–62
funding instability examples, 63
goals of, 58–59, 61–62
impact on access to postsecondary
education, 66–67
impact on college completion, 68–69
impact on retention, 67–68
impact on the likelihood that a student
will attend college, 66–67
last-dollar programs, 65
lessons learned about, 217
locations, 56–57
scalability of the programs, 70–72
social returns sought, 72–73
sources of funding, 62–64
summary of noteworthy programs, 64
sustainability of the programs, 69–70
types of postsecondary institutions that
are subsidized, 57–59
typical subsidy schedules, 60

Raise Labs, 80, 81
Reimagining Aid Design and Delivery, 9
research agenda design
actionable knowledge need, 14–15, 216
case studies and observational studies,
27–28
categories of needed research and
development, 217
demonstrations that are evaluated and
documented, 28–29
experimental studies, 29
focus on a search for value and, 26
limits of current experimentation and
research, 8–9
policy design and prototyping, 28
program monitoring, review, and
assessment, 29–30
rigorous evidence collection need,
216–218
targets for an actionable knowledge
research program, 30–31
theory and hypothesis development and
articulation, 27
See also financial aid program
performance
Rethinking Student Aid, 9
risk pooling IBLs, 136–137
risk profiles and indexes, 179–180
risk sharing IBLs, 137–138
Rivlin, Alice, 200
Roosevelt, Franklin, 39

Sanders, Ted, 48
Schools App, 84
administrators' and staffs' role in
advocating use of social media,
98–99
categories of topics in financial aid
exchanges, 89–91
community colleges in the study, 87
data sources and analysis, 88
demonstration of potential of social
media to help the aid process, 100
evidence of federal policy's failure
to account for non-traditional
students, 99–100
exposure of problematic complexity of
the aid process, 97

Schools App *(Cont.)*
  issues due to accuracy of information,
    94–95
  issues due to understaffing of financial
    aid offices, 93–94
  need for ongoing levels of engagement,
    92–93
  opportunities afforded by the platform,
    98
  purpose and approach used, 81, 87–88
  staff resistance to social media as a tool,
    95
  student difficulties due to a link
    between academics and aid
    qualification, 95–96
  student difficulties due to federal
    prioritizing of students with a
    dependent-status, 96–97
  student exposure to and valuing of
    technology's importance, 91–92
  usefulness of staff availability to
    respond, 90–91
  value derived by non-active users, 93
  value of a student-based site, 98
SEOG (Supplemental Educational
  Opportunity Grant), 37
Shapiro, Morton, 204
Shiller, Robert, 177
Single Stop USA, 213
social media
  financial aid information pilot program
    (see Schools App)
  promise of, 100
  reshaping of how students
    communicate, 76–77
  tangential benefits from using, 79
Social Security Student Benefit Program,
  66, 68
Sparkman Scholarship Foundation, 58, 61
Spellings, Margaret, 2
Stafford loans, 7, 132
staged experiments, 29
state financing of higher education
  decline in state-level support for higher
    education, 5–6
  importance of state investment and
    oversight of affordability, 194–195
  incentive-based grants and, 125

  response to federal initiatives, 18
  shift towards federal versus state funded
    aid, 5
state merit aid programs, 59
State Student Incentive Grant program,
  37, 201
Studentaid.ed.gov, 80
student financial aid
  actionable knowledge need, 14–15
  attainment gaps between income
    groups, 6
  basis on which to build reforms,
    220–221
  decline in affordability of college, 3–4
  decline in state-level support for higher
    education, 5–6
  federal *(see* federal government and
    financial aid)
  fundamental problems with current
    system, 2
  funding by Pell Grants, 3, 5
  history of, 5, 13, 39
  institution-focused approach *(see*
    institution-focused federal student
    aid)
  institution-initiated approach *(see*
    institutional aid)
  lessons learned about, 216–222
  need for experimentation and research
    (see research agenda design)
  path towards meaningful reform, 9–10
  performance of programs *(see* financial
    aid program performance)
  policy debates, 7–8
  presidential-level calls for reform, 2–3,
    4
  problem of complexity, 97
  reform challenges *(see* financial aid
    policy reform; income-based
    student loan system reform)
  relationship to rising tuition costs, 6
  shift towards federal versus state funded
    aid, 5
  size of the student debt load, 1
  size of the system, 14, 101
  state support of, 5–6, 18, 194–195
  status of student debt and delinquency
    rates, 7

student progress and completion
emphasis need, 221–222
student loan debt
average amount of, 173
delinquency situations and repayment
plans, 132–133
need to consider student views on
incurring, 213
size of the student debt load, 1
status of student debt and delinquency
rates, 7
student performance due to incentive-
based grants
amount earned versus amount eligible
for, 116, 118
credit accumulation after one year,
117–118
credits earned and degree attainment,
119–120
effect size estimates across studies, 116,
117
GPA in first and second years, 119
matriculation findings, 110, 116
meeting academic benchmarks, 116–
117, 118
summary table, 111–115
students and parents
access and completion goals in an
income-based system, 174–175
aid considerations for low-income
students (*see* lower-income
students)
assumptions made in projections of
benefits from aid programs, 16
current knowledge of effectiveness of
programs and approaches, 20–23
economic value and loan repayment
adjustment in an income-based
system, 175–177
examples of technologies designed to
inform college choice process,
82–83
examples of technologies designed to
motivate college-going behaviors,
84–85
FAFSA requirement, 9, 61, 163
family income's relationship to college
attainment, 192

federal policy's failure to account for
non-traditional students, 99–100
institutional aid's effect on persistence
and degree attainment by students,
162
lifetime earnings impact of college
attendance, 173–174
need to decrease the cost of accessing
pricing information, 167
need to encourage students to attend
higher-quality schools, 169
percent of American children expecting
to attend college, 193
performance-based aid results (*see*
student performance due to
incentive-based grants)
plausible positive behavioral changes
due to a new model, 142–143
price sensitivity of college attendance,
161
shortcomings of the current
distribution of aid, 196–197
using social media to help inform (*see*
Schools App)
value of a college degree, 172–173, 174
Supplemental Educational Opportunity
Grant (SEOG), 37

tax credits for higher education
AOTC, 43, 47
challenges from relying on the tax code,
46–47
complaints over reporting
requirements, 44–45
Hope Scholarship, 43–44, 45
level of support from higher education
advocacy groups, 45–46
Lifetime Learning, 43, 44, 164
start and expansion of programs, 43
structure of, 43–44
Taxpayer Relief Act (TRA), 44, 46
Taxpayer-Teacher Protection Act (2004),
51
technology's role in financial aid
advantages of technological solutions,
81, 100
assumptions made about technology, 77
benefits from using social media, 79

technology's role in financial aid *(Cont.)*
  case study on the use of social media
    (*see* Schools App)
  challenges of technological solutions,
    81, 86
  existing research on the issue, 86
  inadequate Internet access for low-
    income students and, 86
  need to improve the whole financial aid
    process, 79
  scope of new technology in use, 75–76
  scope of research needed, 86
  social media's reshaping of student
    communication, 76–77
  students' preferred means of receiving
    financial aid information, 78
  technological solutions for financial
    aid/college funding, 80
  technologies designed to inform college
    choice process, 82–83
  technologies designed to motivate
    college-going behaviors, 84–85
  usability problems with college Web
    sites, 78
Title I programs, 211
Title IV programs, 48, 194, 202
TRA (Taxpayer Relief Act), 44, 46
Tractus Insight, 81, 82
Treasury Department, 45
tuition and fees
  analysis of institutional aid's buffering
    effects on cost increases, 152–154
  correlation between available aid and
    college cost increases, 163, 195,
    200
  current institutional autonomy to
    determine cost of attendance, 191
  disincentive for institutions to keep
    tuition affordable, 209
  financial aid's relationship to rising
    tuition costs, 6

  growth in the cost of college, 3, 149, 152
  institutional aid's implications for
    affordability and access, 150–151
  institutional aid's role in the college
    affordability discussion, 169–170
  lack of institutional accountability for
    controlling costs, 2, 3–4, 192–193,
    195–196, 213–214
  need for incentives for institutions to
    keep tuition affordable, 218–219
  need for institutional responsibility for
    cost setting, 195–196
  need to decrease the cost of accessing
    pricing information, 167
  net price of college, 151
  rise at both public and private colleges,
    6
  shift in financial responsibility from
    states to individuals, 5–6

United Kingdom, 137, 138
University of Amsterdam, 108, 117
Upjohn Institute, 56
Uversity, 87

Venegas, Kristan, 77

War on Poverty, 197
Weisbrod, Burton, 199
West Virginia, 68
Wolf, Charles Jr., 17
wordclouds, 88, 89
Working Families Success Network, 213

Yale University, 128, 136–137
Yudof, Mark, 204

Zell Miller Scholarship, 71
Zombie College, 84